Civilians at War

CIVILIANS AT WAR

From the Fifteenth Century
to the Present

Edited by Gunner Lind

Museum Tusculanum Press
University of Copenhagen
2014

Civilians at War: From the Fifteenth Century to the Present
Gunner Lind (ed.)

Composition, layout and cover design: Erling Lynder
Set with Adobe Caslon and printed by Specialtrykkeriet Viborg
ISBN 978 87 635 4063 6

This volume is published with financial support from
The Danish Council for Independent Research – Humanities

Museum Tusculanum Press
Birketinget 6
DK-2300 Copenhagen S
Denmark
www.mtp.dk

MIX
Paper from responsible sources
FSC® C104608

Contents

Preface

War is an eminently social activity. The parties of war are states, clans, tribes, political parties, congregations, or other large, coherent social entities. If the parties are not large, other terms will be used: piracy, feud, duel, murder. If the units are not coherent, they will not be able to wage war at all. Social solidarity is a basic hidden theme whenever people speak about war. All are concerned, because it is *us* and *them* who are fighting, winning, losing, suffering. War divides the world into insiders and outsiders, and the outsiders into enemies and neutrals.

Seen from the inside, however, war does not really concern all to the same degree or in the same way. As we know, the warring parties will immediately split into groups with radically different roles and conditions. Broadly speaking, each warring society will be divided into two: the active combatants and the rest. In practice the division will be much more complicated. There will be many degrees of activity, and many different ways to be more or less immune from some or all the effects of war. Some may be almost untouched by the war raging around them, or at least, in an ideal world, regarded as being outside of it.

We also partition the enemy. As objects of our hostility, the enemy population will split into three: the targets of our weapons; the victims of exploitation, looting and abuse; and the rest, whom we keep outside of the war. This division will probably have some relation to the internal division recognized by the enemy society, but not in any simplistic way. It will not be the same people who are seen as outside of the hostilities by the two parties, and still less who will actually be safe from any hostile acts.

War, then, does create a huge number of social distinctions, and much will depend on these distinctions: respect or contempt, safety or suffering, life or death. The fundamental modern word when discussing these divisions is *civilian*. It is an important technical term for lawyers and social scientists as well as a common expression in everyday language. The word is also the carrier of an ethos – the obligation to restrict hostile activities to the soldiers, leaving the enemy civilians alone; and a corresponding obligation to make the border between civilians and military distinct and easy to recognize. In other words, we must subsume our division of the enemy from the outside to how the enemies divide themselves into military and civilians; and we must establish social divisions among ourselves which are easy to interpret along the conventional civilian-military lines. The prominence of the civilian-military dichotomy implies that the many distinctions observable in practice ought to be reduced to this simple line, even if civilians are not always untouchable according to current international humanitarian law.

This ethos surely has an impact, not least because concentrating hostile acts on the active combatants among the enemies has practical advantages. But it may also be advantageous to act otherwise, for example to target the unarmed and victimize the undefended. There is no strong coupling between the systems of division used from the inside and the outside. They are fundamentally independent, creating a permanent ambiguity. As we all know, even in the most "civilized" of modern wars, the division between civilians and military will be blurred in many ways.

If we consider all the ways people are divided by war, current or historical, the complexity is overwhelming. It is possible to be an actor in many ways; one can change one's status back and forth voluntarily, or be forced to do so. Individuals can desire to cross a dividing line, or it can be forced upon them. They can disagree with the social role assigned to them, seeing themselves as not really a soldier, or maybe as a combatant without arms. Neither is there agreement on the proper behaviour of any group. The only stable thing is the fact of division.

This complexity of the distinction between participants and non-participants is a challenge for those who are involved in war, for those who want to regulate war, and for those who desire to understand war. Exploring this distinction, and how more complex divisions relate to the simple dichotomy, must however be part of our approach. All actions towards people we do not know individually are governed by categorization. We determine "who" they are and adjust our behaviour accordingly. Understanding how we divide other people in the context of war is, thus, fundamental.

In the present volume, the social divisions surrounding war are explored through a number of case studies. Lars Bo Kaspersen opens with an examination of classical and recent social theory. It has often been remarked that social theory does not provide an adequate understanding of war. Kaspersen examines the common assumptions lying at the root of this failure and outlines how social theory may be renewed through the inclusion of concepts drawn from Hegel and Clausewitz. This chapter thus provides an explanation of why it has been so difficult to understand how war relates to the internal structure of warring societies.

Gunner Lind follows the long-range advance of the concept "civilian" and the distinction between military and civilian in the Western world, both as a practical social division and as a norm. This chapter thus explores the genesis of the division seen as fundamental today, and often used without any consideration of the modern Western origin of the concepts.

Jeppe Büchert Netterstrøm examines the earliest stage of the historical development of the civilian-military dichotomy in the case of Denmark – a fairly typical Western European example. This chapter focuses on the warlike phenomena inside what we would call states and the relations between social groups and feuding.

The final three chapters examine how civilians may be at war through three twentieth-century cases. Palle Roslyng-Jensen studies how civilians may conceive of themselves as imagined participants, relating to the events of war through the news media and their own interpretation and commentary in relation to these events. His case is Denmark during the Second World War, occupied by Germany and torn between perspectives of accommodation or resistance. Robin May Schott deals with the civilian as victim: how violence, and especially rape, may be directed purposefully toward civilians, women most of all. Her material mostly comes from the wars in the former Yugoslavia. Finally, Steffen Jensen and Finn Stepputat examine how soldiers who were once pulled out of civilian life pass the dividing line, formally becoming civilians again. Their cases are drawn from late twentieth-century Africa and South America.

The texts explore a number of common questions. How do people become combatants and how do they cease to be combatants? How does the treatment of civilians develop in the dynamic setting of war? How well do actual roles fit with the civilian-military dichotomy? How do individual identities change as combatants are recruited or demobilized? How do social roles and subjective identities interact? How clear, to themselves and to others, are the varying roles people may have? All the essays focus on actual processes in recent or older history, and all the texts aim to draw general insight from the actual cases.

The essays have their origin as papers given at the seminars of the research network on *War Experiences* financed by the Danish Research Council for the Humanities during the years 2005–2007. Members of the network work with many different themes, but it became clear that one theme of special importance was the borderline defining zones of relative peace in times of war. The studies presented here have been rewritten for this volume, expanding and improving on the original papers. They deal with specific developments in time and place. But it is our hope that they will contribute to a better general understanding of war, which is rooted in most strange and controversial human behaviour.

Gunner Lind

War and Social Theory
A Critique of the Fusion Theory in Social Theory

Lars Bo Kaspersen

The Problem

In the history of social theory, we find relatively few theorists addressing the issues of violence and warfare. Since sociology as a variant of social theory became institutionalized at the end of the nineteenth century, the mainstreams of social theory in particular neglected warfare and its implications for the social organization of human life. One exception is Julien Freund, who offers some important reflections in his book *Warfare in the Modern World* (1996). Since societies are either in a state of war or a state of peace – and as there is a constant tension between these two states – it is important to study warfare. Another major feature also concerns the fact that all modern nations have their origins in warfare, whether directly or indirectly. Thus, war is both destructive and constructive at one and the same time. War is an instrument of man's domination by man, alongside such other issues as power, ideology, or the economy. It is also a particular kind of social relation: it resorts to weapons, that is to say means of attack and defence which are devised to kill.

Warfare is not only a particular social relation; this very relation also has a deep impact on the overall social organization of society. Given the fact that war is a conflict between two political entities, it is directly linked to their structure – that is to say, to the social organization, political constitution, economic systems and their value system in general. Military activity is attuned to the other activities. Consequently, the manner in which a war is waged depends upon the particular culture of the potential belligerents at any given stage in time. Thus, war is as much an expression of civilization as are works of art, economic systems or religion.[1] Moreover, as it is

1 Paul Hirst, *War and Power in the Twenty-First Century* (Cambridge: Polity, 2001).

waged by means of weapons, each war is affected by technology and its development.

War is one of the few great constants in human affairs and predates recorded history and organized states. Almost all societies have engaged in some form of combat against others. In other words, there are good reasons for social theory to pay attention to warfare. This has not been the case however. Of course, historians have written about wars and their implications, as well as security studies scholars who concentrate on wars, but we find very few social theorists who theorize on war and its relation to and embeddedness in larger societal structures. Despite some recent interest, especially among comparative and historical sociologists, warfare has been largely ignored. The question is, why?

There could be several explanations for the neglect of warfare in social theory. It is beyond the scope of this chapter to discuss a long list of potential explanations; instead, I will bring forward the claim that there is a relationship between a particular dominant conception of society in social theory and the limited interest in warfare as a social phenomenon. This particular conceptualization of society involves a specific understanding of the state – an understanding which prevents warfare from being conceptualized properly.

Social theory has developed various definitions of the concept of society, which have subsequently been the occasion of intense debates and polemics. Since the state is conceived of as a natural extension of society, there has, likewise, been strong disagreement as to what the state is and what its role is in relation to society. In spite of the disagreements among the various theories, there are some basic points of resemblance, and these are the point of departure for discussion here. Functionalism, structuralism, the sociology of action and Marxism are all based on the same implicit configuration of society and state. Society (and the state) is thought of as a unification or fusion of individuals, institutions or classes, while the state – understood as an administrative apparatus and a political power institution – is derived from society as a superstructure necessary for the maintenance of order. The purpose of this chapter is to analyze this tacit assumption, on which sociology constructs its theory of society and state, and to discuss some of the problematic implications, including the almost complete neglect of warfare.

The dominant theoretical streams in sociology (Marxism, functionalism, structuralism and the sociology of action) assume that there is a plurality of societies/states in the world and that these are distinguishable from each other. The main problem of most social theory is that it cannot account for why society is demarcated, and what determines this demarcation in relation to other societies. The structure of these theories themselves does not include concepts, or relations of concepts, and thus no definitions that may point out and transcend these difficulties. It is always problematic when a theory cannot account for its own preconditions; and it becomes even more so if inconsistencies prevent the possibility of a theory from becoming an analytical tool. The foundation of the ruling social theoretical paradigms within the said configurations of society and the state has grave implications for social theory in terms of analyses of social order and social transformation. Here, the shape and content of state and society are determined primarily by the elements that exist within state and society. If social theory is to contribute to an understanding of the structure and development of a society – and, moreover, of why different societies exist and are demarcated in relation to each other – it is necessary to rethink and redefine the concepts of state and society. My claim is that the concept of the state is the starting point of this redefinition. Instead of an extension of the civil society, the state must, I shall argue, be seen as a political entity *sui generis* with the most developed autonomy compared to all other organizations and social entities. The state provides specific conditions for the development of society, and thus the state determines the demarcation of a society. It is important to include the importance of the mutual relations of the states in the states system. Thereby, the mutual struggle – and, in the last instance, the war – for recognition of the states becomes a crucial aspect of the structure and the development of the single state and the civil society belonging to it.

The chapter is structured as follows: the first part focuses on the configuration of state and society in the writings of selected classical sociologists (including, Karl Marx, Emile Durkheim and Max Weber). Showing the characteristics of the configurations and their immanent theoretical problems. The second part takes a closer look at the implications of those configurations for studies of social order and social transformation. Part three examines more recent sociological theories (represented by Michael Mann) and their attempts to include the state and its external relations in the studies of social transformation processes. Finally, some limitations and problems in Mann's conceptions are demonstrated and as a possible source of inspiration for further work on this issue, ideas from the works of Hegel and Clausewitz, as interpreted and further developed by Anders Boserup, are also presented.

From Marx to Weber and Durkheim

In the following, I examine how the problem of society, and, in particular, that of the state, is to be localized in the thought of classical sociology.

KARL MARX

In Marx's (1818–83) writings, society is the primary concern and the state is treated as something peripheral. Marx's primary focus is the analysis of the capitalist mode of production and social formation; the state, once more, is something derived from society. Society consists of the social formation and the modes of production; the latter consisting of the relations between, for example, labour and capital. These relations form the fundamental structures of society, and consequently the Marxist conception of society is endogenously conditioned. The mode of production is not in itself limited by any political or military border. A mode of production is an all-economic concept; politics is merely a mirror of the antagonism between economic classes. Consequently, using the idea of the mode of production as the key concept, Marx's conception of society also leads to the problem of demarcation. Marx does not explain why some modes of production become limited by, for example, English or German political borders. This, therefore, also has a bearing on the problems of the state, which, in consequence of the conception of society (social formation and the concepts of modes of production), are rarely dealt with specifically. Throughout most of Marx's writings there are hints at what may be the character of the state, but there is no developed theory of the state. In spite of this, it seems reasonable to assume that there are two different configurations of the state to be found in Marx:

1. A state which possesses "relative autonomy" in relation to classes. This interpretation may be supported by texts such as "The Eighteenth Brumaire of Louis Bonaparte" and "A Contribution to the Critique of Hegel's Philosophy of Right."
2. The state is conceived of as an instrument of the ruling class. Here, there is no clear-cut distinction between politics and economics. Texts supportive of such a reading are, for example, *The Communist Manifesto.*

With regard to the first point, the "Brumaire" text may be regarded as an illustration of the way in which Marx deals with the problem of the state. This text is very complex, but it is one of Marx's more direct attempts to describe the relation between the classes and the state. Here, the state is not conceived of as a direct tool of the ruling class. The state and the bureaucratic apparatuses have a variety of forms and they constitute a power factor that possesses a certain measure of "relative autonomy" in relation to the various classes. In a superior way, the state simultaneously secures the reproduction of society to the advantage of the general interests of the dominant classes. We see how the various factions within the ruling class are fighting between themselves and how Napoleon III successfully manages to perform his coup d'état and establish himself as ruler. This comes about, however, with the aid of the peasantry. Marx goes on to describe how the executive power of the state, including the bureaucratic and military organization, takes on independent power (relative autonomy):

> [The] executive power with its enormous bureaucratic and military organization, with its ingenious state machinery, embracing wide strata, with a host of officials numbering half a million, besides an army of another half million, this appalling parasitic body, which enmeshes the body of French society like a net and chokes all its pores, sprang up in

the days of the absolute monarchy, with the decay of the feudal, which it helped to hasten.[2]

But there are limits to the possibilities for Louis Napoleon, since the state in a capitalist society cannot renounce its dependence on society (the civil society) and the process of production. If the general politics of the state is not in accordance "with the objectives of manufacturers and traders, otherwise civil society and the stability of the state itself are jeopardized."[3]

With regard to the second point about the state as an instrument of the ruling class, this mode of reading the configuration of the state does not alter much about the basic assumption of the state being derived from society. In most of Marx's writings, as well as in Engels's (in *The Communist Manifesto*, for example), the state is regarded as a direct instrument of the ruling class.[4] Here we are back at the model of a basic superstructure, where the state is the superstructure erected on the basis of the economic/social relations. In *The Communist Manifesto*, Marx and Engels emphasise that "political power … is merely the organized power of one class for oppressing another."[5]

Marx's famous thoughts on the "*Aufhebung*" of the state in communist society is a further illustration of how the state is conditioned by the class society, and therefore the logical consequence of this is that the classes themselves can abolish the state through the victory of the proletariat in the revolution, since the proletariat possesses the privilege of being the subject of history.

Unlike many other social theorists – such as Thomas Hobbes and Jean-Jacques Rousseau, who had a strong focus on the individual in their work – Marx begins with the classes as his point of departure. As a consequence, society and the state are conceived as constituted "from within" and "from below"; in other words, the classes are the building bricks. Society consists

2 Karl Marx, "The Eighteenth Brumaire of Louis Bonaparte" [1852], in Karl Marx and Friedrich Engels, *Selected Works in Two Volumes* (London: Lawrence & Wishart, 1958), 293.
3 David Held, ed., *States and Societies* (Oxford: Martin Robertson, 1983), 28.
4 Ibid., 26.
5 Karl Marx and Friedrich Engels, *The Communist Manifesto* [1848], (Harmondsworth: Penguin Books, 1969), 105.

of classes and the state is a superstructure. Marx says very little about the origin or genesis of the state; for this, one has to turn to Engels. In Engels's *The Origin of the Family, Private Property, and the State*, for example, it is stated that it is the emergence of the classes that conditions a concept of the state. This creates a problem since the classes are regarded as a condition of social transformation. How could a transformation occur from primitive communism to a kinship-based mode of production when there is no battle between the classes in primitive communism?

To summarize, then, one could say that no matter which reading has been undertaken of the society and the state configuration of Marx, they are obvious configurations constructed "from within," but Marx focuses on the structure of society, with the point of departure in the relations of classes.

EMILE DURKHEIM

Emile Durkheim's (1858–1917) explicit aim is to constitute a science of society. Durkheim regards society as a "thing," a reality *sui generis.* For him, society consists of individuals, the things that surround them and of which they make use; for example, buildings and ways of communication.[6] The fundamental element, therefore, of his concept of society is the individual. However, for Durkheim, society is more than the sum total of individuals, and so society cannot be traced back exclusively to the individuals and the other physical elements. In other words, society has specific properties different to those of the individual. According to Durkheim, the state is not the means of binding together the various parts of society. He operates with two types of society, based on different types of solidarity: mechanical and organic. Mechanical solidarity is found in the so-called traditional societies, where the force of cohesion consists of a collective solidarity (conscience collective). In modern societies, with a progressed division of labour, in each single individual there is no deeply rooted collective consciousness. "Organic solidarity … links the individual to society via the separate parts of society, organic solidarity is mediated solidarity."[7]

6 Emile Durkheim, *Suicide: A Study in Sociology* [1897], (London: Routledge & Kegan, 1952), 307.

7 Dag Østerberg, *Emile Durkheims samfunnslære* (Oslo: Pax Forlag, 1983), 42.

The functional division and differentiation of modern society is in itself only the means of binding the individuals together and makes a society possible; the greater the differentiation and specialization, the greater the interdependence among individuals.

Only in connection with modern society and organic solidarity does the state emerge as a result of the increased division of labour and of specialization. The state, at first, is defined as a political society with a clear distinction between authority and submission to authority, between rulers and the ruled. This definition of a political society might also relate to the family, and in order to avoid a confusion of concepts Durkheim adds a further characteristic to the state: the presence of secondary groups/corporations that are subject to the authority of the state, as are the individuals.

We should, then, define the political society as one formed by the coming together of a rather large number of secondary social groups who are subject to the same one authority, which is not itself subject to any other authority duly constituted.[8] Political society is one side of the state. The other, more narrowly defined, is related to the bureaucracy and the employed functionaries:

> The state … is a group of official *sui generis*, within which representations and acts of volition involving the collectivity are worked out, although they are not the product of collectivity. It is not accurate to say that the State embodies the collective consciousness, for that goes beyond the State at every point … The State is the centre only of a particular kind of consciousness, of one that is limited but higher, clearer and with a more vivid sense of itself.[9]

Thus, the state is a small and specific form of collective consciousness that is present in modern organic society all the same. Durkheim regards the state as "the brain" in an organism, in which its task is to be a thought organ aiming at practical goals. The state is not in itself an active agent, but

8 Emile Durkheim, *Professional Ethics and Civic Morals* [1922], (London: Routledge, 1992), 45.

9 Ibid., 50.

is attempting, as an organ of social thought, to guide and lead collective behaviour.

The thoughts of the state point in the direction of an increase of power and a taming of the power of the secondary groups, leading to increased freedom for the individual. As differentiation increases, the thoughts and actions of the individual are liberated from the collective consciousness. Durkheim's thesis may seem paradoxical in that the increasing differentiation and a state emerging with increasing power mean greater individual freedom. In *The Division of Labour in Society* (1893) and *Professional Ethics and Civil Morals* (1922), Durkheim tried to prove that this is not a paradox. Here, the state becomes the primary institution which implements and secures the rights of the individual in modern society.[10] Durkheim opposes Hobbes's and Rousseau's concept of the innate rights of the individual. The task of the state is to allot and distribute these rights.[11] This is why Durkheim regards the growth of a state as progressive, for this is regarded as an expression of the institutionalization of greater rights for the individual.

In order to achieve freedom for the individual, the state has to counteract all the forces trying to absorb the personality and individuality of the members – such as, for example, the secondary groups of the family, the church, trade organizations and the trade unions. "The state must therefore enter into their lives, it must supervise and keep a check on the way they operate and to do this it must spread its roots in all directions."[12] The role of the state, therefore, has a moral character.

Analogous with Marx, Durkheim conceives of society as developed "from within"; it is seen as a fusion of its internal elements. The state is regarded as an outcome of the societal development, with increasing division of labour, etc., and is directly conditioned by the development of society. The state has a moral obligation in the political society (in which the state operates) the instance that it creates and institutionalizes the rights that enable the increased freedom of the individuals. Only at this stage in the theory can Durkheim's society and state be confronted with other societies/states. Durkheim is aware that the external environment of a society

10 Ibid., 57.
11 Ibid.
12 Ibid., 65.

– i.e. other societies – may limit the moral role of the state, and, thus, each society's possibilities of development. The moral obligations of the state can be carried out only if society exists without pressure from the environment. We have not (yet) reached this stage of development; in other words, there is still war and strife among societies. The state has to defend itself, since the primary obligation of the state is to preserve society as a collective being. War means another kind of moral discipline, the aim of which is no longer the individual but a national collectivity.

The past never vanishes completely, says Durkheim. This means that obligations such as, for example, defence against external enemies – and, thus, another kind of moral disciplining of the individual – will survive for some time. But the obligation of the state to defend itself in war will become more secondary as development progresses. Previously, the actions of the state pointed outwards, now the obligations are increasingly directed internally. This happens because the state can only achieve its moral aims in relation to the individual, and her or his liberty, if its focus is on the internal.

Apparently, Durkheim finds himself in a dilemma that cannot be solved. The moral aim of humankind has to be universal freedom; the wider the distribution and generalization of this universal, the greater the individuality and freedom. Confronted with this aim, we are living in a society with national ideals and patriotism, the immediate effect of which is to undermine the conditions of the universal. Here there is a problem, since man is only a moral being; because he lives in specific societies with a state, or, more precisely, a nation-state. The presumption of living in a society is a sense of patriotism. It is patriotic feelings that tie together a specific individual and a society. If patriotism disappears, where could the individual find its moral authority?[13]

Durkheim's proposal to solve the paradox takes its point of departure in the specific states and societies. Ethics exists in each state and society, but the aim has to be that each state must promote a set of ethics which point in the direction of general humanism and individual freedom. The aim of the state must be the maintenance of order in its own house. Instead of an

13 Ibid., 73.

urge for expansion and hostile actions towards other societies, the problem of "internal order" has to be solved first. If the primary purpose of the state is to make human beings into good citizens, civic and moral obligations will only be a particular form of the general obligations of mankind. The more societies there are that concentrate their energy on the internal, the more they will avoid the struggles that create the clashes between cosmopolitanism and patriotism:

> As they grow in size and get greater complexity, so will they concentrate more and more on themselves. Here we see how the advent of societies on an even bigger scale than those we know will constitute an advance in the future.[14]

The solution is that patriotism has to become a fragment of world patriotism. And, as the quotation illustrates, the logical implication of Durkheim's conception of society is, in the last instance, that the increased differentiation creates, in the long run, a world society in which universal freedom is materialized. If each state aims to work towards justice instead of wealth, all particular differences are broken down and a world society will become a reality.

MAX WEBER

The works of Max Weber (1864–1920) may be roughly divided into two groups. One consists of his explicit theoretical – and, according to Weber, also scientific – work (definitions of categories and concepts, and historical comparative analyses by means of ideal types); the other consists mostly of his political writings. The reason I draw attention to this grouping of Weber's production is that it is also the source of discrepancy in his conception of state and society.

The central point in Weber's sociology is social action and not society as such. Weber's methodological individualism implies that he, like Hobbes, starts out from the individual as the first and most important unit in the construction of society. Society consists of the actions of individuals and

14 Ibid., 75.

nothing more. Compared to Durkheim's collective consciousness, there is no common moral which binds individuals together in Weber's sociology. On the contrary, social interactions are characterized as relations of power, and society is bound together not by contractual relations (Rousseau and Spencer), or a moral consensus (Durkheim), but by the exercising of power.

As in Hobbes's work, it is the state that creates cohesion among acting individuals. The state, as a particular kind of political organization, aims at controlling a particular territory and its inhabitants. This control implies a willingness to use physical power, including arms. The state is regarded as a collective actor consisting of individuals and their actions:

> [F]or the subjective interpretation of action in sociological work these collectivities (states, corporations, etc.) must be treated as solely the resultants and modes of organization of particular acts of individual persons, since these alone can be treated as agents in a course of subjectively understandable action.[15]

Weber emphasizes that the state is defined in relation to its means, not to its aims. The state's monopoly of exercising force and violence within a given territory, supported by the administrative force of the state, is its main characteristic:

> A compulsory political organization with continuous operations will be called a "state" insofar as its administrative staff successfully upholds the claim to the monopoly of the legitimate use of physical force in the enforcement of its order.[16]

The potentially violent social actions of the state are aimed at opponents inside as well as outside the borders of the territory. Yet violence as a means of coerciveness primarily points inwards towards the members of the society because,

15 Max Weber, *Economy and Society* [1922], 2 vols., ed. Guenther Ross and Claus Wittich (Berkeley: University of California Press, 1978), 13.
16 Ibid., 54–55.

> the political community, even more than other institutionally organized communities, is so constituted that it imposes obligations on the individual members which many of them fulfil only because they are aware of the probability of physical coercion backing up such obligations.[17]

As can be seen, for Weber, some obligations are forced on the members of society, but unfortunately he does not elaborate further on the kinds of obligations or on the cause of why the members have to be forced into these particular obligations. What is lacking in his definition of the state is an explicit explanation of the aims of the state as regards the exercise of violence and force.

Moreover, the state may possess a certain autonomy, since the bureaucrats, the officers or the kings may act out of motivation for prestige and honour, which may lead to an expansive foreign policy. The more power and prestige the state achieves in the eyes of the world, the greater prestige is achieved by the actors themselves, which could facilitate their possibilities of promotion and career. The state as a collective actor, therefore, may accomplish actions that are in conflict with the interests of other members of society.

Weber's configurations of society and the state as presented in his sociological writings can be designated as "created from within" and "from below," as in the work of other theorists. Weber notices the external relations and the participation of the state in a system of states, but it has no effect on the theoretical explanation of the concept of society and state; this still consists of the active actors inside the territory.

This endogenous configuration of the state is also found in Weber's political writings. Here, however, he is more ambiguous, since the external relations of the state carry more weight, and the internal conditions – such as constitutional matters and political ideologies – are regarded as a means of the state to increase its power. It is very much on Weber's mind, given the time and location in which he was writing, to account for the strengthening of Germany as a national state and its place on the world map. The state is allotted a greater deal of autonomy in these writings, thus it does

17 Ibid., 902.

not stand out clearly as an entity derived from society. The state has ends of its own, the achievement of which society contributes to with means. This configuration of the state, however, marks a break with the endogenously conditioned one which is otherwise predominant in sociology generally, and in Weber's own sociological theory in particular.

The state pursues its own interests, and whereas the implication of economic development to the functionalists and the victory of the proletariat to the Marxists were a redundancy of the state, this can be seen to be in opposition to Weber. Here, a strengthened national state is a precondition for a strong German national economy. The external politics of the state has the direct purpose of pursuing German interests.

Society and State: A Fusion Perspective

This examination of selected parts of classical sociology has demonstrated how society (and the state) is thought of as a fusion of the internal composite parts of society. The state is derived from society, thus society is, in other words, the precondition of the state. The composite parts of society – be they individuals, institutions or classes – are allotted a priori characteristics and properties, needs and/or behaviour. They are born good or evil, they require regulation, or they act only on the basis of values, for example "the will to power." The state often enters as a regulating instance in relation to these individuals or as a tool of the ruling class. The concept of society is thought of as a closed, demarcated system that is easily identifiable – the modern nation state, for example. This demarcation is made exclusively by an empirically based argument; the argument is never based on theory.

Social contract thinkers such as Thomas Hobbes presume as a given that when humans transfer sovereignty to a Leviathan, or enter a social contract, it takes place with groups of human beings inside specific territorial boundaries. Logically, then, all human beings should be able to make one contract globally. But the possibility of a covenant or social contract apparently comes to a halt at the border. The problem remains unsolved. Why does the possibility of entering a covenant or social contract come to a halt at the borders of the state? How come society is demarcated by the borders of the state?

There is no explanation in Hobbes; neither is there one in Marx, Weber or Durkheim. The logically necessary consequence of the structure of these theories makes it impossible to conceive of the state and society as something demarcated. Durkheim's conception of society as an organism consisting of contractual relations between human beings, bound together by a common set of ethics (represented by the state in modern organic societies), contains no mechanism that explains why we can find different organisms that can be contrasted and distinguished from each other. It is true that Durkheim mentions that different societies with different traits of patriotism and national sentiments are observable, but the implication of the organism metaphor is a development towards one society and one state, and one set of ethics. The boundaries of the state are therefore virtually non-existent.

Marx's studies of modes and cycles of production provide us with the same picture. Modes of production are transnational since economy knows no boundaries. Capital moves to countries with low production costs in order to maximize profit, and as a consequence an increasing part of the population will become a proletariat. This proletariat will go through a process of "pauperization," which will create a common class consciousness. According to Marx this will lead to social and political mobilization and, eventually, a world revolution, which will mean the victory of the proletariat and the abolition of war between the classes whereby the state will wither away. Because of Marx's explanation, his theory – like that of functionalism – contains no tool for understanding why economy is limited within specific state societies. But the state has not withered away, and we still see states fighting each other to improve their national economies; the states, in other words, have restrained the transcending dynamics of the modes of production.

Weber's work is more ambiguous, but the construction of his sociological theory harbours the same problems as the other classical thinkers. When the basic structure of a theory consists of individuals (actors) where the aggregate of the actions of individuals make up society, the logical conclusion is that all actors act, and that the sum total of all social actions in principle makes one society. But Weber also cannot explain why social actions are demarcated by different state boundaries.

Weber seems to be more useful in relation to his political writings in which the state, exercising a monopoly on violence within a given territory, has a prominent place as an "autonomous" political agent. The state demarcates a given society, implying that the state enforces certain conditions on society. This is why the state does not appear as a direct extension of society, but pursues interests and aims of its own. Weber's conception of the state in his political writings has to do with his involvement in what was happening in contemporary Germany. He sees how the superpowers on the European stage act as something different and bigger than the sum total of the actions of individuals. The state achieves an existence of its own, but this consideration appears to be an unintended consequence of his empirical work rather than a logical result of his sociological theory. But it is this observation, as we shall see in the following, that has been a source of inspiration to several more recent sociologists who have problematized this perspective of the fusion theory.

As has been pointed out, society, in sociology, is predominantly conceived of in a fusion perspective, which makes it impossible to clarify the problem of the demarcation of society. But the configuration of society is not the only problem for sociology if we want to reflect on the issue of demarcation (of society) and the exogenous conditions. Also the concept of the state implies many theoretical problems because it is partly conceived of as derived from society and partly as a product of a (social) evolution. In Marx, Weber and Durkheim, the state is an outcome of the development of history. When society reaches a certain stage, states are developed – often conceived of as an apparatus of government and power. It could be said that the state is generally reduced to a question of social and/or economic order.

The Consequence of the Fusion Theory for Sociological Analysis

Anchoring sociology in a fusion theory leads to two problems. As mentioned before, this theoretical approach prevents a theoretical explanation of the presence of more than one society. Why is the world split into innumerable societies? What determines the demarcation between these societies? The other problem, dealt with briefly in the following, is the implications for a sociological analysis of social order and transformation.

To provide a more coherent explanation of these problems, we have to turn to the concept of the state and politics; sociology has to undertake theoretical considerations of the political dimension of the state. A fusion conception of state and society prevents sociology from developing a theoretically tenable determination of politics – to be understood, first of all, as the external political and military relations of the state. Only when this is included is it possible to determine the conditions of demarcation of a society. The defence of the territory of the state is the key to understanding the problem. It is precisely the defensive capability of the state that becomes decisive for the demarcation of society. The state acquires an independent "structuring" role in relation to civil society. An acknowledgment of the state's political military role in relation to the greater system of the state implies that the state is conceived of as an autonomous being, thereby imposing conditions on civil society. The struggle of the state to maintain its domain and the external pressure has significance for the internal order and structure of civil society.

The second problem, briefly stated above, is the implications of a fusion approach to a sociological analysis of order and transformation. A consequence of the present conception of the state in sociology is that it "narrows" the conception of social reproduction and transformation. Social change is often defined as related to factors within civil society. Marx speaks of class struggle and the development of the forces of production; Durkheim writes of the division of labour, the density and volume of the population; and Weber mentions religion and rationalization as essential causal variables when explaining, for example, the transition from feudalism to capitalism.

The external relations of the states and war are important factors when social change is on the agenda. War and a change in relations between states have great significance for the internal conditions in the state. This has, to a large extent, been neglected by sociology, although, as we shall see, the situation has changed in recent decades. When external conditions are included in explanations, these are often reduced to deductions from internal conditions. For example, in many Marxist writings, warfare is considered as being directly derived from the economic conditions in civil society. The autonomy of the state in relation to the classes of civil society cannot be achieved, since the state is defined as a superstructure and a mere reflection of civil society.

Such external conditions must have an independent theoretical place within sociology if analyses of the development of modern societies are to be more adequate. This has been attempted in some recent sociological studies, illustrated here by an example from Michael Mann's work in the following.

The State in Recent Sociological Theories

As has been shown, social theory, and in particular sociology as a discipline, contains a problem when taking its point of departure in conceptions of society and the state as a fusion of pre-existing subjects (individuals/classes/institutions). Fortunately, in recent decades, some sociologists have attempted to break away from such an approach. Several empirical studies have pointed to the necessity of rethinking the problem, including the autonomous character of the state, its external relations, the monopoly on violence, warfare and the significance of military defence to the internal conditions of the state and society. Consequently, in order to overcome this problem, comparative historical sociologists such as Michael Mann, Charles Tilly, Thomas Ertman, Theda Skocpol and Brian Downing have turned to a group of "neo-Machiavellian thinkers" for inspiration. This term covers scholars such as Gaetano Mosca, Robert Michels, Max Weber, Otto Hintze, and geopoliticians like Halford J. Mackinder, Ludwig Gumplowicz and Gustav Ratzenhofer. These are all very different thinkers, but they resemble each other in one or several of the following points:[18]

1. They are critical of the optimistic "conclusions" of Marxism and industrialism with a subsequent "transnational pacifism."
2. They are also critical of economic reductionism and attempt to overcome evolutionism.

18 Clive Ashworth and Christopher Dandeker, "Warfare, Social Theory, and West European Development," *Sociological Review* 35 (1987): 3–4.

3. They emphasize the significance of the politics of power and relations among states to societal development.
4. Social conflicts and the ever-present potential for war are fundamental features of human society.
5. Warfare plays a significant role in providing opportunities for structural social change.

These five main points have served as a platform for Mann, Tilly, Ertman, Downing and others, in an attempt to develop concepts of the state, power, and social transformation with the purpose of analyzing the specific sociological changes in Western Europe with the emergence and development of the nation-state and capitalism. Weber's definition of the state, with its focus on the territorial aspect and on violence, has, in particular, served as a source of inspiration to this wave of historical and comparative sociologists.

As indicated above, it is rather doubtful whether Weber solves the problem of the conceptualization of the state, since, in his sociological theory, the state is constructed "from within." He does notice more clearly, however (and in contrast with the other "classics"), that there is an interdependence between the internal and the external conditions of the state.

In order to illustrate the move towards another conceptualization of the state, I shall introduce the work of Michael Mann as representative of the group of comparative and historical sociologists who have worked on the problem of demarcation and the challenge of explaining structural social changes. Mann addresses explicitly the problem of the state.

Michael Mann

The state – and the autonomy of the state – is central in Mann's works. He has, in several of his works, dealt with the state-society problematic, both theoretically and empirically.[19] Below I shall concentrate on his definition of the concept of the state.

19 Michael Mann, "States, Ancient and Modern," *Archives Européennes de sociologie* 18 (1977); "The Autonomous Power of the State: Its Origins, Mechanism, and Results," *Archives Européennes de sociologie* 25 (1984): 185–213; *The Sources of Social Power,* vol. 1, *A History of Power from the Beginning to AD 1760* (Cambridge: Cambridge University Press,

Mann's project should be regarded as an attempt to break with the evolutionism and, in particular, the reductionism that characterizes liberal, Marxist and functionalist theories, in which the state is reduced to pre-existing structures in civil society. Mann tries to complete the most fruitful elements of classical "fusion" sociology with aspects of the "neo-Machiavellian" thinkers. Hereby a configuration of the state emerges which is conditioned both endogenously and exogenously. The state has two dimensions: one has to do with the economic and ideological conditions of civil society; and the other with the state's international military conditions. The state responds to two kinds of interests/pressures (both internal and external), generating a particular autonomous "space" where the state-elite may manoeuvre and play off the classes against each other. This dual conception of the state is one that Mann shares with Skocpol and Tilly, and it is conceived as a step away from reductionism. But Mann does not stop here; he suggests a further radicalization in order to avoid reductionism. The state is only an arena, a space; and this is the source of the autonomy of the state.

THE DEFINITION OF THE STATE

Broadly, Mann subscribes to a Weberian definition of the state as a point of departure for an understanding of the state.[20] This includes four parts:

1. A *differentiated* set of institutions and staff, forming
2. *centrality*, defined as political relations, radiating outwards from a centre to cover
3. a *territorially demarcated* area, over which is exercised
4. a monopoly of *authoritatively binding rule making*, backed up by a monopoly of physical means of violence.

To Mann, the essential thing is the centralized institutions of the state containing a high level of power possessed by the state elite. The power of the state elite and the centralized institutions has two dimensions. One is called a *despotic power*, which is the direct potential and range of action

1986); *States, War and Capitalism* (Oxford: Oxford University Press, 1988); *The Rise and Decline of the Nation-State* (Oxford: Oxford University Press, 1990).

20 Mann, *States, War and Capitalism*, 4.

of the state elite. Actions may be carried out without any kind of routine negotiations with groups of the civil society.

The other kind of power is *infrastructural power*, which is the capacity of the state to penetrate civil society and to implement political decisions within a given territory. Infrastructural power has made it increasingly possible for states to subject the everyday life of the population to an extended level of control and surveillance. The capacity of surveillance has increased such that we are controlled from the cradle to the grave; it is this form of power that dominates modern capitalist democracies.

THE ORIGIN OF AUTONOMOUS POWER

The possession of despotic and infrastructural power gives the state autonomy. This power and autonomy have their origin in three conditions:

1. The necessity of the state;
2. The multiplicity of the functions of the state; and
3. The territorial centralization of the state.

Concerning the *necessity* of the state, Mann takes his point of departure in a Hobbesian conception of society. The existence of a society is conditioned by the presence of rules that are capable of protecting life and property. These rules originate from a monopoly. Moreover, it is said that states always exist in a system of states which also imposes certain rules of behaviour onto each state. The autonomous power of the state proceeds from this necessity; "necessity is the mother of state power."[21]

In contrast to the reductionist theories of the state, Mann claims that the state has *several functions*. The state as a "binding rule making authority" covers several areas, each of which are functional with respect to different areas within society. These are divided into four main categories:

1. The maintenance of internal order.
2. Military attack/aggression. The external functions of the state.

21 Ibid., 196.

3. The maintenance of infrastructure (of communication). For example: roads, rivers, coinages, weights and measures, and message systems.
4. Economic redistribution. An authoritative distribution of scarce material resources between various age groups, sexes, regions, classes, etc. Moreover, there is also an international element, since it is the state that regulates the relations of trade and currency exchange along the borders.

These four kinds of tasks, necessary either to society as a whole or to certain groups of interest within society, are undertaken by the state. Thus, the state has several functional relations with various groups. The state's room for manoeuvre exists between all these different groups, and this space can be used to play off the various groups against each other.

Mann's conclusion is that this room for manoeuvre is the birthplace of state power. But this insight does not capture the distinctiveness of the state as a social organization.

As can be seen in the definition of the state given above, the state's *institutional, centralized and territorial nature* is included as an element. This particular element is the precondition of the unique autonomous power of the state. Only the state has a particular inherent centralized authoritative power over a specific territory. In contrast to economic, ideological and military groups in civil society, the resources of the state elite radiate authoritatively outwards from a centre which only comes to a halt at a territorially defined border: "The state is, indeed, a place – both a central place and a unified territorial reach."[22]

It is precisely this property that distinguishes the state from other powerful societal groups such as businesses, capital owners, the church or the nobility. The autonomous power of the state proceeds precisely from the difference in the organizational structure and socio-spatial conditions. "Territorial centralization provides the state with a potentially independent basis of power mobilization being necessary to social development and uniquely in the possession of the state itself."[23]

22 Ibid., 198.
23 Ibid., 201.

The autonomy of the state consists therefore of its necessity, the plurality of functions and territorial centralization. The power of the state elite cannot be reduced to the power of any group and it is thus autonomous in relation to civil society.

INFRASTRUCTURAL POWER AND THE DEMARCATION OF SOCIETY

Mann maintains that the state power, the infrastructural power in particular, is decisive when we speak about demarcated societies. Whenever a state regulates – normatively and with power – certain social and territorial relations and boundaries are set up in relation to what is external.

Moreover, the delimitation of borders is significant with respect to social change. When the state extends its territoriality in certain areas of social life, this may simultaneously influence societal changes which would not have occurred otherwise.

The development of an active state with great infrastructural power extends territorialization, thereby also the demarcation of society. The development of the European nation-states will be used as an example. Two processes in European development contributed to a further degree of centralization and territorialization from the twelfth century onwards: the first is the military development which required more capital (for mercenary soldiers), and later also men skilled in the use of arms (conscripts). Both of these demands could best be fulfilled by territorially centralized states. The other process concerns the increasingly capitalist economic development. In order to increase growth and wealth, capitalism posed certain requests which were best met by the territorial states. The states could provide, for example, military protection against external enemies, a common jurisdiction with legal regulation of property and a guarantee of the currency. Capital was looking for the security and conditions of existence provided by these states:

> Thus European states gradually acquired far greater infrastructural powers: regular taxation, a monopoly over military mobilization, permanent bureaucratic administration, a monopoly of law-making and enforcement … The nation-state system of our own era was not a product of capitalism (or, indeed, of feudalism) considered as pure modes

> of production. It is in that sense "autonomous." But it resulted from the way expansive, emergent, capitalist relations were given regulative boundaries by pre-existing states.[24]

Mann concludes that the state and its autonomous power is the primary condition of understanding societal development in Europe until today. In many ways this is a radical alteration and differentiation of the traditional sociological conception of the origins of capitalism, industrialism and the nation-state. Moreover, the results of Mann's studies indicate that the sociological concept of society should be seen in a historical perspective. Society, as a demarcated and definite entity, is an outcome of the development of the state. Only in the case of the nation-state does it make sense to regard society as something clearly demarcated. Society is conditioned by the infrastructural power of the state, and this power causes an extended territoriality as the nation-state develops. Mann can therefore not subscribe to the use of the concept of society within traditional sociology which is often temporally and spatially universalized. His concept of society is historically specific and belongs to the period of the nation-state.

From Fusion to Fission

Mann is a predominant representative of that movement within sociology which, with increasing force during the last two to three decades, has been highly critical of the one-sided focus on society within sociology. The works of Mann, Tilly, Downing, Ertman and others should be regarded as an attempt to criticise the so-called fusion theory in which society and the state are regarded as endogenously conditioned and a fusion of internal elements (individuals, classes or institutions). Their attempts at a synthesis between classical sociology and "neo-Machiavellian" thought is a means to link the dualism whereby state and society are regarded as both endogenously and exogenously conditioned. They want, simultaneously, to prove that society and the state condition each other, and that the state has an autonomy which creates a demarcation of society.

24 Ibid., 209.

Consequently, the state must necessarily be the starting point of an understanding of (modern) society. Thus, in other words, the concept of the state – and not that of society – should be the point of departure of sociology. This would enable sociology to pay more attention to the autonomy of the state – an autonomy which exists both in relation to other states, and in relation to the various classes and powerful groups in civil society. Moreover, it is an autonomy that determines the conditions of existence of society.

In their sociological analysis, Mann, Tilly and others attempt to link both the dual state – with its autonomous power directed both inwards towards the civil society and outwards towards the state system – and the relations in civil society as such. In particular, in their empirical analyses, these historical and comparative sociologists achieve much in the development of a fruitful concept of the state, but they do not, however, transcend theoretically the endogenous configuration of it. Michael Mann, Charles Tilly and Thomas Ertman are all inspired by Weber's definition of the state, which regards the state as an institution with a personnel/stratum of civil servants acting on the basis of values. In the last instance, therefore, the state consists of actions carried out by individuals and/or collectives (which, in their turn, are aggregates of individuals). In doing so, they still draw on the traditional sociological concept of society which – as emphasized – is constituted "from within" and "from below" by the social relations of individuals. The state is a product of history developed over time and reflects the evolution of society. When the state is conditioned by society, there is still no theoretical explanation of why and how the state may achieve its autonomy. Mann, Tilly and Ertman do not take the last step and draw the full consequence of their otherwise excellent and illustrative empirical analyses. War and the struggle for recognition are conspicuous in their empirical studies as an essential factor in understanding the constitution of society and the state. War (and politics) is regarded as a decisive driving force, and it seems as if war and the struggle for recognition implicitly constitute the state. But with a theoretical point of departure in Hintze and Weber, etc., they come to the opposite conclusion; war becomes the outcome of the action and manoeuvres of the state/the state's elite – "a will to power" (Mann). Mann and the others lack a stronger theoretical understanding of the relation between war and societal development in general, and between war and state in particular.

The inadequate understanding of the state-war relation leads to another decisive, theoretical problem which these theorists do not deal with explicitly in their work. The presence and significance of war to social change is noted, but they still owe an answer to the question of a possible termination of war. Michael Mann's theories, and those of most of the other comparative sociologists, admit two possible answers:

1. If the Weberian aspect of power is emphasized in their theories, then war will always exist since it is a general feature of human society. They are critical of Weber's "will to power" as an explanation of the presence of war, but they do not themselves give any reason for the dominating role of war in history. Further, one wonders whether war has always existed, how is it that it has not been possible for one state to conquer all the other states and thereby create a global reign and install world peace.
2. If war is the outcome of the actions of states/individuals, then the states, and their elites, could terminate war by establishing a global pact. This has not happened. Why not?

They do not follow up on this problem, which remains unsolved. The problem of war, and their inspiration from Weber concerning the concept of the state, illustrate that they remain embedded in a fusion theory. In spite of their efforts to break with the fusion theory, they, too, encounter the same theoretically basic problem as the classical sociologists.

Clausewitz, Hegel and Boserup: A Contribution to a Theory of Fission

It is difficult to point to a definitive solution to this basic theoretical problem, but a fruitful contribution may be found in the works of Karl von Clausewitz and G.W. F. Hegel, further developed by the peace and conflict researcher Anders Boserup.

Instead of conceiving of the state as a fusion of its elements, Anders Boserup, by combining Clausewitz and Hegel, conceives of it as the outcome of a fission process. Relations between states are constituent to the individual state. Thus, the state may be said to originate in a fission of the state system. I shall try to repeat the argumentation of the foundation of the fission theory.

In his article "The State, Society, and War in Clausewitz" (1986), Boserup extracts elements from Clausewitz and Hegel in an attempt to develop the foundation of a different theory of the state. He tries to address such problems as the demarcation of society, the state-society relation and the significance and position of war in social theory by rethinking concepts such as the state, war, society and sovereignty so that these concepts achieve a position of their own in a self-determined theoretical structure. The core of Boserup's theory is the connection between Clausewitz's concept of war and Hegel's concept of recognition (*Anerkennung*) in *The Phenomenology of Spirit*.

CLAUSEWITZ'S CONCEPT OF WAR

Clausewitz's concept of war is the point of departure for Boserup. Before proceeding with this concept, it is important to establish that the purpose of war is determined by the political. Clausewitz says nothing about the character of the political will involved, but merely emphasizes that war is a means, and thus only an instrument of politics. His concept of war can be specified on three "levels": the "explosive," the "virtual," and the "moderate" war.

In the explosive war, the purpose of politics is repressed to the advantage of the real end of war: winning a victory/avoiding defeat. Here, there is complete polarity between the two opponents since both have the same unambiguous, universal and diametrically opposed end. This leads to an explosive and unlimited war in which hesitation can mean losses and/or defeat. This state of war is rarely to be found in the real world, but it still throws light on central features of war.

The next form is a modification of the explosive war, called the "virtual war." This concept explains why there is often a stand-still in war. A pause occurs, conditioned by the breaking of the polarity between the opponents. Clausewitz explains this by introducing two forms of fighting: offensive and defensive. The defensive forms of fighting are, in principle, always stronger than the offensive, which is why wars come to an end. Had this not been the case, history would have looked totally different. If the offensive forms of fighting were the strongest, history would appear as an uninterrupted state of war that would only be terminated when the world was united under one global reign.

The argument for the superiority of the defensive is rooted in the condition that the offensive only possesses means that can be freely mobilized ("the army"), whereas the defensive possesses these as well as having its own purely defensive forces at its disposal. These forces consist of a series of means that are only raised in consequence "of the progress of the offensive itself and can only be mobilized by this, such as mountains and rivers, the resistance of the civilian population, and the support from those countries that fear the future strength of a victorious attacker."[25] Thus, the defence has the possibility of strategically combining geography, civilian population etc. and its freely mobilized forces, whereas the offensive part is only capable of operating with freely mobilized forces in its strategy.

The superiority of the defensive is thus the reason why there may be a real *pause*, and the length of the pause is conditioned by the strength of the defensive. But during this pause,

> the war is continued as a virtual war, for the action of war has ceased, it is true, but the war "goes on" in a particular sense, viz., as an always present possibility that is only not actual for as long as the conditions of the pause are maintained. The pause is only a precarious, temporary balance, conditioned by the forces keeping each other in check, and thus, therefore, even if the war is only "virtual," it imposes real claims on the two antagonists.[26]

The moderate war is the third form and here political motives are once again brought into the picture. During the pause, war may "take on more limited forms where the antagonists only go for small gains that offer

25 Anders Boserup, "Staten, samfundet og krigen hos Clausewitz," in *Om krig*, by Carl von Clausewitz, vol. 3, ed. and trans. Niels Berg (Copenhagen: Rhodos, 1986), 921.
26 Ibid., 915.

themselves, and where both parties may be said, in a certain sense, to be in the defensive!"[27]

The concept of virtual war makes possible a concept of peace based on the superiority of the defensive. In other words, Boserup, therefore, is capable of demonstrating theoretically why wars are interrupted by pauses. Mann, Tilly and Downing, etc., are capable of showing empirically that this is so, but they lack a theoretical explanation. Boserup demonstrates that it is the disparity of force between the defensive and the offensive that makes "peace" possible during which societal and state units can exist and develop.

THE STATE

Boserup's interpretation of Clausewitz's theory of "the pause" is essential to develop an alternative understanding of the concept of the state, but this requires that the concept of recognition in Hegel is included. Boserup argues that both Clausewitz and Hegel deal with the same logical configuration, but in two different contexts. The inspiration is found in Hegel's *The Phenomenology of Spirit*, in which the struggle for recognition is central as a means of achieving self-consciousness, and hence recognition (*Anerkennung*). What is decisive is

> that Hegel regards "self-consciousness" as an external, social condition, and not as something derived from internal, psychological events. Self-consciousness is to be achieved only in a mutual struggle for recognition where this is centred on the recognition of the other as identical with oneself. The recognition of the other is thus a simultaneous recognition of oneself in the other (from which follows self-recognition and self-consciousness). It is also the recognition of the other's corresponding recognition of oneself, and soon, in an infinite relation of mirroring.[28]

The argument in favour of it being a social relation is illustrated with the

27 Ibid.
28 Ibid., 923–24.

possessive "mine" as an example. What is "mine" cannot be conceived of without making a distinctive line between "mine" and "not mine." This line must necessarily be drawn externally by someone else.

In order to think the exclusion of others from what is "mine," I therefore have to experience my own exclusion, and then laterally inverse the relation.[29] Boserup connects this configuration with the state, about which he says:

> In its purest most abstract form the state has to be understood as others' recognition of it as a fully valid member of a system of states, recognition which is always uncertain and preliminary … Recognition is, also according to Hegelian thought, recognition of the ability of the state to defend itself, to compel respect.[30]

Consequently, the state, according to Boserup, is defined by the preparedness and capability to defend the status of the state "as a free and sovereign member of the system of states." Only in this way can the state achieve recognition from the other states in the society of states. This struggle for recognition continues as a "virtual" war during the pause. The struggle for recognition itself is the key to understanding the war, hence the state. The theory says nothing about the concrete causes of war themselves (nor has it any intentions thereof), as this varies from one situation to the next. But the presence of war, in the shape of an "explosive," a "virtual" and a "moderate" war can be explained as an inherent potential dimension of the struggle of recognition. This is absent in Mann's work.

The struggle for recognition as a universal feature of the history of states may explain why the system of states is of fundamental importance to their construction. The struggle for recognition is a life and death struggle. States that are unable to maintain an adequate ability of defence will often be swept away by stronger powers. Moreover, the concepts of virtual war and pause explain that even during that which we usually call peace, an "invisible" war is going on. It is this particular situation that makes specific

29 Ibid., 924.
30 Ibid.

demands on the economic, political and ideological structures of the state. This is brilliantly illustrated in several passages in the works of Mann, and it is in this sense that he and other more recent historical and comparative sociologists mentioned above foster new thoughts compared with classical sociology, although the theoretical explanation is still absent.

Instead of thinking of society and the state as a fusion created "from the inside," consisting of its internal components, Hegel and Clausewitz conceive of it as constituted in a struggle for recognition, in relation to other states. Boserup's theory makes it clear that it is impossible to understand the state as a fusion, for reasons which are, in principle, logical. The state cannot be generated first by individuals, and then enter a state system as something already developed. The concept of the state itself becomes absurd without at least two states recognizing each others' realm of sovereignty, and thus the borders.

Clausewitz's concept of pause makes a situation possible in which states have compelled respect because of the superiority of the defensive, abstain from war and instead recognize each other as free and sovereign states. Hereby, different states and their domains of sovereignty are recognized, and it is at this point in the theory that it becomes possible to speak of societies as demarcated entities. Thus, the pause, the struggle for recognition and the state become the necessary conditions for the demarcation of society.

SOVEREIGNTY

The concept of sovereignty itself is also defined differently by Boserup than by, for example, Hobbes. According to Hobbes, the individual is born with rights which he/she then passes on to the state; however, according to Boserup, sovereignty is not primarily a relation between the state and the individuals within the domain of the sovereignty of the state, but a relation between other states and the realm of sovereignty of the state concerned.

Generally speaking, it is obvious that sovereignty is neither a "right" nor a "domination"; and there does not have to be any ability on the part of the state to do anything with its realm of sovereignty. Maintaining sovereignty is not to manage and "intervene," but to prevent others from doing so.[31]

31 Ibid., 929.

The essence of the state is not internal constitutional law and order, but external "law." Only then is it possible to comprehend the internal conditions in the state, for example the constitution, the construction of institutions, etc.[32]

Boserup's theory transcends the fusion theory, and is based instead on the idea of fission. He emphasizes that the theory of fission does not imply a postulate of existence, or an account of the genesis of the state in this sense. It consists, at first, of purely theoretical concepts, requiring further specification, so that the concrete historical forms of the state can be analyzed.

The basic concept in Boserup is the system of states conceived of as a self-contained theoretical construction, consisting of mutual relations of recognition among states. States are thus fissioned by the system of states as a consequence of the mutual struggle for recognition. Whereas the state and individuals constitute war and the state system in Mann's theory, this relation is inverted in Boserup: the struggle for recognition, and therefore the war, constitutes the states and this relation generates certain conditions to the construction and development of states and societies.

Conclusion

I have demonstrated how classical sociology conceives of society and the state as a fusion. This implies the problem of the demarcation of society. Michael Mann attempts to transcend this problem by reconsidering the state as something conditioned both endogenously and exogenously. Inspired by "neo-Machiavellian" thinkers, Mann includes warfare, the state, the monopoly on violence, territorial conditions, and the external relations of the state in a synthesis of theory, in an attempt to create a more adequate analysis of the nation-state and the development of capitalism in Western Europe. However, as we can see, Mann is not capable of overcoming the problems of the fusion theory.

By examining the ideas of Hegel and Clausewitz, Boserup succeeds in radically redefining the concept of the state. Although this contribution

32 Ibid.

does not substitute the perspective on society and the state of traditional sociology, it does at least supplement it. He proves the necessity of conceiving of the state as part of a social relation which includes a multitude of states. The demarcations of the state are only conceivable in relation to another state, since the demarcations are always imposed from without. This is why the state is always a social relation, and not a private one (i.e. "created from within"). Thus, the concept of virtual war becomes central in order to understand the character of the relation among states.

Mann operates with a concept of the state which is historically conditioned and where the state is a result of a specific historical development. State and society for Boserup are general concepts. The state constituted as a relation of recognition between two states is a simple and abstract relation. Further work is needed to elaborate on this theory so that it can become applicable to concrete sociological analyses. Only here will it be possible to assess the strength of the theory.

References

Ashworth, Clive, and Christopher Dandeker. "Warfare, Social Theory, and West European Development." *Sociological Review* 35 (1987): 1–18.

Avineri, Shlomo. *The Social and Political Thought of Karl Marx*. Cambridge: Cambridge University Press, 1968.

Badie, Bertrand and Pierre Birnbaum. *The Sociology of the State*. Chicago: University of Chicago Press, 1983.

Boserup, Anders. "Staten, samfundet og krigen hos Clausewitz." In *Om krig*, by Carl von Clausewitz. Vol. 3, edited and translated by Niels Berg, 911–30. Copenhagen: Rhodos, 1986.

Boserup, Anders, and Robert Neild. *The Foundations of Defensive Defence*. London: Palgrave Macmillan, 1990.

Creighton, Colin, and Martin Shaw. *The Sociology of War and Peace*. London: Macmillan, 1987.

Durkheim, Emile. *The Division of Labour in Society* [1893]. London: Macmillan, 1984.

———. *Suicide: A Study in Sociology* [1897]. London, Routledge and Kegan Paul, 1952.

———. *Professional Ethics and Civic Morals* [1922]. London: Routledge, 1992.

Evans, Peter B., Dietrich Rueschemeyer and Theda Skocpol, eds. *Bringing the State Back In*. New York: Cambridge University Press, 1985.

Freund, Julien. *Warfare in the Modern World: A Short but Critical History*. Washington, D.C.: Plutarch Press, 1996.

Gerth, H. H., and C. Wright Mills. *From Max Weber: Essays in Sociology*. London: Routledge and Kegan Paul, 1985.

Giddens, Anthony. *Nation-State and Violence*. Cambridge: Polity, 1985.

———. *Durkheim on Politics and the State*. Cambridge: Polity, 1986.

Hall, John A., ed. *States in History*. Oxford: Blackwell, 1986.

Held, David, ed. *States and Societies*. Oxford: New York University Press, 1983.

Hirst, Paul. *War and Power in the Twenty-First Century*. Cambridge: Polity, 2001.

Hobbes, Thomas. *Leviathan (or the matter, forme and power of a commenwealth ecclesiasticall and civil)* [1651]. New York: E. P. Dutton, 1962.

Mann, Michael. "States, Ancient and Modern." *Archives Européennes de sociologie* 18 (1977): 262–98.

———. "The Autonomous Power of the State: Its Origins, Mechanism and Results." *Archives Européennes de sociologie* 25 (1984): 185–213.

———. *The Sources of Social Power.* Vol. 1, *A History of Power from the Beginning to AD 1760*. Cambridge: Cambridge University Press, 1986.

———. "War and Social Theory: Into Battle with Classes, Nations and States." In *The Sociology of War and Peace*, edited by Colin Creighton and Martin Shaw. London: Macmillan, 1987.

———. "The Roots and Contradictions of Modern Militarism." *New Left Review* 162 (1987): 35–50.

———. "Ruling Class Strategies and Citizenship." *Sociology* 21 (1987): 339–54.

———. *States, War and Capitalism: Studies in Political Sociology*. Oxford: Blackwell, 1988.

———. *The Rise and Decline of the Nation-State*. Oxford: Blackwell, 1990.

Marx, Karl. "The Eighteenth Brumaire of Louis Bonaparte" [1852]. In Karl Marx and Friedrich Engels, *Selected Works in Two Volumes*. London: Lawrence & Wishart, 1958.

Marx, Karl, and Friedrich Engels. *The Communist Manifesto* [1848]. Harmondsworth: Penguin Books, 1969.

Mommsen, W. J. *Max Weber and German Politics 1890–1920*. Chicago: University of Chicago Press, 1984.

Østerberg, Dag. *Emile Durkheims samfunnslære*. Oslo: Pax Forlag, 1983.

Parkin, Frank. *Max Weber.* London: Ellis Horwood and Tavistock Publications, 1982.

Rousseau, Jean-Jacques. *The Social Contract* [1762]. Middlesex: Penguin, 1968.

Shaw, Martin. *Dialectics of War: An Essay on the Social Theory of War and Peace.* London: Pluto Press, 1988.

———. "War and the Nation-State in Social Theory." In *Social Theory of Modern Societies: Anthony Giddens and His Critics*, edited by David Held and John B. Thompson, 129–46. Cambridge: Cambridge University Press, 1989.

———. *The Post-Military Society: Militarism, Demilitarization and War at the End of the Twentieth Century.* London: Polity Press, 1991.

Shaw, Martin, ed. *War, State and Society.* London: Macmillan, 1984.

Skocpol, Theda. *States and Social Revolutions: A Comparative Analysis of France, Russia and China*. Cambridge: Cambridge University Press, 1979.

Tilly, Charles. *Coercion, Capital, and European States, AD 990–1990*. Oxford: Blackwell, 1990.

Tilly, Charles, ed. *The Formation of National States in Western Europe*. Princeton: Princeton University Press, New Jersey 1975.

Weber, Max. *Makt og byråkrati*. Oslo: Gyldendal, 1971.

———. *Economy and Society* [1922]. 2 vols. Edited by Guenther Ross and Claus Wittich. Berkeley: University of California Press, 1978.

———. *Gesammelte Politische Schriften*. Tübingen: J. C. B. Mohr, 1991.

Williams, B. "World-State or State-World: Thomas Hobbes and the Law of Nations." In *Hobbes: War among Nations*, edited by Timo Airaksinen and Martin A. Bertman. Aldershot and Brookfield (USA): Avebury, 1989.

Genesis of the Civilian in the Western World, 1500–2000

Gunner Lind

In modern Western societies, being inside or outside of war is conceived as the product of two dichotomies: between war and peace, and between military and civilian. The distinction between war and peace is found in almost all human cultures, past and present. The distinction between military and civilian, however, is relatively recent and distinctly Western in origin.

This may come as a surprise. Speaking about civilians is ubiquitous in the discourse about war, as it is also when dealing with historical and non-Western cultures. It may even invade the discourse about violence resembling war, as when a journalist describes bystanders in clashes between criminal gangs as "civilians." But this obscures the fact that military-civilian is only the current conception of how different members of warring societies are involved in war in varying degrees. Such a distinction is indeed universal, but it has been formulated in many different ways. The concept "civilian" is particularly worthy of attention. Labels for subgroups, such as "military," are common, but it is extraordinary to have a specific term for the rest, the non-military. Ecclesiastical-lay is the only parallel in regular use. This makes it worthwhile to examine the predecessors and historical origins of this modern concept pairing.

The Current Dichotomy

Today the distinction between military and civilian in war is enshrined in law, both national and international, notably in the Fourth Geneva Convention (1949) "Relative to the Protection of Civilian Persons in Time of War" and the Additional Protocol I to the Geneva Conventions (1977).[1] The large number of signatories gives these documents global significance. The international conventions deal with behaviour in times of war, but the distinction between military and civilian is also clearly visible in times of peace. Distinctive institutions in society delimit what is military, and military professionalization shapes the behaviour and outlook of individuals. The trivial division by organization and employment has both been elevated as law and has taken root as an important social institution.

Being civilian is the default status. People are born as civilians and remain so unless they enter the military as a result of specific social actions. Other acts transform the soldier into a civilian again. These acts may be improvised and minimal – such as when volunteers join the fight against an invader, for example – but they must be present. A main point of the international conventions is to minimize ambiguity about status. At any point in time, the military-civilian dichotomy must cleave humanity sharply in two. Defining the one defines the other. In war, it is the privilege and duty of the military to signal its status through flags, colours and uniforms and by bearing arms openly. In peace, policies vary between states. However, uniforms and other symbolic indicators make it easy to recognize the soldier, at least when on duty, and to recognize buildings and objects as belonging to the military establishment.

In war, military or civilian status is supposed to govern the relationship between enemies. Civilians are not allowed to damage the enemy. On the other hand, the enemy must minimize damage to civilians as far as it does not make it impossible for them to fight their armed adversaries. In short, civilians are neither allowed to be active nor to be targets, still less to be victimized. International law extends special protection to certain elements of the civilian population, such as children and the sick, but this is less important than the general obligation to minimize the implications of war for civilians. Grey areas do, of course, abound in the real world. What is minimal damage? When and how do civilians acquire military status? And so on. But this does not diminish the clarity or wide acceptance of the basic

1 Authoritative texts of these and related documents can be found at the International Red Cross website, http://www.icrc.org.

principles. Compared with the vast dimensions of military activities, the grey areas are not overly large.

In times of peace, being in the military is an occupation. It is not a standard job, as can be seen from a number of special traits, varying from state to state, such as garrison life, military courts or conscription. Even in extreme cases, however, it is only one of many specialized professions. Describing this with such unusual language as the military-civilian dichotomy points to the importance of conditions outside of contemporary everyday life. The current military-civilian distinction has been shaped by two partially interdependent developments: changing ideas about classes of people in times of war; and the development of the dividing line surrounding the military institution and military trade within peaceful societies.

The Hierarchy of Arms

Around the year 1500, the military as a permanent state institution did not exist, or almost did not.[2] Most rulers limited their military establishment to court and castle guards, numbered in the hundreds. The kings of France and Spain maintained permanent field units, but even these were only a tiny fraction of later French and Spanish armies. Rulers and republics fought their wars with armies assembled for the occasion. These armies were a mixture of three classes of warriors: firstly, there were the soldiers; that is, mercenaries organized by a military entrepreneur and hired for as short a time as possible, due to the high costs. Secondly, there were the nobles: members of the hereditary warrior estate who followed their lord and were accompanied by their own armed followers. Finally, there were the armed subjects of the lower orders who owed their obedience to the warring lord. Despite the existence of specialized warriors, other men did regularly possess weapons and were expected to take part according to their ability. The duty to participate in local defence was recognized everywhere,

2 Neither, some will argue, did the state, following a narrow definition such as that of Max Weber. Max Weber, *Wirtschaft und Gesellschaft: Grundriss der verstehenden Soziologie*, ed. Johannes Winckelmann (Tübingen: J. C. B. Mohr, 1976), Part I: § 17. However, I will follow the majority of scholars who adhere to less strict definitions such as that offered by Charles Tilly (Charles Tilly, *Coercion, Capital, and European States, A.D. 990–1992*, rev. ed., Oxford: Basil Blackwell, 1995, 1).

but it was also not rare to see armed burghers or select peasant militias participate in more ambitious undertakings.[3]

Instead of a single line dividing the fighting men from the rest, we see a hierarchy of arms. Simplified, it had three levels:

- those whose social role it was to be a warrior, such as noblemen and mercenaries;
- the rest of the male gender, excluding the very poor and sometimes the clergy;
- women and children.

The hierarchy had more levels, when looked at in more detail. The nobility was of varying size and composition in different European regions. At the individual level, the hereditary warriors were not warriors to the same degree, even if they all posed for their portrait wearing swords and even armour. Mercenaries were real fighting men; but some contemporaries challenged the legitimacy of the warrior status of the low-born among the professionals. Among the rest of the male gender, we find a progression according to wealth. Everybody had to find their own arms and equipment; one needed money to own weapons, so therefore the rich were more likely to do so and were more likely to be trained in their use and to carry the arms they owned. The head of the household had more and better weapons than the household's other male members. He would arm himself first and was likely to be the owner of the arms with which his sons and servants were equipped. Burghers were better armed and were more likely to engage in war than the peasants, and wealthy peasants more likely to do so than the poor. Both within and between the estates, the hierarchy of arms was to a high degree also the hierarchy of money, status and power, from the king down to the women. Few armaments were exclusively instruments of

3 Some of the many major works on the military of this era are, for example: Eugen von Frauenholz, *Entwicklungsgeschichte des deutschen Heerwesens*, 5 vols. (Munich: C. H. Beck Verlag, 1935–1941), vols. 1–2; Philippe Contamine, *La guerre au Moyen Age* (Paris: Presses universitaires de France, 1980); J. R. Hale, *War and Society in Renaissance Europe 1450–1620* (London: Fontana, 1985), André Corvisier, ed. *Histoire militaire de la France*, 4 vols. (Paris: Presses Universitaires de France, 1992–1994), vol. 1.

war. They were general instruments of power and were likely to be deployed in conflicts of all kinds, both at the top and the bottom of the social scale.

Such a hierarchy of arms was not new. There were long-term trends such as, for example, towards a greater specialization of roles for the nobility, towards an increasing use of mercenaries and towards internal pacification, thus making arms less relevant for the common man. These trends accelerated during the sixteenth and seventeenth centuries, but the basic pattern can be followed back for centuries and weakened only very gradually.

Expressing the Hierarchy of Arms

In such a society, there was nothing that resembled a "military." Instead, we find a wealth of gradations. Even in specific situations in war it was often not at all clear to what degree the people of the enemy society ought to be regarded as adversaries. No standard symbolic indicators distinguished the different levels in the hierarchy of arms in the same obvious way as the uniform distinguishes the modern military. The men at the top of this hierarchy, both nobles and mercenaries, went around armed, normally with a sword. Others might do so, however, when travelling, for example, or out of a sense of ambition. Restrictions on owning or bearing arms were rare. Such restrictions had specific aims, such as the repression of street violence in cities, or to prevent poaching, and access to arms was rarely protected as a privilege before the eighteenth century.[4] Much more legislative effort was expended on the futile attempts to keep the silks and velvets of the nobility away from commoners.[5] Belonging to the hereditary warrior estate was signalled by the combination of arms and costly dress, forcing the poorer noblemen into problematic spending and making it possible for others to assimilate their appearance to that of the nobility.

Some mercenaries developed special dress styles. The German *Landsknechten* and the Swiss *Reisläufer* of the late fifteenth and early sixteenth

4 André Corvisier, ed., *Armées et sociétés en Europe de 1494 à 1789* (Paris: Presses universitaires de la France, 1976), 19. Joyce Lee Malcolm, *Guns and Violence: The English Experience* (Cambridge, Mass.: Harvard University Press, 2002), 14–89.

5 For example, in France. See Daniel Roche, *The Culture of Clothing: Dress and Fashion in the Ancien Régime*, trans. Jean Birrell (Cambridge: Cambridge University Press, 1994), 49, 56.

centuries are famous for their fanciful costume. This fitted well with the strong sense of a separate collective identity among these elite combatants. Exaggerated dress – at once costly, sensational and outside of mainstream taste – signalled their pretence of independence and their lack of subordination to the general social hierarchy.[6]

Others may have been dressed in livery. These could have included servants and subordinates, perhaps even nobles themselves, in the courts of the princes and great lords; or they might be other followers who were not in daily service. Liveries might be worn as a regular feature, or for special occasions. The wearer of a livery was quite likely to be warlike, as princes and lords were followed by many fighting men; but liveries signified service, not warrior status as such.[7]

Many, perhaps most, mercenary soldiers were not dressed in any specific way. Arms and armour were combined with everyday costume corresponding to their means, preferably adapted to the demands of the job. Strong shoes, hats and mantles, leather breeches for horsemen, perhaps some feathers or other pretence at sharing the style of the noblemen, did not add up to any great divergence from the dress of others.[8] Neither did carrying a sword, as swords were so common.

Like the symbolic language of dress, spoken and written language did not express any simple division such as the military-civilian dichotomy. Instead, we find a large number of terms in contemporary texts which correspond to the many elements in the hierarchy of arms. Such terms might be used in a concrete way, such as, for example, the halberdiers, the gunners, the soldiers (in the original meaning of the designation, as professionals serving for pay) or the noblemen. They might also be used less realistically, as when panegyrics praised the hereditary nobles as the *bellatores,* the *Wehrstand*, the warriors or defenders of society, as if they were the only fighting

6 Reinhard Baumann, *Landsknechte. Ihre Geschichte und Kultur vom späten Mittelalter bis zum Dreißigjährigen Krieg* (Munich: C. H. Beck Verlag, 1994), 39–45; Andrea Denny-Brown, "Rips and Slits: The Torn Garment and the Medieval Self," in *Clothing Culture, 1350–1650*, ed. Catherine Richardson (Aldershot: Ashgate, 2004), 223–37.

7 Liveries and lords have been best studied in connection with the English developments often called bastard feudalism, see e.g. Michael Hicks, *Bastard Feudalism* (London: Longman, 1995). For the liveries of servants, see Roche, *The Culture of Clothing*, 100–1.

8 Roche, *The Culture of Clothing*, 221.

men. Equally unrealistic was the use of "man" as a code for "warrior," as if every man was a fighter. This was strongly embedded in everyday language; "manliness" meant "martial courage" in many, if not all, languages, and weapons were standard codes for the "spear side" in art and in speech.

European languages also possessed two classes of general terms. There was one for the en masse group who were actually conducting war, such as the "army," "armée," "Heer," "hær"; and there was another for the actual people in the army, as a class or as individuals. This class of labels were derived from the word "war": "war-man," "warrer," "warrior," "guerrier," "Kriegsmann," "Kriegsleute," "krigsfolk," and so on. The latter label (a man or person of war) might be used for any group or conglomerate of groups whose business was war – very useful considering the mixed nature of most actual fighting forces.[9]

In contrast most attempts at describing the group of non-warriors seem to be catalogues or lists. A good example can be taken from the contemporary ballad on the Danish victory at Falkenberg in 1570: "[A] Christian prince waging war … may strike freely at those who are causing him damage. He may persecute his enemies and men capable of defence but women, children and habitable land ought to be protected. It is often said that a warrior should not be merciful, but this must be understood correctly if he desires to fight with honour. [He must show his strength against his enemies,] but he will gain small honour from murdering poor innocent children and other people, or miserable women, with his dagger and pike."[10]

The vague contours of the group we would call civilians are drawn by superimposing several dividing lines. It is made clear by repetition that women and children form the core. Gender and age are not the only criteria, however. A division can be made according to intent (those who are

9 Dictionaries consulted: (English) *The Oxford English Dictionary* (1888–, http://dictionary.oed.com); (Danish) *Ordbog over det danske Sprog* (1918-1954, http://ordnet.dk/ods/); *Ordbog til det ældre danske Sprog (1300–1700)* (1881–1907, http://www.hist.uib.no/kalkar/). (French) *Dictionnaires d'autrefois. French dictionaries of the 17th, 18th, 19th and 20th centuries* ([1606–1935], http://www.lib.uchicago.edu/efts/ARTFL/projects/dicos/). (German) *Deutsche Wörterbuch* (1852–, http://www.dwb.uni-trier.de/). (Swedish) *Ordbok över svenska språket, utg. av Svenska akademien* (1898– , http://g3.spraakdata.gu.se/saob/).

10 "Slaget ved Falkenberg," in *Danske Viser fra Adelsvisebøger og Flyveblade 1530–1630*, 1–7, ed. H. Grüner-Nielsen (Copenhagen: Gyldendal, 1912), 1: 113–24, 4: 62–76. The ballad addresses this theme because the Swedes are accused of such crimes.

not enemies), or according to ability (those who do not cause damage or those who are incapable of bearing arms[11]). The status of men is vague; they are likely to be enemies, but they may be friendly, or they may be poor or otherwise incapable of defending themselves. With so many dividing lines, coherence becomes a question. Are all women really innocent, or are all those who might be poor incapable of doing damage? Specifying who among the enemy were not real enemies was an exercise in ambiguity.

The Innocent

The text of the ballad quoted above attempts to define the "civilian" group because the author – clearly not a fighting man himself – exhorts those who are fighting to protect those on the list from the wrath of war. He was not alone. Learned men routinely taught that the "innocent" ought to be spared. This term was central in the discussion of what came to be called the *jus in bello,* the limits of legitimate violence in war – a discussion which expanded rapidly in scope and importance over the sixteenth and seventeenth centuries.[12] Within this specialized discourse, the term "innocent" came close to being a general label for the non-warriors.

The term "innocent" was important because it formed a link to the traditionally more important discussion of the *jus ad bellum*, the right to wage war. Since Augustine, it had been established doctrine in the Christian world that making war was not by definition sinful, but wars had to be just according to criteria which were reasonably clear in theory even if less easy to apply in practice. In practice, everybody tended to assume that their war was just and that therefore, logically, the enemy was waging an unjust war. If you do what is not just, you are guilty. So the innocent were those who for some reason did not share in the guilt, despite being associated with the enemy party, and so ought to be spared the hard fate of the guilty.

Scholars differed in their definition of the innocent and the amount of protection they demanded for them. The most famous theorist of the sixteenth century, the Spaniard Francisco de Vitoria, declared that children

11 The original uses the word "værhaftig."

12 Richard Shelly Hartigan, *The Forgotten Victim: A History of the Civilian* (Chicago: Precedent, 1982), 82–102.

were always innocent, as were women, except for "any individual woman who is certainly guilty."[13] He continued to proclaim "harmless agricultural folk … innocent until the contrary is shown." Likewise, "clerics and members of a religious order … are presumed innocent unless the contrary be shown, as when they engage in actual fighting."[14] Vitoria went even further when he specified that the women and children of the infidel Turk were innocent too, and when he asserted that the innocent ought not only be spared from death but also from violence, enslavement and looting. It might be acceptable in a just war that the innocent get hurt, but the risk of such collateral damage should mean that military leaders must exercise restraint.

Despite the variations, the scholarly discourse had a considerable common core that was shaped by the traditional concepts of justice and innocence. Part of this core was the realization that the degree of involvement of adults in war meant that they had to be judged by their actual acts, by their ability to act, even by their intent. Visible social status, such as gender and age, could only provide a hint. The scholarly texts described a hierarchy of innocence which resembled the complex and vaguely delimited hierarchy of arms. But it was not a mirror image, as the focus was more on acts and intent, and less on fighting potential and social status. The label "innocent" stressed the element of intent. Scholars sometimes struggled to find a term appropriate for the description of non-combatant men. Vitoria writes "pubes togati" when describing grown men who are as harmless as poor peasants[15] – an allusion to ancient Rome, where the unpractical toga had to be exchanged for other dress, probably armour, before a man could fight.

How well did practice conform to the ideas of the scholars? The protection of women, young children and clergy was an oft-repeated item in military statutes of the influential German tradition, beginning with the 1508 Articles of Emperor Maximilian I. This clause, or clauses to the same effect, was adopted by most German states and several of Germany's neigh-

13 Franciscus de Victoria, *De Indis et de iure belli relectiones*, ed. John Pawley Bate, Ernest Nys and Herbert F. Wright (Washington, D.C.: Carnegie Institution, 1917), 179.

14 Ibid.

15 Ibid., 270, 89. Literally, grown men wearing the toga. Also "gens togata et pacifica": ibid., 288.

bours.[16] In well-disciplined armies, transgressors may have been punished. With or without such attempts at discipline, the narratives of war provide abundant evidence that those fighting did not destroy without distinction. The innocent might be targeted, even explicitly as a strategy of terror, but as routine only in connection with bombardments. This relative protection may be connected with the question of honour that was so prominent in the worldview of a profoundly hierarchical society. The innocent were poor and miserable; they must be spared out of pity, not out of respect. If respect was involved, it was self-respect. To show mercy was to show domination: a source of honour and pride. But it was also expedient to minimize the number of armed adversaries and create a pacified population where necessities and plunder might be found. If the innocent were not targeted as adversaries, they were victimized on a large scale. All classes of warriors tended to regard the conquered enemy as booty – not only their possessions, but also, in many ways, their bodies. Apart from the clergy, those labelled "innocent" were the subordinate of early modern societies, the "poor and miserable" as they were so often called. Little honour could be gained from killing them because they had no honour themselves. If they were shown mercy, it was as objects of contempt; and such contempt might also lead to their destruction.

In brief, the hierarchy of innocence was visible in practice; but for the fighting men, "innocent" in the meaning of "not harmful" was much more important than "not guilty," the crucial distinction for the scholars. The innocent should be spared, but as harmlessness was associated with subordination, innocence offered little protection against plunder and abuse. Who counted as innocent, and thus as the nearest equivalent to what would later be called civilian, was extremely fluid and negotiable, dependent on the situation and on individual acts and interpretations, not because of a lack of observation or analytical rigour, but because of the realities in a

16 [J.F.S.], ed., *Corpus Juris Militaris. Darinnen insonderheit Das Churfürstliche Brandenburgische Krieges-Recht und Artickels-Brieff, von neuen übersehen und verbessert, wie auch verschiedener anderer hohen Potentaten Kriegs-Satzungen und Observationen enthalten* (Frankfurt and Leipzig: Rupert Völcker, 1687), part 1: 3, 6, 35, 52, 60–61, 68, 69, 192–93, 98, 258, 355, 406, 51–52, part 2: 96, 107, part 3: 3, 12, 20–21, 29, 97–98, 279–80.

society where weapons were privately owned and widely disseminated and where warrior status was assigned according to several principles.

The Military of the State

The social organization of warfare changed dramatically during the sixteenth and seventeenth centuries. This transformation was pioneered by Spain, Sweden and the Netherlands in the sixteenth century, spread to many other states at the time of the Thirty Years' War, and became almost universal in western Europe during the wars of Louis XIV. The transformation has been the subject of much debate, and is indeed difficult to subsume under a single heading.[17] So many aspects of war and its organization changed: tactics, technology, military organization and governance, the social composition of armies and navies. What matters in our context is the establishment of armies and navies as large, permanent state institutions, financed by taxes, governed by bureaucrats and bureaucratic regulation, and consisting of hired soldiers equipped with arms issued by the state. If these armies used conscripts – and many did – they were equipped, trained and organized as much like professionals as possible. The military entrepreneurs who recruited and commanded earlier mercenaries were gradually changed into career officers, becoming military variations on the theme of the bureaucratic state servant.[18]

Some of these traits could also be found in earlier permanent establishments, but the scale had changed. Army strength in times of peace was now somewhere between a half and a fifth of the strength in times of war, instead of a tiny fraction. At the same time, the trend was towards larger armies. Permanence was costly, but it made the new military hugely successful. Permanence on this scale transformed armies and navies into "containers" preserving competence between wars.[19] When war came, trained and competent soldiers could be deployed immediately, could be managed

17 An overview of the controversies can be found in Clifford J. Rogers, ed., *The Military Revolution Debate: Readings on the Military Transformation of Early Modern Europe* (Boulder: Westview Press, 1995).

18 Jan Glete, *War and the State in Early Modern Europe: Spain, the Dutch Republic and Sweden as Fiscal-Military States, 1500–1660* (London: Routledge, 2002), 10–66.

19 Ibid., 63, 214.

better and serve as instructors and cadres for new men. This gave a huge qualitative advantage over old-fashioned warriors of all kinds. The new armies were better, perhaps not man for man, but unit for unit; and the high costs produced more efficient violence for each pound, dollar or ducat.

This extensive shift towards the ideal type of the "state monopoly of violence" gradually made other warrior types irrelevant. From the sixteenth to the eighteenth century, noble uprisings and peasant revolts became dramatically fewer and had less and less chance of success. Local men turning out with their own arms for local defence were no longer able to confront the threats which were probable in war. Noble levies ceased to be mobilized in war, even in states where they had been modernized along professional lines. The Danish *rostjeneste* appeared for the last time in 1675, the French *ban et arrière-ban* in 1697.[20]

Few of the steps in this transformation process were conceived as system changes. Mostly rulers acted *ad hoc* in response to perceived needs or opportunities. Many important changes were quantitative shifts rather than clear cut transformations. But the net effect was a comprehensive change in the social organization of war and a redistribution of the potential for violence, both in times of war and in times of peace. The old hierarchy of arms was not abolished with one stroke, but it did disappear from the centre stage. Noble or gentle birth was a career advantage inside the military, but even gentlemen were now assumed to need training and incorporation into the state military before they were useful. The ownership of arms still had few restrictions and was probably quite widespread, but the equipping of armies now came from the state. Housing and clothing the soldier became a state responsibility. This enabled recruitment from all classes, including the poorest. Wealth and status heavily influenced military career prospects, but poverty was no longer a bar to military participation. Gender was the only traditional category still standing. Soldiers were supposed to be male – but men were less and less supposed to be warriors; when women enlisted, they did so disguised as men.[21]

20 Otto Vaupell, *Den danske Hærs Historie til Nutiden og Den norske Hærs Historie indtil 1814*, 2 vols. (Copenhagen: Gyldendal, 1872), 2: 583. John Lynn, *Giant of the Grand Siecle: The French Army, 1610–1715* (Cambridge: Cambridge University Press, 1997), 371.

21 On the military of this age, see, for example: Frauenholz, *Entwicklungsgeschichte*, vols.

Establishing the Civilian

These changes made the dividing line between professional soldiers and others the only division really relevant in war. Other men could be lumped in with the women and children. The dividing line was sharp. Becoming a soldier requires enlisting in a fighting unit acting under the licence of a political authority, and a soldier returns to civilian status again by being discharged. The social division could be read with precision from the rolls of the military bureaucracies that recorded formal and often public acts.

The changes made it highly desirable to find simple terms for those inside and outside the new large institution in society. The systematic use of the neo-Latin terms "military" and "civilian" may well have originated among lawyers. Lawyers needed to speak about the special law codes and the courts of law of the professional armies, and they traditionally labelled what was general, not specialized, with words stemming from the Latin *civilis*. The Latin *miles* (soldier) had been in continuous use since antiquity to describe the various classes of fighting men. Other early adopters of the terms were administrators and politicians who wanted to distinguish between civilian and military officers and budgets, etc. An example of how the words spread can be taken from Swedish, where it is particularly well documented. In Swedish, "military" is first documented as describing the state army as a sector of society in 1626, appropriately enough in a text written by King Gustavus Adolphus himself. In 1635, a political document speaks about the "civilian and military ordinary budgets." The "military estate" as a group in society is mentioned in 1661; "civilian office" as opposed to military in 1663; "civilian and military officers" in 1664; the "civilian establishment" (i.e. administration) in 1671; and "civilian person" in 1730.[22] "Military" often supplanted older compound words based on the

3–5; Corvisier, ed., *Histoire militaire de la France*, vols. 1–2; Jeremy Black, *A Military Revolution? Military Change and European Society, 1550–1800* (Basingstoke: Macmillan Education, 1991); Jeremy Black, *European Warfare, 1660–1815* (London: UCL Press, 1994).

22 *Ordbok over svenska språket utgiven av Svenska Akademien*, s. v. "Militia," "Militär," "Civil I," "Civil II," "Civil III," "Civilist" and combinations. "Civilist" is the noun form in Swedish.

root "krig" (war).[23] Swedish was the language of a society in the forefront of military change, but development in other languages seems to be similar both in chronology and in the ways in which the words were used.[24]

The conceptual dichotomy was thus established by specialists dealing with the new state military, such as lawyers, administrators and politicians. In the language of the seventeenth century it was typically used when speaking of particulars, in compound words and set phrases, and about institutions, organizations, laws, etc., rather than people. Speaking of "civilian" and "military" as a general quality of persons came later, in around 1700 or during the first decades of the eighteenth century. "Civilian" had still not become a noun, however, and "military" described the institution rather than the men, except when used as an adjective.

The new concept pair was only used to describe institutions of society seen from the inside, i.e. in a peaceful context. In speaking of war, and especially when discussing the enemy, the terms were not "military" versus "civilian," but "the soldiers" or "the army" versus "the population" or "the inhabitants," to be understood as specific groups of people rather than general categories.[25] In learned discourse, which did focus on classes of people in general, "innocent" was still the most important term for seventeenth-century scholars, including Hugo Grotius.[26] He described the innocent in traditional terms as children first, then women, then many men. Like Vitoria a century before, he clearly lacked a term for what he clumsily described as "males, whose modes of life are entirely remote from the use of arms."[27]

23 S. A. Nilsson, *På väg mot militärstaten. Krigsbefalets etablering i den äldre Vasatidens Sverige* (Uppsala: Historiska institutionen, 1989), 13–15.

24 For other languages, see footnote 9.

25 For dictionaries: see footnote 9. Language use has been additionally studied by searches for the relevant terms in *Early English Books Online* (http://eebo.chadwyck.com/) and *Gallica, bibliothèque numérique* (http://gallica.bnf.fr/).

26 Hartigan, *Forgotten Victim*, 82–100.

27 "de maribus quorum vitae genus ab armis abhorret." Hugo Grotius, *Hugonis Grotii De iure belli ac pacis libri tres in quibus ius naturae & gentium: item iuris publici praecipua explicantur* [1652], ed. B. J. A. de Kanter-van Hettinga Tromp (Leiden: E. J. Brill, 1939), 754. The translation follows the version printed in London 1814, cf. http://www.constitution.org/gro.

The Dominance of the State Military

The eighteenth century saw the disappearance of most of the old hierarchy of arms – not as an element of the social order, but as a practical instrument in the preparation for war. A sign of the times was the reconstitution of local defence. Coastal and regional defence arrangements had always rested on the mobilization of the best-equipped part of the male population under the leadership of local dignitaries. The duty to serve might be prescribed by royal decree, but organizations were not really guided or governed by the state. Now local associations and independent volunteer services went into decline as fighting units, even if they continued as social symbols of upper class manliness. New militias were constituted as part-time branches of the state army; they were divided into regiments, had officers with military titles, and standardized arms and uniforms. Officers and men might even be paid. In all cases they formed a subgroup of the soldiery when under arms, and individuals often moved between militia and army. The distinction between military and civilian had to take the degree of mobilization into account, but it could be made, and along the same principles as when dealing with the full-time military.[28]

During the eighteenth century, men who were not military began to be exempted from service if they did not own or use arms. The practice of duelling came under severe criticism, and in some countries tended to be seen as an element of military culture, not a social institution relevant for all men of honour.[29] The sword was still a necessary element of fashionable male dress until the middle of the century, but then men of indisputable wealth, power and status began walking around unarmed, notably in England. The walking stick replaced the sword as the mark of social respecta-

28 Claude C. Sturgill, *La formation de la milice permanente en France (1726–1730)* (Paris: Service historique de l'armée de terre, 1975); Yvonick Danard and Armelle Gautier, "La Milice de l' Ancien Régime en Bretagne," *Revue Historique des armées,* no. 205 (1996): 115–25; John R. Western, *The English Militia in the XVIIIth Century: The Story of a Political Issue 1660–1802* (London: Routledge and Kegan Paul PLC, 1965); Stephen Conway, *War, State, and Society in Mid-Eighteenth-Century Britain and Ireland* (Oxford: Oxford University Press, 2006), 56–66.

29 Sune Christian Pedersen, *På liv og død. Duellens historie i Danmark* (Copenhagen: Gyldendal, 2003), 134–36, 80–88.

bility.[30] Like the sword, the stick could only be worn with difficulty if you had to work with your hands. So it did demonstrate wealth and rank; but it was a symbol of authority, not of warlikeness, and only vaguely hinted at the possible enforcement of authority through the personal exercise of violence.

On the other side of the civilian-military divide, the military uniform triumphed as a symbolic expression of the separateness of soldiers. Uniforms for private soldiers became the norm during the second half of the seventeenth century, combining the heraldic colours of liveries with the functional traits of soldier costume. Regimental distinctiveness was soon subordinated to a national basic pattern. Officers began to wear uniforms around 1700, and uniforms as daily wear for officers was enforced by regulation in many states during the eighteenth century. For some decades around the middle of the century, the visual distinction between civilian and military was almost total. Even naval officers were issued uniforms.[31] This testified to the prestige of the uniform both as a livery of the state and as the mark of the armed man. This prestige was so high, however, that other servants of state and court demanded and got uniforms during the last decades of the eighteenth century, typically also including sidearms. Among elite men, warrior connotations were surely still attractive and this made it difficult to maintain the outward separation of the military man; but symbolic details may have helped in this respect.[32]

30 Aileen Ribeiro, *Art of Dress* (New Haven: Yale University Press, 1995), 36, 78.

31 Paul Martin, *European Military Uniforms: A Short History* (London: Spring Books, 1967); Erik Bellander, *Dräkt och uniform. Den svenska arméns beklädnad från 1500-talets början fram till våra dagar* (Stockholm: Norstedts, 1973); Erik Borg, *Den danske marines uniformer gennem tre århundreder* (København: Strubes Forlag, 1974); Brian Lyndon, "Military Dress and Uniformity, 1680–1720," *Journal of the Society for Army Historical Research* 54, no. 218 (1976): 108–20; Roche, *The Culture of Clothing*, 221–58; Amy Miller, *Dressed to Kill: British Naval Uniform, Masculinity and Contemporary Fashions, 1748–1857* (London: National Maritime Museum, 2007); Gunner Lind, "Uniform and Distinction: Symbolic Aspects of Officer Dress in the Eighteenth-Century Danish State," *Textile History* 41, Supplement (2010): 49–65.

32 *Uniformen für's Zivile. Zur Geschichte uniformer Kleidung als symbolischer Kommunikation* (Krefeld: Deutsche Textilmuseum, 2002); Philip Mansel, "Monarchy, Uniform and the Rise of the Frac 1760–1830," *Past and Present*, no. 96 (1982); Lind, "Uniform and Distinction."

In the realm of language, the word pair military-civilian spread outside the circles of the specialists. The words began to appear as shorthand labels for persons. At some point during the last decades of the eighteenth century or the first decades of the nineteenth, the *noun* "a civilian" comes into use in many languages. It is first recorded in Swedish in 1799; in English in 1829.[33] Already in 1830, it was denounced as the "fashionable and most childish use of this word now current" because it clashed with the older meaning, an expert in Civil Law.[34] But a generation later, a student of language noted about the new use of the word that "its prevalence is well nigh universal" and that "as we needed, in soldier, a substantive of military, so we needed a substantive of civil, as contrasted with military."[35] This need was so dominating that older uses of "civil" and "civilian" often retreated into oblivion, except for a few combinations such as "civil law." The new use had gained the field, demonstrating how important the military-civilian dichotomy had become in discourse in general. The dichotomy might even be expressed in old-fashioned terms as two estates: "Who does not belong to the military estate, belongs to the civilian estate."[36]

The word pair had become common when speaking about social life under peaceful conditions, but it was still not preferred when dealing with groups of people in times of war. It was probably not even used at all. One example is the prominent eighteenth century theorist of war, Emerich de Vattel. De Vattel is very conscious of the recent transformations which had created a sharp dividing line: "Formerly, every one capable of carrying arms became a soldier when his nation was at war, and especially when it was attacked. … At present, war is carried out by regular troops."[37] Accordingly

33 *Svenska Akademiens Ordbok,* s.v. "civilist"; *Oxford English Dictionary,* s. v. "Civilian." In French, the first dictionary definition even of the adjective is from the 1832 dictionary of the Académie, *Dictionnaires d'autrefois,* s. v. "civil." In French, the noun form is often replaced by compound terms or the word "bourgeois" – a translation of the Latin term into the modern French equivalent.

34 *Oxford English Dictionary*, s.v. "Civilian." The condemnation was issued by Thomas de Quincey.

35 Fitzedward Hall, *Recent Exemplifications of False Philology* (New York: Scribner, Armstrong and Co., 1872), 10.

36 "Wer nicht zum Militairstande gehört, gehört zum Civilstande." Fr. von Sengespeik and Chr. von Schneider, *Der Officier. Eine Anleitung fur junge Leute, welche diese Benennung verdienen und im Militairstande Glück machen wollen* (Glückstadt, 1810), 146.

37 Emer de Vattel, *Le droit de gens ou principes de la loi naturelle, appliqués à la conduite et*

he describes one side of the dichotomy in specific terms as "soldiery" or "regular troops." But the non-soldiers are still described by a very varied vocabulary, sometimes as a list: "the people, the peasants, the citizens"; "the unarmed inhabitants."[38]

Even if he did not use the word "innocent," de Vattel closely followed the discussion of Vitoria and Grotius. Like them, de Vattel wrote first about the restrictions on violence against children, women and old men, then of the clergy and other groups with a traditional claim to immunity, followed by peasants and other peaceful inhabitants of occupied areas. It is only in the last paragraph that reflection upon the recent changes in the practice of war stimulates new ideas about the way in which war divides people into groups with different roles.

The rich debate in enlightenment Europe produced a range of viewpoints, not necessarily as conservative as that of de Vattel. Among the most radical was Rousseau, who defined war as a relationship between states, where the soldiers of each state were the only enemies, and even then not fully so as they were also citizens and men.[39] Yet Rousseau had no concept for the non-soldiers; he comes closest when speaking of "particuliers" (private) as people outside a relation to the state.[40]

The Nineteenth-Century Codification of Humanitarian International Law

In discarding "innocent," de Vattel had nothing that resembled a general term for the non-soldiers – an early example of a trend. Some eighteenth century theorists, such as Jean-Jacques Burlamachi, did still speak of "innocents" (mixed with a catalogue of other expressions, like de Vattel),[41] but

aux affaires des nations et des souverains, ed. P. Pradier-Fodéré, 3 vols. (Paris: Guillaumin, 1863), 3: 14–15. French terms are: "troupes reglées," "le people, les paysans, les bourgeois", "habitants désarmés."

38 Ibid., 14–15.

39 Geoffrey Best, *Humanity in Warfare: The Modern History of the International Law of Armed Conflicts* (London: Weidenfield and Nicolson, 1980), 54–58.

40 Jean-Jacques Rousseau, *Du contrat social ou principes du droit politique* [1762], (Paris: Libraire de la Bibliothèque Nationale, 1894), 23–24.

41 Jean-Jacques Burlamaqui, *Principes du droit de la nature et des gens*, ed. M. Dupin, 2nd ed., 5 vols. (Paris: Warée, 1820–1821), 5: 116–71.

this terminology was disappearing, and there was no immediate replacement.

The many major texts on the law of war which were written during the nineteenth century use a large number of terms. Henri Dunant writes of *soldats*, *combattants*, *militaires*. He uses the term *vie civile*, but the general population is never called "civilian" or given any other general label.[42] Several terms are used in the influential *Instructions for the Government of Armies of the United States in the Field* issued in 1863 and authored by Francis Lieber.[43] Here, a number of paragraphs deal with "the distinction between the private individual belonging to a hostile country and the hostile country itself, with its men in arms." In parallel with the "private individual," Lieber writes "the unarmed citizen," "[p]rivate citizens," "the inoffensive individual," "the inoffensive citizen." The counterpart is "the soldier" but also "the belligerent."[44] Lieber uses "civil" solely to distinguish state servants not of the military *profession*, such as "civil officers," "civil or diplomatic service," as had been current since the seventeenth century. At one point, Lieber makes a general dichotomy, but uses other words: "All enemies in regular war are divided into two general classes – that is to say, into combatants and non-combatants, or unarmed citizens of the hostile government."[45] This word pair, made by adding a new negative to the old word "combatant," had been used in military parlance for a generation or two for another purpose: to distinguish between true soldiers and unarmed members of the armed forces, such as surgeons or clerks.[46] Now it was drafted into service as a first attempt to impose a general dichotomy in relation to a people in war.

At this point in time, "civilian" and "military" were established as the standard terminologies in times of peace, both in English and in German, Lieber's mother tongue. But Lieber never uses these words as a pair. The difference in war is described by several concepts representing a number of

42 Henri Dunant, *Un souvenir de Solférino* (Geneva: CICR, 1986 [1862]).

43 Edited and commented in Richard S. Hartigan, *Lieber's Code and the Law of War* (Chicago: Precedent, 1983). Text available as "General Orders No. 100: Instructions for the Government of Armies of the United States in the Field," http://avalon.law.yale.edu/19th_century/lieber.asp.

44 "General Orders No. 100," §§ 22, 23, 25, 57.

45 Ibid., § 155.

46 *Oxford English Dictionary*. s.v. "Combatant," "Non-combatant."

distinctions: the individual as different from the (warring) state; the presence or non-presence of arms; the harmless as distinct from the dangerous; the fighting as different from being at peace. Such persons are distinguished from those of the military profession, but also from "those fighting" without any explicit presumption about the relationship of the latter to the state military establishment. Implicitly, however, the frequent use of "private" and "individual" reveals that the non-combatant is conceived as not linked to the state and vice versa, reflecting the extreme dominance of the state military in the actual fighting during wars of this era.

Like earlier theorists and lawmakers, Lieber, and his political backer Abraham Lincoln, wanted to limit targeting and victimization. But Lieber's code did also contain a type of prohibition which was new in such a formal context. This was that men committing hostilities "without being part and portion of the organized hostile army" were to be treated as robbers or pirates. Summary punishment, including death, was also the fate of "persons within an occupied territory who rise in arms against the occupying or conquering army."[47]

The Lieber code was not intended to create new rules, but to codify current best practice. Less complete and authoritative expressions of the same ideas can be found from the second half of the eighteenth century, if not earlier.[48] The code contains numerous references to the difference between the "modern" and "European" way of war and those of former times or barbarous nations. The change is attributed to "civilization" and to "principles of justice, faith, and honor."[49] But most of all, it reflects how military considerations had shaped the routine of state armies. Considerations of military efficiency made it desirable to target none but the soldiers of the enemy, but not to spare anybody in the way of operations. Considerations of supply and discipline made it desirable to suppress random violence and plunder. Operating along these lines also demanded that enemy soldiers could be clearly identified. Civilians engaging in hostile acts thus appeared as transgressors, not only enemies.

47 "General Orders No. 100," §§ 82, 83, 85.
48 Best, *Humanity in Warfare*, 59–74, 112–26.
49 "General Orders No. 100," §§ 22–30.

The Lieber code had considerable influence on the international agreements made from the mid-nineteenth to the early twentieth century which saw the establishment of laws of war as multilateral treaties for the first time. However, these conventions were much less verbose on the relationship between the armies of the warring states and private individuals and did not share the vocabulary. The nineteenth-century Geneva resolutions and conventions on the wounded in war mention the "inhabitants of the country" and use the word "military" in many connections, but they are basically silent on the military-civilian distinction as such.[50] The nineteenth-century international codification of the law of war that culminated in the Hague Conventions of 1899 and 1907 use a single term: "belligerent." Individuals may be belligerent as a consequence of states being belligerent, and it is a principal issue to establish a clear borderline between "les individus dont se compose 'la force armée' et les autres ressortissants d'un Etat."[51] These others are not named, however – not even as inhabitants. What comes closest is the phrase "the population of occupied territory." The *Convention Respecting the Laws and Customs of War on Land* (1907) does distinguish between "military" and "non-military" but only in a paragraph on spies, who may be both.[52] "Combatant"

50 "Résolutions de la Conférence internationale de Genève, 26 au 29 octobre 1863," in *Droit International Humanitaire – Traités & textes*, http://www.icrc.org/dih.nsf/FULL/115?OpenDocument; "Convention de Genève du 22 août 1864 pour l'amélioration du sort des militaires blessés dans les armées en campagne," in *Droit International Humanitaire – Traités & textes*, http://www.icrc.org/dih.nsf/FULL/120?OpenDocument; "Articles additionnels à la Convention du 22 août 1864. Genève, 20 octobre 1868," in *Droit International Humanitaire – Traités & textes*, http://www.icrc.org/dih.nsf/FULL/125?OpenDocument; "Convention pour l'amélioration du sort des blessés et malades dans les armées en campagne, Genève 1906," in *Droit International Humanitaire – Traités & textes*, http://www.icrc.org/dih.nsf/FULL/180?OpenDocument. The French original writes "habitants du pays."

51 The phrase comes from Gustave Moynier, "Manuel des lois de la guerre sur terre. Oxford 1880," in *Droit International Humanitaire – Traités & textes* (accessed September 2008), http://www.icrc.org/dih.nsf/FULL/140?OpenDocument, article premier. This text was the product of a "think tank" with great influence on the international diplomatic process.

52 "Convention (IV) concernant les lois et coutumes de la guerre sur terre et son Annexe: Règlement concernant les lois et coutumes de la guerre sur terre. La Haye, 18 octobre 1907," in *Droit International Humanitaire – Traités & textes* (accessed September 2008), http://www.icrc.org/dih.nsf/FULL/195?OpenDocument, §29.

and "non-combatant" are used in the old manner to describe armed and unarmed members of the armed forces.[53]

The personnel of the armed forces and their interaction are the focus in these texts. Others appear as background, as depersonalized objects, even in the few sentences that set limits to any violence directed against them: "Family honours and rights, individual lives and private property, as well as religious convictions and liberty, must be respected. Private property cannot be confiscated."[54] Implicit in these first attempts at an official codification of the laws of war was the division of humanity in two: the "belligerents" and the remainder. This remainder have characteristics. Being individual and private, it is implicit that such individuals are not strongly connected to the state; but they are so inconspicuous in the texts that they are not labelled in any explicit way.

The focus on the state military continued to fit well with the practice of war in the Western world during the nineteenth and early twentieth centuries. Wars were fought by state armies. When populations rose up against occupation, as the Spanish did in 1808 and the French in 1870, they were repressed as criminals. The greatest change in the way of war from the late eighteenth to the early twentieth century was the increasing use of conscription. Conscription blurs cultural borderlines. Civilians may be "militarized," identifying themselves with their military service as reservists and veterans or as future soldiers in proto-military youth movements. Conversely, conscripts may conceive of themselves as civilians at heart even in the heat of battle. But conscription does not muddle the formal dividing line between military and civilians. Clearly defined symbolic acts transform the civilian into a soldier and back again; and the huge size of conscript armies made irregulars even less relevant in war.

53 All these terms are used in a uniform way from the early "Projet d'une Déclaration internationale concernant les lois et coutumes de la guerre. Bruxelles, 27 août 1874," in *Droit International Humanitaire – Traités & textes* (accessed September 2008), http://www.icrc.org/dih.nsf/FULL/135?OpenDocument. to "Acte final de la Conférence internationale de la Paix. La Haye, 29 juillet 1899," in *Droit International Humanitaire – Traités & textes* (accessed September 2008), http://www.icrc.org/dih.nsf/FULL/145?OpenDocument, §46.

54 "Acte final 1899," §46.

Industrial warfare provided the means to target civilians on a larger scale than ever before, but it were rarely applied before the First World War. Even then, unrestricted submarine warfare and the occasional bombardment of cities from the air or by artillery produced a very limited number of casualties compared with the losses among the soldiers. Civilians were also still victimized, but less so than ever before, at least in the wars in the West. The propaganda war on the atrocities committed by the German army in Belgium in 1914 demonstrates how unacceptable and uncommon the victimization of civilians had become.[55]

The Civilian in Twentieth-Century Laws Governing War

The first decades of the twentieth century also seems to have been the era when the use of "civilian" became commonplace when speaking about people in war. Judging from the pages of *The Times* of London – one of the few places where language change can be followed in detail – this development had been coming for some time. During the Boer war, reporters routinely wrote about the "civilian population" or "civilian element" instead of simply "inhabitants" or "population." Casualty lists carried the subheading "Civilians" in parallel with the names of regiments.[56] From there it was only a short step to the language used during the Great War. Then "civilian" and "civilians" became everyday words, whether these civilians were targets, victims, irregular participants, supporters or bystanders.[57]

The experience of the First World War shaped the new conventions on the conduct of war made during the next decades. The 1922 convention on the use of submarines and poison gas speaks of "non-combatants at sea."[58] For the first time in international humanitarian law, a single term, taken from Lieber, was used for those who were to be protected. The same term,

55 John Horne and Alan Kramer, *German Atrocities 1914: A History of Denial* (New Haven: Yale University Press, 2001), part III.

56 "*The Times* 1785–2006," http://infotrac.galegroup.com/itweb/. Quotations from 11 April 1900: 4; 9 May 1900: 7.

57 Examples: ibid. Jan. 2, 1917: 7; Jan. 9, 1917: 5; Jan. 13, 1917: 9.

58 "Treaty relating to the Use of Submarines and Noxious Gases in Warfare. Washington, 6 February 1922," in *International Humanitarian Law – Treaties & Documents*, http://www.icrc.org/ihl.nsf/INTRO/270?OpenDocument.

non-combatants, is also found in "Rules concerning the Control of Wireless Telegraphy in Time of War and Air Warfare (1922–1923)",[59] which never became a treaty. Soon after, the word "civilians" first appeared in the modern sense in an authoritative text on international humanitarian law. This was in the *Final Act* of a diplomatic conference in 1929 in Geneva, which called for "an international convention regarding the condition and protection of civilians of enemy nationality in the territory of a belligerent or in territory occupied by a belligerent." Such a convention was drafted in Tokyo in 1934. The first paragraph dealt with the definition of "Enemy civilians" as "persons … not belonging to the land, maritime or air armed forces of the belligerents."[60] The "Draft Convention for the Protection of Civilian Populations against New Engines of War (1938)" defined "civilian population" almost in the same way, as "all those not enlisted in any branch of the combatant services nor for the time being employed or occupied in any belligerent establishment." The last clause was intended to permit classifying industries as "belligerent establishments": such as, for example, munitions factories, airplane workshops and the like.[61]

These texts never became international conventions but they testify to the shift in terminology. "Civilian" had now become the word of choice, linking peacetime social structure with wartime activity. "Civilian" became the core concept when new treaties were written after the Second World War. The fourth Geneva convention of 1949 uses this word in the title: "Convention relative to the Protection of Civilian Persons in Time of War". It has become an important treaty, one of the few international agreements adopted by essentially all states.[62] The convention does not define

59 "Rules concerning the Control of Wireless Telegraphy in Time of War and Air Warfare (1922–1923)."

60 "Draft International Convention on the Condition and Protection of Civilians of enemy nationality who are on territory belonging to or occupied by a belligerent. Tokyo, 1934," in *International Humanitarian Law – Treaties & Documents* (accessed December 2008), http://www.icrc.org/ihl.nsf/FULL/320?OpenDocument.

61 "Draft Convention for the Protection of Civilian Populations against New Engines of War. Amsterdam, 1938," in *International Humanitarian Law – Treaties & Documents* (accessed April 2008), http://www.icrc.org/ihl.nsf/FULL/345?OpenDocument.

62 Other texts from the corpus of international humanitarian law using the term is the "Agreement for the Prosecution and Punishment of the Major War Criminals of the European Axis, and Charter of the International Military Tribunal. London, 8 August 1945," in *International Humanitarian Law – Treaties & Documents*, http://www.icrc.org/

"civilian persons." Implicitly, they are described as the sum of a number of groups accorded different types of protection. The most prominent are the protected persons "who … find themselves … in the hands of a Party to the conflict or Occupying Power of which they are not nationals" without engaging in hostile activities. "[T]he whole of the populations of the countries in conflict" is also mentioned, but protection against targeting is only extended to certain places, such as hospitals, and certain subgroups such as the sick, the aged, children, medical or religious persons.[63] It resembles the older category of the innocent. Compared with earlier centuries, the main difference, however, is the abolishment of any special protection of women. Mothers of young children are protected as mothers, but women as such are no longer presumed to be outside of war by virtue of their gender. The 1949 convention, therefore, adopts a new terminology when it speaks about "civilians," but only as a convenient label for several categories to be protected in different contexts. The word is not used as part of a military-civilian dichotomy.

Since then, "civilian" has been widely used in international humanitarian law. The most important text after 1949, the 1977 "Protocol … relating to the Protection of Victims of International Armed Conflicts" defines the term – but in more than one way.[64] In the preamble, humanity is divided into "civilians and combatants," that is, with respect to their activities in war. Later, a number of categories such as the wounded and sick are described as "persons, whether military or civilian." Here the dichotomy is

ihl.nsf/FULL/350?OpenDocument., "Principles of International Law Recognized in the Charter of the Nüremberg Tribunal and in the Judgment of the Tribunal, 1950," in *International Humanitarian Law – Treaties & Documents* (accessed April 2008), http://www.icrc.org/ihl.nsf/FULL/390?OpenDocument., and the "Draft Rules for the Limitation of the Dangers incurred by the Civilian Population in Time of War. ICRC, 1956," in *International Humanitarian Law – Treaties & Documents* (accessed April 2008), http://www.icrc.org/ihl.nsf/FULL/420?OpenDocument. All of these use the combination "civilian population." In the French version: "populations civiles."

63 "Convention (IV) relative to the Protection of Civilian Persons in Time of War. Geneva, 12 August 1949," in *International Humanitarian Law – Treaties & Documents* (accessed April 2008), http://www.icrc.org/ihl.nsf/FULL/380?OpenDocument, article 4 and 13.

64 "Protocol Additional to the Geneva Conventions of 12 August 1949, and relating to the Protection of Victims of International Armed Conflicts (Protocol I), 8 June 1977," in *International Humanitarian Law – Treaties & Documents* (accessed April 2008), http://www.icrc.org/ihl.nsf/FULL/470?OpenDocument.

used in the original way with a focus on the military institution. In the section on combatants, the "armed forces" are defined broadly as all organized armed groups under a command responsible to one of the warring parties. It is stated that their members (other than medical personnel and chaplains) "are combatants, that is to say, they have the right to participate directly in hostilities." In the large section on the protection of civilian persons and objects, we find the "basic rule" that "[p]arties to the conflict shall at all times distinguish between the civilian population and combatants and between civilian objects and military objectives."[65]

In practical terms, the Additional Protocol sometimes defines the civilian as the non-military, sometimes as different from the broader category "armed forces." Changes from the nineteenth-century "combatant" and "non-combatant" may seem marginal. But the text as a whole is evidence of a reversed world view. Civilians are now the central category of people and the bulk of the text deals with their protection. Their status is elevated by the lofty language and by the long list of duties towards them (even if the practical difference from earlier best practice is marginal). Being civilian is declared the default state of human beings: implicitly, by being everybody who is not military; and explicitly, when dealing with the grey area: "In case of doubt whether a person is a civilian, that person shall be considered to be a civilian."[66] Here the definition is reversed. The military becomes the residual after subtracting everybody who may be called civilian.

The reversal of priorities shows how the rights of the civilian according to the Additional Protocol are conceived along the pattern of universal human rights. The innocents of earlier times and the non-combatants of the nineteenth century were a subcategory of the enemy. The late twentieth-century civilian is the fundamental human being before the world is divided into friend and foe. A rapid transition has taken place from the first appearance of the idea of the general protection of civilians in the

65 Ibid., Article 48. A further definition that "A civilian is any person who does not belong to one of the categories of persons referred to in Article 4 (A) (1), (2), (3) and (6) of the Third Convention and in Article 43 of this Protocol" refers to definitions of "armed forces."

66 Ibid., Article 50, 1.

1920s and the concomitant appearance of "civilian" in the twentieth-century sense in connection with war.

Triumph and Erosion

It is a common observation that this triumph on paper has been accompanied in practice by an erosion of the dividing line between military and civilian.

The dichotomy has held up well inside and within societies. State militaries operate as before with bureaucratically defined membership and strong symbolic expression of their unique qualities. Uniforms are at least as distinctive as before, even if their special qualities are now derived from the new style of field uniforms rather than from the heraldic heritage. When states support or deploy grey-zone combatants, be they guerrillas or military contractors, they take pains to avoid confusion within their own borders.

In war, however, the line has been eroding in several ways. Industrial mass production and technical prowess has made it possible to target whole populations, a capability that was demonstrated during the Second World War and the potential of which was developed even further during the Cold War. Victimization of civilians exploded on the Eastern front in World War II and continues in the conflicts in the third world. Wars involving weak states, insurgents and popular movements have weakened the dominance of state armies in the field. The Geneva Protocols try to create clear lines by classifying all who take up arms as military if there is the least resemblance to regular soldiers. Nonetheless, when civilians are allowed to turn themselves into soldiers and back again in a quick and easy way, the distinction between military and civilian is blurred.

Boundaries have also been blurred by changes in the character of civilians. Industrial war has linked the war effort very directly to the productive capacity of the civilian population. Targeting civilian producers has become more relevant and easier to defend as a legitimate act of war. The dependence of irregulars on the material support of the civilian population has the same effect. Mass politics – whether authoritarian or democratic – has also made the enemy citizen of the twentieth century less innocent than the enemy subject of the past. Wars have become conflicts between masses with a political status, often with real power in the political process and conceiving of themselves as nations or political parties. Democracy, the rule of a political nation, has been linked convincingly with ethnic cleansing.[67] It also links the political nation as such to the wars it conducts. The unarmed are less innocent than in times past.

The difference in relation to the past must not be exaggerated. Even at the high point of nineteenth-century "civilized" warfare, targeting and victimizing of civilians was widespread, and non-soldiers participated in fighting. We must take into account that there is still a clear conflict between the direction of changes in actual war and the way the military-civilian dichotomy has triumphed in the discourse, both in formal and informal contexts. Projecting this internal dichotomy of peaceful societies into a general division of humanity maximizes the claims to protection made on behalf of everybody who is not under military command.

The mixture of strongly pacifist commitments to peace and the fiercely bellicose glorification of war that was typical of the decades around 1900 has been described as schizophrenic.[68] Two world wars have made open praise of war rare. But the increased focus on the protection of civilians, and specifically the increased centrality of the military-civilian dichotomy in discourse, can be described as an equally heroic attempt to contain conflicting realities and ambitions. This is much too large a phenomenon to have a single explanation, but a strong impulse clearly comes from the combination of two twentieth-century developments: on the one hand, the growing political power of the masses; and on the other, the terror of being targeted. The first attempts at creating protection for civilians, and labelled as such, were linked to the experience of unlimited submarine warfare and the perspective of large-scale aerial bombardment. The obliteration of almost all distinction by strategic nuclear weapons after the Second World War created a push in the same direction. The more difficult it becomes to maintain the distinction in actual warfare, the more is done to re-establish it by decree.

67 Michael Mann, *The Dark Side of Democracy: Explaining Ethnic Cleansing* (Cambridge: Cambridge University Press, 2005).

68 Best, *Humanity in Warfare*, 130.

Conclusion

The dichotomy between military and civilian emerged in the discourse during the seventeenth century, but only became general and important three centuries later. Beginning as the division of social sectors in peacetime, the dichotomy has become fundamental also for creating distinctions between people during war. It is enshrined in national and international law, is expressed in dress and other symbolic language, and has been fine-tuned to create clarity in grey areas such as the use of conscripts.

Within societies, the distinction is very realistic. It corresponds to the social division of labour which is so fundamental to modern life. Across the front in times of war, the distinction is not realistic at all. Civilians are continuously targeted, habitually victimized, and are frequently active participants, making their designation as civilians ambiguous. If anything, the trend has been towards a widening of the gap between the viewpoint expressed in the military-civilian dichotomy and the reality of war. The modern laws of war offer weaker protection to civilians than is commonly imagined by those same civilians. Yet the more complex and vague conceptual dividing lines applied in earlier times gave a more realistic image of actual conditions then than our conceptualization does of conditions now.

When the conceptual division of humanity into military and civilian is imported into the language describing war, realism is sacrificed to ambition. Using these concepts carries an implicit message: that everybody not belonging to the military of the state must be protected from becoming a target or a victim. It serves as a tool in the struggle to limit the most terrifying ability to wage war found in human history by maximizing the number of protected people and by carrying the message that being a civilian is the default status of a human being. The message is the same in everyday discourse and in international humanitarian law.

Projecting the terminology back into history is even less realistic. It obscures that the past did not only use other words, but often divided people along other lines, both in theory and in practice, and in both peace and war. Applying modern terminology may sometimes be analytically meaningful, but often not. It also obscures how recent current terminology is, especially in the full scope of its application.

Pointing this out does not invalidate any argument for the protection of civilians. But it shows how historically changing our conceptions are, including the conceptions of who may and who must fight, who may be targeted or in other ways involved in war. We still live under this variability, a condition of both threats and hope.

References

[J.F.S.], ed. *Corpus Juris Militaris. Darinnen insonderheit das Churfürst:. Brandenburgische Krieges-Recht und Artickels-Brieff, von neuen übersehen und verbessert, wie auch verschiedener anderer hohen Potentaten Krieges-Satzungen und Observantionen enthalten*. Frankfurt and Leipzig: Rupert Völcker, 1687.

"Acte final de la Conférence internationale de la Paix. La Haye, 29 juillet 1899." In *Droit International Humanitaire – Traités & textes*. http://www.icrc.org/dih.nsf/FULL/145?OpenDocument (accessed September 2008).

"Agreement for the Prosecution and Punishment of the Major War Criminals of the European Axis, and Charter of the International Military Tribunal. London, 8 August 1945." In *International Humanitarian Law – Treaties & Documents*. http://www.icrc.org/ihl.nsf/FULL/350?OpenDocument.

"Articles additionnels à la Convention du 22 août 1864. Genève, 20 octobre 1868." in *Droit International Humanitaire – Traités & textes*. http://www.icrc.org/dih.nsf/FULL/125?OpenDocument.

Baumann, Reinhard. *Landsknechte: Ihre Geschichte und Kultur vom späten Mittelalter bis zum Dreißigjährigen Krieg*. Munich: C. H. Beck Verlag, 1994.

Bellander, Erik. *Dräkt och uniform: Den svenska arméns beklädnad från 1500-talets början fram till våra dagar*. Stockholm: Norstedts, 1973.

Best, Geoffrey. *Humanity in Warfare: The Modern History of the International Law of Armed Conflicts*. New York: Columbia University Press, 1980.

Black, Jeremy. *A Military Revolution? Military Change and European Society, 1550–1800*. Basingstoke: Macmillan Education, 1991.

———. *European Warfare, 1660–1815*. London: UCL Press, 1994.

Borg, Erik. *Den danske marines uniformer gennem tre århundreder*. Copenhagen: Strubes Forlag, 1974.

Burlamaqui, Jean Jacques. *Principes du droit de la nature et des gens*. Edited by M. Dupin. 5 vols. Paris: Warée, 1820–1821.

Contamine, Philippe. *La guerre au Moyen Age*. Paris: Presses universitaires de France, 1980.

"Convention (IV) concernant les lois et coutumes de la guerre sur terre et son Annexe: Règlement concernant les lois et coutumes de la guerre sur terre. La Haye, 18 octobre 1907." In *Droit International Humanitaire – Traités & textes*.

http://www.icrc.org/dih.nsf/FULL/195?OpenDocument (accessed September 2008).

"Convention (IV) relative to the Protection of Civilian Persons in Time of War. Geneva, 12 August 1949." In *International Humanitarian Law – Treaties & Documents.* http://www.icrc.org/ihl.nsf/FULL/380?OpenDocument (accessed April 2008).

"Convention de Genève du 22 août 1864 pour l'amélioration du sort des militaires blessés dans les armées en campagne." In *Droit International Humanitaire – Traités & textes.* http://www.icrc.org/dih.nsf/FULL/120?OpenDocument.

"Convention pour l'amélioration du sort des blessés et malades dans les armées en campagne, Genève 1906." In *Droit International Humanitaire – Traités & textes.* http://www.icrc.org/dih.nsf/FULL/180?OpenDocument.

Conway, Stephen. *War, State, and Society in Mid-Eighteenth-Century Britain and Ireland.* Oxford: Oxford University Press, 2006.

Corvisier, André, *Armées et sociétés en Europe de 1494 à 1789.* Paris: Presses universitaires de France, 1976.

Corvisier, André. ed. *Histoire militaire de la France.* 4 vols. Paris: Presses universitaires de France, 1992–1994.

Danard, Yvonick, and Armelle Gautier. "La Milice de l'Ancien Régime en Bretagne." *Revue historique des armées* 205 (1996): 115–25.

Denny-Brown, Andrea. "Rips and Slits: The Torn Garment and the Medieval Self." In *Clothing Culture, 1350–1650*, edited by Catherine Richardson, 223–37. Aldershot: Ashgate, 2004.

Deutsche Wörterbuch. 1852–. http://www.dwb.uni-trier.de/.

Dictionnaires d'autrefois. French dictionaries of the 17th, 18th, 19th and 20th centuries [1606–1935]. http://www.lib.uchicago.edu/efts/ARTFL/projects/dicos/.

"Draft Convention for the Protection of Civilian Populations against New Engines of War. Amsterdam, 1938." In *International Humanitarian Law – Treaties & Documents.* http://www.icrc.org/ihl.nsf/FULL/345?Open Document (accessed April 2008).

"Draft International Convention on the Condition and Protection of Civilians of Enemy Nationality who are on Territory Belonging to or Occupied by a Belligerent. Tokyo, 1934." In *International Humanitarian Law – Trea-*

ties & Documents. http://www.icrc.org/ihl.nsf/FULL/320?OpenDocument (accessed December 2008).

"Draft Rules for the Limitation of the Dangers Incurred by the Civilian Population in Time of War. ICRC, 1956." In *International Humanitarian Law – Treaties & Documents*. http://www.icrc.org/ihl.nsf/FULL/420?Open Document (accessed April 2008).

Dunant, Henri. *Un souvenir de Solférino* [1862]. Geneva: Comité international de la Croix-Rouge, 1986.

Frauenholz, Eugen von. *Entwicklungsgeschichte des deutschen Heerwesens*. 5 vols. Munich: C. H. Beck Verlag, 1935–1941.

"General Orders No. 100: Instructions for the Government of Armies of the United States in the Field." http://avalon.law.yale.edu/19th_century/lieber.asp.

Glete, Jan. *War and the State in Early Modern Europe: Spain, the Dutch Republic and Sweden as Fiscal-Military States, 1500–1660*. London: Routledge, 2002.

Grotius, Hugo. *Hugonis Grotii De iure belli ac pacis libri tres in quibus ius naturae & gentium: item iuris publici praecipua explicantur* [1652]. Edited by B. J. A. de Kanter-van Hettinga Tromp. Leiden: E. J. Brill, 1939.

Grüner-Nielsen, H., ed. *Danske Viser fra Adelsvisebøger og Flyveblade 1530–1630*. 7 vols. Copenhagen: Gyldendal, 1912–1931.

Hale, J. R. *War and Society in Renaissance Europe 1450–1620*. London: Fontana, 1985.

Hall, Fitzedward. *Recent Exemplifications of False Philology*. New York: Scribner, Armstrong & Co., 1872.

Hartigan, Richard Shelly. *The Forgotten Victim: A History of the Civilian*. Chicago: Precedent, 1982.

———. *Lieber's Code and the Law of War*. Chicago: Precedent, 1983.

Hicks, Michael. *Bastard Feudalism*. London: Longman, 1995.

Horne, John, and Alan Kramer. *German Atrocities 1914: A History of Denial*. New Haven: Yale University Press, 2001.

Lind, Gunner. "Uniform and Distinction: Symbolic Aspects of Officer Dress in the Eighteenth-Century Danish State." *Textile History* 41, Supplement (2010): 49–65.

Lyndon, Brian. "Military Dress and Uniformity, 1680–1720." *Journal of the Society for Army Historical Research* 54, no. 218 (1976): 108–20.

Lynn, John. *Giant of the Grand Siecle: The French Army, 1610–1715*. Cambridge: Cambridge University Press, 1997.

Malcolm, Joyce Lee. *Guns and Violence: The English Experience*. Cambridge, Mass.: Harvard University Press, 2002.

Mann, Michael. *The Dark Side of Democracy: Explaining Ethnic Cleansing*. Cambridge: Cambridge University Press, 2005.

Mansel, Philip. "Monarchy, Uniform and the Rise of the Frac 1760–1830." *Past and Present* 96 (1982): 103–32.

Martin, Paul. *European Military Uniforms: A Short History*. London: Spring Books, 1967.

Miller, Amy. *Dressed to Kill: British Naval Uniform, Masculinity and Contemporary Fashions, 1748–1857*. London: National Maritime Museum, 2007.

Moynier, Gustave. "Manuel des lois de la guerre sur terre. Oxford 1880." In *Droit International Humanitaire – Traités & textes*. http://www.icrc.org/dih.nsf/FULL/140?OpenDocument (accessed September 2008).

Nilsson, Sven A. *På väg mot militärstaten: Krigsbefalets etablering i den äldre Vasatidens Sverige*. Opuscula Historica Upsaliensia. Uppsala: Historiska institutionen, 1989.

Ordbog over det danske Sprog. 1918–1954. http://ordnet.dk/ods/.

Ordbog til det ældre danske Sprog (1300–1700). Edited by Otto Kalkar. Copenhagen: Thieles Bogtrykkeri, 1881–1907. http://www.hist.uib.no/kalkar/

Ordbok över svenska språket utgiven av Svenska Akademien. 1898–. http://g3.spraakdata.gu.se/saob/.

The Oxford English Dictionary. 1888–. http://www.oed.com.

Pedersen, Sune Christian. *På liv og død: Duellens historie i Danmark*. Copenhagen: Gyldendal, 2003.

"Principles of International Law Recognized in the Charter of the Nüremberg Tribunal and in the Judgment of the Tribunal, 1950." In *International Humanitarian Law – Treaties & Documents*. http://www.icrc.org/ihl.nsf/FULL/390?OpenDocument (accessed April 2008).

"Projet d'une Déclaration internationale concernant les lois et coutumes de la guerre. Bruxelles, 27 août 1874." In *Droit International Humanitaire – Traités & textes*. http://www.icrc.org/dih.nsf/FULL/135?OpenDocument (accessed September 2008).

"Protocol Additional to the Geneva Conventions of 12 August 1949, and Relating to the Protection of Victims of International Armed Conflicts (Protocol I), 8 June 1977." In *International Humanitarian Law – Treaties & Documents*. http://www.icrc.org/ihl.nsf/FULL/470?OpenDocument (accessed April 2008).

"Résolutions de la Conférence internationale de Genève, 26 au 29 octobre 1863." In *Droit International Humanitaire – Traités & textes*. http://www.icrc.org/dih.nsf/FULL/115?OpenDocument.

Ribeiro, Aileen. *Art of Dress*. New Haven: Yale University Press, 1995.

Roche, Daniel. *The Culture of Clothing: Dress and Fashion in the Ancien Régime*. Translated by Jean Birrell. Cambridge: Cambridge University Press, 1994.

Rogers, Clifford J., ed. *The Military Revolution Debate: Readings on the Military Transformation of Early Modern Europe*. Boulder: Westview Press, 1995.

Rousseau, Jean-Jacques. *Du contrat social ou principes du droit politique* [1762]. Paris: Libraire de la Bibliothèque Nationale, 1894.

Sengespeik, Fr. von, and Chr. von Schneider. *Der Officier: Eine Anleitung fur junge Leute, welche diese Benennung verdienen und im Militairstande Glück machen wollen*. Glückstadt, 1810.

Sturgill, Claude C. *La formation de la milice permanente en France (1726–1730)*. Paris: Service historique de l'armée de terre, 1975.

Tilly, Charles. *Coercion, Capital, and European States, A.D. 990–1992*. Rev. ed. Studies in Social Discontinuity. Oxford: Basil Blackwell, 1995.

"*The Times* 1785–1985." http://infotrac.galegroup.com/itweb/.

"Treaty relating to the Use of Submarines and Noxious Gases in Warfare. Washington, 6 February 1922." In *International Humanitarian Law – Treaties & Documents*. http://www.icrc.org/ihl.nsf/INTRO/270?OpenDocument.

Uniformen für's Zivile. Zur Geschichte uniformer Kleidung als symbolischer Kommunikation. Krefeld: Deutsche Textilmuseum, 2002.

Vattel, Emer de. *Le droit des gens ou principes de la loi naturelle, appliqués à la conduite et aux affaires des Nations et des Souverains*. Edited by P. Pradier-Fodéré. 3 vols. Paris: Libraire de Guillaumin, 1863.

Vaupell, Otto. *Den danske Hærs Historie til Nutiden og Den norske Hærs Historie indtil 1814*. 2 vols. Copenhagen: Gyldendal, 1872.

Victoria, Franciscus de. *De Indis et de iure belli relectiones*. Edited by Ernest Nys. Translated by John Pawley Bates and Herbert Francis Wright. The Classics of International Law. Washington D.C.: Carnegie Institution of Washington, 1917.

Weber, Max. *Wirtschaft und Gesellschaft: Grundriss der verstehenden Soziologie* [1922]. Edited by Johannes Winckelmann. 5th revised edition. Tübingen: J. C. B. Mohr, 1976.

Western, John R. *The English Militia in the Eighteenth Century: The Story of a Political Issue, 1660–1802*. Studies in Political History. London: Routledge and Kegan Paul, 1965.

Military and Civilian in Fifteenth- and Sixteenth-Century Denmark

Jeppe Büchert Netterstrøm

Present-day international war law is built on a sharp distinction between military and civilian, between combatants and non-combatants. Wars should be fought by soldiers, while the civilian population should play a passive role and be left alone. In times of war it is permissible to kill enemy soldiers, but it is forbidden to kill civilians or harm them unnecessarily unless civilians turn themselves into hostile combatants by virtue of their own actions. The distinction between combatants and non-combatants made by international law reflects the differentiation between military and civilian within the society at war: in war as in peace a firm line is drawn between the military and the rest of society, between soldiers and civilians. This demarcation within every society would appear to arise from the state, and likewise laws governing war arise from the existence of an international community of states. It is the state which determines when there is war and when there is peace. And it is the state which defines who is a military person and who is a civilian and when the members of a society switch between these roles. One characteristic of a modern state is precisely its monopoly on the use of legitimate force, including military force. Thus it makes sense to investigate the origins of the present-day dichotomy between military and civilian in the emergence of the modern state. Furthermore, the protection of the civilian population stipulated by modern war law appears to be based on a concept of universal human rights that has its roots in the Enlightenment.

The actual concept of a distinction between combatants and non-combatants, however, is not a product of modern Western society. Many historical societies had a special group of warriors that were distinct from the rest of society, and many societies operated on the basis of culturally determined rules of warfare that included the moderation of actions towards members of the population who were not warriors. For example, in all parts of the world, both among civilized societies as well as "primitive" tribal societies, and in every historical epoch, a widespread norm has been the protection of women and children from the horrors of war. In Europe, the concept of a distinction between combatants and non-combatants has existed at least since the time of the Romans; it existed among the Germanic peoples of the time of the Migration Period and it was recreated and reshaped throughout the Christian Middle Ages and the Renaissance. This essay investigates how the sharp distinction between the military and the civilian that underpins modern international war law is rooted in pre-modern, pre-nation-state Europe. At the same time it also considers how the pre-modern distinction between combatants and non-combatants differed significantly from the modern dichotomy between military and civilian, both in theory and in practice. In the process, we will naturally examine the question of how and why we progressed from medieval to modern distinctions and norms. However, this chapter does not consider these problems in their full temporal and spatial breadth, or in their full complexity, but instead focuses on a case from a certain period and a certain geographical area that cannot claim to be representative for the whole of Europe and is only one part of a long development within the region. The region investigated is the Kingdom of Denmark, and the period examined is the fifteenth and sixteenth centuries. According to traditional Danish historiographical periodization, the Middle Ages ends with the Lutheran Reformation in 1536 and is followed by the early modern era. Both sides of this periodical transition will be analyzed here and an attempt made to determine to what extent the Reformation brought about any significant change in the relationship between military and civilian in Denmark. Can we, for example, generally identify a development in the direction of greater "modernity" in the course of the sixteenth century? The section on the late Middle Ages focuses on feuds and other forms of private/non-state violence, while the section on the post-Reformation period focuses on the Seven Years' War between the Kingdom of Denmark and the Kingdom of Sweden (1563–1570).

Before turning our attention to Denmark in the fifteenth and sixteenth centuries, we will look at the etymological aspects of both the dichotomy between military and civilian, as well as the European medieval background to the distinction between combatants and non-combatants.

Concepts of Military and Civilian

The actual word "military" – the first element of the dichotomy between military and civilian – is relatively new, although it does derive from classical Latin. The word comes from the Latin adjective *militaris,* which comes from the noun *miles* (soldier; *milites* in the genitive case). Thus, *militaris* means "that which concerns soldiers, or serving in battle." It was not until the seventeenth to eighteenth centuries that the noun "military" evolved in modern European languages (German *Militär*; French *militaire*), although the word was already employed as an adjective in the early sixteenth century. The word "civilian," which goes further back in time than the word military, derives from the Latin noun *civis* (citizen) and is also used adjectivally in classical Latin (*civilis*, concerning the citizens). In the Middle Ages, *civis* often designated a person who lived in a town (*civitas*), as opposed to a peasant (*rusticus*), who lived in the country. *Civilis* in this context is used in connection with town life or citizenry. *Civilis* is also used as the opposite of ecclesiastical or clerical, such as the opposites of secular and religious law (*juris civilis*, *juris canonici*). When the word *civis* or *civilis* is used in the Middle Ages as meaning the opposite of *militaris* or other words related to *miles*, it is not done in the same way as in the modern dichotomy between military and civilian. It is more in the sense of townspeople, understood as a social group (such as the clergy or peasants), as opposed to a warrior class. In other words, *civis/civilis* does not as such mean non-military or non-combatant. Words such as *militaris* and *miles* are simply not the main antonyms of words such as *civilis* and *civis* in medieval usage. The dichotomy between military and civilian first took on its present-day meaning at the close of the early modern era.[1] The emergence of powerful military states, permanent armies and the ensuing clear division of society into a

1 Otto Brunner, Werner Conze and Reinhart Koselleck, ed., *Geschichtliche Grundbegriffe*, 4, Art. "Militarismus," 2–3, 7. Norbert Angermann et al., ed., *Lexicon des Mittelalters* (1983), Art. "Bürger, bürgertum," col. 1010.

military sphere and a non-military sphere offers an explanation for the creation and spread of the dichotomy precisely at this point in time.

The Middle Ages: Estates, Peace Movements and Just War

From a longer and broader historical perspective, the specific dichotomy between military and civilian is of fairly recent origin. As mentioned above, this does not mean that prior to this dichotomy no distinction was made between those whom we would call military or civilian, respectively. In Europe of the Middle Ages, the demarcation line was simply somewhere else. There was no modern state to define the separation of society into military and civilian. Instead, society was divided into three estates, which was partly based on a distinction between combatants and non-combatants. The distinction between soldiers and other members of the population was, thus, not anchored in the state but was an integral part of a homegrown social order, the development of which was in fact due to the disintegration of a state, namely the Carolingian state, in the ninth century.

From about the year 1000, society was divided into three groups: those who prayed (*oratores*), those who fought (*bellatores*) and those who laboured (*laboratores*). According to this medieval tripartite division of society, each group had its own very specific social function. Those who prayed were meant to strive for salvation for all the members of society through prayer and piety. Those who fought were meant to use brute force to defend those who prayed and those who laboured. Those who laboured were responsible for the upkeep of those who prayed and those who fought in battle.

The division of society into three estates (French *etats*; German *Ständen*) was a product of so-called feudal anarchy (or, alternatively, feudal revolution) around the year 1000. The disintegration of the Carolingian Empire and the development of new military technologies led to the growth of an aristocracy of professional warriors. This perceived tripartite division of society, which reflected actual developments, while certainly also simplifying social relations, legitimized this positioning of feudal knights of the nobility in society. In the Carolingian realm, the social divide was more between men who were free and men who were not free. Now the knights of the nobility constituted a separate estate, distinct from the estate of townsmen and peasants, which included free men as well as serfs. The bipartite division of the secular sections of society was added to an older dichotomy between priests and laymen. This gave rise to the tripartite social model, which (in some places with townsmen and peasants separated into two independent estates) persisted right up to the nation states and revolutions of the modern era.[2]

Another outcome of the feudal anarchy that was linked to the birth of the three estates was the peace movement of the church, which from the end of the tenth century began to preach and proclaim the peace of God, *Pax Dei*. As a reaction against the brutality of the "feudal anarchy," the early *Pax Dei* movement demanded that the knights refrain from violent acts towards the clergy, the peasants, merchants, the poor and women and children. This was done by ecclesiastical leaders issuing local proclamations under pain of excommunication and other religious penalties. The stipulations of *Pax Dei* were replaced during the course of the eleventh century by proclamations about the Truce of God, *Treuga Dei*, which completely prohibited violence among Christians at certain times, such as on Sundays, at Whitsun, Christmas, etc. These prohibitions applied to all Christians, but were in practice directed mostly at feuding knights. After some time, the countless efforts of the *Pax Dei* movement to restrain violence proved to be fruitless as the religious penalties that were intended to support the peace proclamations were not sufficiently heeded. The aims and rules of the movement were, however, adopted by the secular power holders (emperors, kings and princes) and were transposed from the twelfth to the thirteenth century onwards into secular law and the so-called Peace of the Land. The purpose of Peace of the Land was first and foremost to limit private feuds between members of the nobility.[3]

The medieval peace movements reinforced the distinction between military and civilian, which was an intrinsic part of the tripartite division of

2 Georges Duby, *The Three Orders: Feudal Society Imagined* [1978], trans. Arthur Goldhammer (Chicago: University of Chicago Press, 1980).

3 Philippe Contamine, *War in the Middle Ages* (Oxford: Oxford Universty Press, 1984), 271–75. Heinz Angermeier, *Königtum und Landfriede im deutschen Spätmittelalter* (Munich: C. H. Beck Verlag, 1966). Christine Reinle, *Bauernfehden. Studien zur Fehdeführung Nichtadliger im Spätmittelalterlichen römisch-deutschen Reich, besonders in den bayerischen Herzogtümern* (Stuttgart: Franz Steiner Verlag, 2003), 12–13.

functions in society. The contrast between the warring nobility and peaceful members of the praying and labouring estates became starker as proclamations of peace branded priests and peasants as victims of the feuds of the warrior aristocracy.

A third element in medieval thinking, which, together with the division of society into estates and the *Pax Dei* movement, served to draw a line between military and civilian, was the theory of just war, *bellum justum*. Originally introduced by Saint Augustine (in the fourth and fifth centuries), but continually reiterated and developed during the course of the Middle Ages, the theory concerned the right to engage in war (*ius ad bellum*) as well as rightful conduct in war (*ius in bellum*). The main points of this theory are outlined here with respect to what it says about the relationship between combatants and non-combatants.[4]

For a war to be a just war there must above all be a just cause. War must always be waged with just intentions. A war waged in defence is always legitimate. An offensive war can be legitimate if it is intended to correct a wrong suffered or to regain lost property or rights. The objective of a just war must be to reinstate the peace and harmony the opponent has destroyed through his actions and war must be the last resort. Firstly, peaceful solutions must be sought through mediation and arbitration. These requirements lend the just war a legal character. The objective of the just war is to re-establish justice, and the ideal conflict is altogether reminiscent of a court case in which the parties make a charge, conduct a case, negotiate, take out a summons, issue a warning and submit to judgement. The just war can be compared to a penalty issued to a criminal or lawbreaker.

Some of the most influential thinkers of the Middle Ages (primarily Thomas Aquinas, c. 1225–74) stated that for a war to be a just war it must be waged by the pope, the emperor, a king or possibly a prince. No other war could ever be just. Other thinkers concede that a just war, at least a so-called smaller war (as opposed to a large war, *bellum universale*), can be waged by people or groups below the level of prince – for example, one

4 For further details on *bellum justum*, see Contamine, *War in the Middle Ages*, 264–65, and 282–95. See also Carsten Selch Jensen, "'Gud vil det' – om retfærdige og hellige krige i middelalderen," in *Retfærdig krig. Om legitimeringer af krig og voldsudøvelse i historien*, ed. Carsten Selch Jensen (Odense: Syddansk Universitetsforlag, 2006), 86–109.

knight against another. In some medieval theories on war and society, this is even seen as allowing subjects to wage a just war against a tyrannical ruler.

The clergy, for whom it is sacrilegious to use violence, may not participate in war. In contrast, all secular persons may do so. In this respect the distinction between combatants and non-combatants in just war differs from the distinction made in the ideology of the estates, and in the peace movement. Persons who according to the ideal of the estates belong to "those who labour" are placed in the same group of potential participants in battle as members of the "warring" estate. Persons who, according to the ideals of the peace movement, belong to the category of innocent victims of the violence of knights are grouped together with precisely these knights.

In other respects, the rules pertaining to just war draw a line between combatants and non-combatants in almost the same place as the ideals of the estates and the peace movement. Thus, some of the medieval interpretations of *bellum justum* state that the clergy, women, children and the poor should be protected from war as under *Pax Dei*. In the case of some thinkers, however, only the clergy, women and children are named as needing special protection, while male non-combatants are, it would seem, legitimate targets in a just war.

The medieval rules pertaining to just war do not actually consider in any detail the question of how combatants should treat non-combatants in areas of war. For the most part, they examine the justification for waging war per se. Some of the rules concerning *ius in bellum* are, however, indirectly relevant to how combatants should behave towards non-combatants. The requirement that war should be conducted with a just disposition is central. War may not be waged out of hatred, revenge, ambition or greed. The combatant may not derive satisfaction from his enterprise or conduct warfare in an uninhibited, impassioned way. He who conducts a just war shall do only what is necessary to achieve the objective of the war, namely to re-establish peace, harmony and justice. As a consequence, the war shall be waged against the enemy's warriors, castles and resources, but non-combatants shall be spared as long as they do not prevent the warrior in his endeavour to achieve the actual purpose of the war.

Another issue related to the just war that is relevant to the relationship between combatants and non-combatants concerns the conscience and sinfulness of the combatant of lower rank. Here, the same medieval scholars who tend to emphasize the authority of the ruler when it comes to warfare believe that the combatant can exercise his profession without committing sin, irrespective of whether the war is just or unjust. In every situation it is the ruler who bears responsibility. As a consequence, the combatant is permitted to use force against non-combatants, at least as long as he is acting upon orders. Only his superiors would be committing sin. However, this contradicts other rules for just war and some medieval thinkers assert that each individual soldier is, indeed, responsible for his own actions. This last viewpoint declined in importance in the late Middle Ages, yielding to a more authoritarian viewpoint, presumably due to the growth of territorial kingdoms. At the same time, the emerging states increasingly disciplined their warriors to refrain from ransacking and acts of barbarism. The ideals of *Pax Dei* and chivalrous conduct were held up as examples. The political motivation was the common interest of the princes in being able to wage moderate wars against each other and each prince's wish to increase control over his warriors.

Let us now sum up. In Europe of the High Middle Ages a distinction was made between combatants and non-combatants. The distinction, however, was not defined by the state. On the contrary, it arose as a reaction to the disintegration (or absence) of state and in many ways differed significantly from the modern-day distinction, partly because it was not based on any notion of universal human rights, but rather on hierarchical distinctions between people within a social ideology of inequality. The medieval distinctions were nonetheless the root of the modern differentiation between military and civilian, and many of today's concrete rules governing the relationship between military and civilian can be traced back to the Middle Ages. Three cultural elements seem to have played a particularly important role (although others might be considered equally important): The ideological division of society into estates, the peace movement and the idea of just war. The first two aspects differentiated between combatants and non-combatants in more or less the same way, and, it would seem, relatively consistently. The varying ideas about just war were in some respects more inconsistent, for example on the question of whether male peasants and townsmen belonged to the category of combatant or non-combatant. A feature common to all three cultural elements was that members of the clergy were regarded as non-combatants. *Pax Dei* and *bellum justum* shared the view that women and children were not legitimate targets in wars and feuds. It goes without saying, of course, that the rules were often violated. Here, however, we are interested in norms and ideologies rather than reality and practice. These norms and ideologies were tremendously important. The importance of the ideals of the peace movements was due to their huge popularity among the commoners (as they offered the weak protection against the strong) and their usefulness to the clergy and later to emerging states. In the case of the ideals of the estates, it was due to their usefulness to the nobility and the clergy. The idea of just war was useful to all larger concentrations of power which needed to legitimize the use of physical force. In the form in which this theory was elaborated by most medieval religious scholars and moralists, it especially served the interests of popes, emperors, kings and princes, although the rules were also used by the nobility in their feuds.

Denmark in the Late Middle Ages

Let us now turn to Denmark in the fifteenth and sixteenth centuries. We will begin in the late Middle Ages, which, according to the conventional periodization in Danish historiography, is the period from 1350 to 1536. The following section focuses on the period after 1450. It is only from that date onwards that the volume and nature of the source material allows a closer study of the phenomena under study. To begin with, we will describe how the three European cultural elements dealt with in the previous section featured in Denmark in the late Middle Ages.

The *estates ideology* was highly developed and constituted the basis of social order. Following Christianization (c. 950–1100), the clergy became a separate, distinct social group whose special status was fully recognized by the mid-thirteenth century at the latest. The origins of the warring nobility presumably reached back to the Iron Age and the Viking Age, and from the twelfth to the thirteenth century their position in society took on the same feudal character as in the rest of Europe. In the provincial laws from the first half of the thirteenth century an estate of so-called *herremænd* (lord's men) become a distinct entity, separate from the rest of the population. A *herremand* was a landowner and had the right to receive dues from his serfs. The main difference between the *herremand* and the other groups is made apparent in the Law of Jutland in 1241. Here *herremænd* are declared exempt from contributing to the mobilization of the kingdom's fleet (the so-called *leding*). In other words, they are exempt from naval conscription and from the levies which could substitute this naval service, unlike freeholders and serfs. According to the Law of Jutland, the justification for this is that *herremænd* pay full dues of their land "since they risk their neck for King and country." The *herremand* must serve "fully armed," as opposed to the peasant who shall merely serve with a shield and "three common weapons" (sword, iron helmet and spear).[5] Even if peasants also help to defend the realm, the law thus argues that the military service of *herremænd* is more perilous and more unlimited. The *herremand* is the vassal of the king and in return for his services as the king's warrior, he is exempt from the payment of levies and taxes. By around 1300 at the latest, this warrior group had developed into an aristocracy with hereditary rights. In the late Middle Ages, the nobility was a closed estate whose special status and more extensive privileges were justified by their military service.

Under the clergy and nobility came the broader population in the countryside and towns. During the Middle Ages the townspeople became a distinct estate of their own, positioned above the peasants in the social hierarchy. The oldest surviving sermon from Denmark, which dates from around 1300, refers to a division into four social classes: clergy, knights, merchants and peasants (*clerici*, *milites*, *mercatores* and *rustici*). A similar division into four groups can be found in the royal coronation charters of 1320 and 1326.[6] In the late Middle Ages the concrete social differences between townsmen and peasants became more clear-cut, while at the same time there was a homogenization of terminology within each group so that

5 Erik Kroman and Stig Iuul, eds., *Danmarks Gamle Love paa Nutidsdansk* (Copenhagen: G.E.C. Gads Forlag, 1945–1948), (Jyske Lov [Law of Jutland], 3rd book §§4, 7 and 18).

6 Aksel E. Christensen, *Ret og magt i dansk middelalder* (Copenhagen: Gyldendal, 1978), 51.

the two main categories now became *borger* (townsman/burgher) and *bonde* (peasant).[7] From the mid-fifteenth century, the four estates (clergy, nobility, townspeople and peasants) were attributed constitutional importance. Denmark, however, never became a fully developed "state of estates" (like the German *Ständestaat*), even though, for example, all four estates occasionally were invoked to legitimize the levying of taxes.[8] The form of rule from the fourteenth century until the absolute monarchy was established in 1660 could be described as monarchic-oligarchic (power was shared among the king, the nobility and, until the Reformation, the clergy).

The European *peace movements* also became very important in Denmark. This can be seen, among other things, from the many rules pertaining to peace contained in the provincial laws, which are directly inspired by *Pax Dei* and *Treuga Dei*. Thus the laws introduce harsh sanctions against acts of violence carried out during certain periods and in certain places and they operate with terms such as *vejfred* (peace on public roads), *tingfred* (peace in the court/assembly), *julefred* (peace at Christmas), etc. Peasants and townspeople are not protected as such but a number of peace rules are clearly aimed at providing special protection to these weaker groups. A telling example is the so-called *plovfred* (peace when ploughing the land). If a peasant is assaulted while ploughing, the penalty is more severe than it would otherwise have been. However, the more severe penalty only applies if the peasant is holding the plough with at least one hand. If he has let go of the plough, he is no longer protected by the *plovfred*. In this case it is clearly the weak (and labouring) peasant who enjoys the special protection of the law. Furthermore, the law contains provisions concerning *markfred* (peace in the fields), *kirkefred* (peace in the church) and *byfred* (peace in the town), which provide protection not only to peasants but also to townspeople and members of the clergy. There are no provisions specifically intended to protect nobles. The intention behind the peace rules is without doubt to protect *oratores* and *laboratores* against *bellatores*. The vocabulary of peace is

7 Bjørn Poulsen, "Forholdet mellem land og by i dansk middelalder," *Historisk Tidsskrift* 109, no. 1 (2009): 1–19.

8 Jens E. Olesen, "Senmiddelalderens danske stændersamfund," in *Konge, kirke og samfund. De to øvrighedsmagter i dansk senmiddelalder*, ed. Agnes S. Arnorsdóttir, Per Ingesman and Bjørn Poulsen (Aarhus: Aarhus Universitetsforlag, 2007), 13–35.

very prominent in the source material extant from late medieval Denmark, such as, for example, national law, local laws, written plaints, penalties, lists of fines, etc.[9]

Finally, Denmark heeded the concept of *just war*. The subject is not particularly well-researched by historians, but there is no doubt that the Danish kingdoms did, in principle, respect common European norms relating to just war and just warfare. There are several examples of these norms being applied in the fifteenth century, as in the wars between Denmark and Sweden, for example, which arose as a consequence of Sweden's attempt to free itself from the Danish-dominated union that was established in 1397. Here, rules pertaining to the legal justification for war, declaration of war, ceasefire, free passage, reprieves, hostages, messengers, protection of peasants, and other concepts which stem from the ideal of *bellum justum*, are invoked and used in different ways.[10]

In late medieval Denmark there was thus an ideological distinction between combatants and non-combatants similar to the one found in other parts of Europe. An entire social group was defined by being warriors, and three social groups were defined, among other things, by not being warriors. The peace rules of the laws show evidence of a similar distinction between warring nobles and peaceful priests, peasants and townspeople, and something similar is seen in connection with concrete wars of the realm. The question, however, is to what extent these ideological constructions coincided with reality. We will look at this question more closely in the next section where it will be shown that the distinction between combatants and non-combatants was not always as clear-cut as presented in the various medieval theories about war, peace and social organization.

It is particularly interesting to examine whether or not it was only the members of the nobility who fought in the wars of the Danish monarchy. It is a matter of considerable debate whether the aforementioned naval conscription, the *leding*, included actual compulsory military service for peas-

9 Ole Fenger, *Fejde og mandebod. Studier over slægtsansvaret i germansk og gammeldansk ret* (Copenhagen: Juristforbundets Forlag, 1971), 341–541.

10 Many examples are available in Jens E. Olesen, *Unionskrige og stændersamfund. Bidrag til Nordens historie i Kristian I's regeringstid, 1450–1481* (Aarhus: Universitetsforlaget i Aarhus, 1983).

ants and townsmen, or whether it had already been permanently converted into a tax prior to the Law of Jutland, from which our knowledge about naval conscription derives. What we do know is that the naval conscription that was stipulated in the Law of Jutland was abolished before 1400 and that the *leding* had been transformed into a tax by the late Middle Ages, paid only by freeholders as a kind of feudal tax to the Crown. Serfs were exempted from the naval conscription tax so that their masters could demand a higher feudal rent from them.[11]

Not a great deal is known about possible military service by peasants and townsmen in the period between 1250 and 1400. There is evidence from the 1400s showing that peasants and townsmen were actually used for military purposes. However, it is extremely difficult to estimate to what degree due to the sparseness of source material. There are instances of peasants and townsmen being conscripted, both in connection with defensive and offensive wars, during the union wars against the separatist Swedes. In 1455, every thirtieth peasant was conscripted, in 1508 every twentieth, and in 1497 as many as every tenth. The townsmen were used in the fleet and on several occasions between 1471 and 1536, 1,500 to 2,000 combatants were conscripted from the Danish towns. We do not know how normal it was for peasants and townsmen to be conscripted in these numbers and we do not know how many actually went to war. Often, instead of conscripting peasants and townsmen for military service, extraordinary taxes or charges were imposed on them to finance foreign mercenaries.[12]

Peasants and townsmen were also used for defence. If the realm was attacked by an enemy, it was the duty of every adult man to leave his home

11 Erik Ulsig, "Landboer og bryder, skat og landgilde. De danske fæstebønder og deres afgifter i det 12. og 13. århundrede," in *Middelalder, metode og medier. Festskrift til Niels Skyum-Nielsen*, ed. Karsten Fledelius, Niels Lund and Herluf Nielsen (Copenhagen: Museum Tusculanums Forlag, 1981), 154–56.

12 William Christensen, *Dansk Statsforvaltning i det 15. Århundrede* (Copenhagen: Det Kongelige Danske Videnskabernes Selskab, C.E.G. Gads Forlag, 1903), 295–99. Bjørn Poulsen, "Med harnisk og hest. Om adel, krig og vold i dansk senmiddelalder," in *Riget, magten og æren. Den danske adel 1350–1660*, ed. Per Ingesman and Jens Villiam Jensen (Aarhus: Aarhus Universitetsforlag, 2001), 44–77, 50–55. Iben Fonnesberg-Schmidt, "Købstædernes militære ydelser før 1570," in *Renæssancens befæstede byer*, ed. Søren Bitsch Christensen (Aarhus: Dansk Center for Byhistorie and Aarhus Universitetsforlag, 2011), 99–144.

and help ward off the attack. This in all probability ancient duty to serve and defend one's country in the militia (*landeværn*) became a system in the late Middle Ages. In coastal areas, at least, peasants had a duty to personally participate in guarding and patrolling the coastline. If an enemy was sighted, a warning system consisting of burning beacons was activated and all men left their homes. According to a declaration by the regional court of Zealand in 1428, any man who remained at home when the beacons were burning was to be hanged from his own beams. During the union wars, peasants were also duty bound to help defend the Scania border with Sweden, and when 244 men from the towns were conscripted for this purpose in 1502, almost three quarters of them came from towns outside of Scania.[13]

One prerequisite for the military conscription of peasants was that they were armed. There does not seem to have been any central arsenal of weapons for use in wars of the realm, and when conscripted, townsmen and peasants were required to bring their own weaponry. There is a good deal of evidence to suggest that it was normal for townsmen and peasants to possess their own weapons and even armour.[14]

Thus, the ideological distinction between noble warriors and peaceful peasants and townspeople did not quite match the reality.[15] Notably, participation in battle by the lower estates was apparently organized by the "state" and not on a feudal level or on the basis of private land ownership. It seems that conscripted peasants not only came from land belonging to the Crown, but also the clergy and the nobility, and the conscripted peasants and townsmen were under the command of a royal official irrespective of their feudal relationship. The same applied to taxation to fund mercenaries. In this respect, the system can be considered to be proto-modern.

However, the nobility undoubtedly remained the warrior estate par excellence. When Denmark was at war, every adult nobleman was essentially duty bound to fight clad in armour and on horseback. Additionally,

13 Christensen, *Dansk Statsforvaltning*, 288–94. On the conscription in 1502, see Fonnesberg-Schmidt, "Købstædernes militære ydelser før 1570."

14 Poulsen, "Med harnisk og hest," 51–52.

15 In this respect the situation in Denmark was no different from the situation in many other parts of Europe, where the peasants occasionally served as soldiers in wars of the monarchy. This fact also explains why the rules on just war did not exclude men from the peasantry serving in a just war (see above).

by the mid-fifteenth century at the latest, nobles were obliged to provide an appropriate number of cavalrymen (generally commoners) commensurate with the size of their estates. Similarly the king's bailiffs (*lensmænd*), who were almost always of noble birth, were to provide ready and able men from the castle fief according to the fief's financial resources. The same applied to bishops, who were usually noblemen. From about 1500, the king occasionally required knights to wear a type of uniform. However, nothing similar applied to combatants from the lower estates.[16]

It is not known precisely how important this noble cavalry (which was known as the *rostjenesten*, or armoured service) was in military terms compared to the peasants, townsmen and mercenaries. From about 1500, its importance was declining, possibly even earlier.[17] It remains to be examined whether the direct military contribution of noblemen was more financially onerous than that of the peasants and townsmen relative to their wealth. It probably was. The fact that the contribution of the nobility was financed through dues paid by peasants is another matter – that was an element of the social division of labour and its ideological structure. The point is that the nobility continued in its role as the warrior estate.

Participation in war by peasants and townsmen modified the distinction made by feudal ideology between combatants and non-combatants and helped to lay the foundation for other, more modern distinctions. However, there was still such a large discrepancy between the military service of the nobility and that of other groups that the old distinction made sense. During the wars with Sweden in the decades between 1450 and 1470, noblemen such as Erik Ottesen Rosenkrantz and Claus Rønnow travelled tirelessly throughout the whole of northern Europe, going to battle in Sweden, defeating subversive noblemen in Denmark and carrying out diplomatic missions in Scandinavia, northern Germany and England to achieve ceasefires and forge alliances.[18] Many noblemen were almost permanently militarized in the service of king and realm, while most peasants

16 Christensen, *Dansk Statsforvaltning*, 299–326.

17 Poulsen, "Med harnisk og hest." Gunner Lind, "Den danske adel og den militære revolution," in *Riget, magten og æren. Den danske adel*, ed. Per Ingesman and Jens Villiam Jensen (Aarhus: Aarhus Universitetsforlag, 2001), 576–603, 578.

18 Harry Christensen, "Rosenkrantz og Gyldenstjerne 1466–1469. Et forsøg," in *Profiler i nordisk middelalder og renæssance. Festskrift til Poul Enemark*, ed. Svend E. Green-Peder-

and townsmen either never were or, at most, only were so for shorter and more well-defined periods.

One phenomenon that very much lessened the distinction between military and civilian in the late Middle Ages in Denmark, and made it different from today, was the many private feuds. As we can see from a statute from 1468 and the coronation charters from 1513 and 1523, a nobleman had the right to declare a feud on another nobleman. He merely had to give him one day's warning and have good reason to do so. The right to wage feuds stemmed from ancient times; the only new aspect was that it had become codified and regulated. Many feuds among the nobility are known from the late Middle Ages in Denmark. The feuds often arose from disputes over property and rights, and there was a political aspect also to many of them. They could be quite prolonged but generally involved relatively moderate acts of violence, often directed against the peasants and men of the opposing side. There were rarely more than one or two fatalities in a feud. Nonetheless, feuds significantly influenced society.[19]

The modern differentiation between the military and the civilian presupposes, among other things, a sharp differentiation between war and peace. In the late Middle Ages, feuds among the nobility meant that the distinction between the two was blurred. There was no clear line separating one type of conflict from another, between what we would now call public and private wars. Noblemen had the right to declare a feud in the same way as the monarchy had a right to declare war. In terms of norms there was very little distinction made between the wars of the king and those of the nobility, and likewise the distinction between public and private was generally vague. The conflicts of the monarchy and those of the nobility shared the same terminology: *feyde* (feud), *tvedragt* (discord), *trætte* (dispute), *uvilje* (ill-will).[20] Until about 1500, there was no specific term to describe wars waged by the monarchy against other sovereign political entities. At the close of the medieval period, words such as *orlog* and *krig*

sen, Jens Villiam Jensen and Knud Prange (Aarhus: Arusia-Historiske Skrifter, 1983), 29–48.

19 Jeppe Büchert Netterstrøm, *Fejde og magt i senmiddelalderen. Rosenkrantzernes fejder med biskop Jens Iversen og Lage Brok 1454–1475* (Kerteminde: Landbohistorisk Selskab, 2012).

20 Ibid., 259–92.

emerged to denote wars between monarchies, but the word *feyde* was used just as often to mean the same thing and continued to be used to denote a private feud, a civil war as well as a rebellion.[21] Likewise the terminology and norms used for peace, peace treaty, ceasefire and safe passage were more or less identical, regardless of whether they concerned a war or a feud.

The Danes of the late Middle Ages were aware, of course, of the difference between a large-scale war involving the mobilization of thousands of troops, major battles and extensive damage and the far more limited private feud, the minor war. However, there were some common traits in the way major and minor wars were conducted in practice. The outcome of major wars was rarely decided in major battles or the military conquest of large areas of land, but largely consisted of raids and looting, which was very akin to the feud practice among the nobility.[22] The men provided by noblemen to fight in the wars of the realm were the same men they used to attack their rivals in private feuds. Attacks on castles were not something that only occurred in large-scale wars; they also occurred in feuds among the nobility.[23]

Furthermore, Denmark was not ravaged to any significant degree by any large-scale wars during the late Middle Ages. The country was seldom invaded by large foreign armies, with the exception of a few short-lived Swedish campaigns in Scania during the union wars, and with the exception of the large-scale invasions during the civil war at the close of the era (*Grevens Fejde*, the Count's Feud, 1534–36). Denmark's wars were generally conducted outside its territory, primarily in Sweden. Thus, for long spans of time, the smaller wars fought between the members of the nobility were more apparent to many Danes than the large wars of the monarchy. Most burghers and peasants presumably had personal experiences with the feuds among the nobility, fewer with the monarchy's feuds with foreign powers.

The difference between times of war and times of peace was therefore not only determined by whether the state was at war. It was also deter-

21 Otto Kalkar, ed., *Ordbog til det ældre danske sprog (1300–1700)* (Copenhagen: Thieles Bogtrykkeri, 1881–1917), s.v. "krig." and s.v. "orlog."

22 Poulsen, "Med harnisk og hest"

23 Netterstrøm, *Fejde og magt,*" 76–77. Jeppe Büchert Netterstrøm, "Den danske stat og voldsmonopolet 1400–1660," *Den jyske Historiker*, no. 116 (2007): 88–119, esp. 95.

mined by whether the nobility were at war with each other. In this respect the difference between what was perceived as military and what was perceived as civilian was not exclusively determined by the state. Legally, there was certainly a difference between times when Denmark as a realm was at war with a foreign power, and times of peace between the realm and its neighbours. In the case of the latter, Peace of the Land prevailed. The feuds of the nobility were only a relative termination of peace in the sense that only the peace between the feuding parties was upset, and even in the case of an open feud the law of the realm and thus the Peace of the Land applied. Only if a man was outlawed for a specific crime (and anyone could kill him with impunity) was there total (but only individual) hostility within a private feud that suspended the general state of law.[24] By contrast, a large-scale war *could* consist of almost all-embracing and complete hostility between two monarchies – not always, however. In the large-scale wars, too, there seem to have been different levels of escalation, with the lowest level being not very different from the regulated and moderate feuds of the nobility. Here, the most chivalrous and humane of the rules of *jus in bellum* seem to have applied.[25]

Moreover, the domestic Peace of the Land, it seems, was not suspended when Denmark was waging war against other monarchies. There was no fully-fledged state of emergency or martial law. All in all, war entailed only a few exceptions to the state of law in times of peace. However, there *were* exceptions. There were special laws which only applied during wartime and/or to "militarized" persons. We have already mentioned the harsh penalty for desertion from the militia. In addition, according to the Law of Jutland of 1241, particularly high fines were charged for killing someone within the *leding* and the laws also contained special stipulations regarding theft within the *leding*.[26] But there does not seem to have been any permanent court martial with jurisdiction over military personnel, either during the period of the provincial laws or in the late Middle Ages. In the fifteenth and early sixteenth century, cases concerning evasion of coastal

24 Netterstrøm, "Fejde og magt," 270–72.
25 Contamine, *War in the Middle Ages*, 288–89.
26 Kroman and Juul, eds., *Gamle Love* (Jyske Lov [Law of Jutland], 2nd book §114 and 3rd book §22.

guard duties by peasants were brought before the same courts as civil cases under secular jurisdiction.[27] Another example of an exception to the general state of law during wars of the monarchy against foreign powers was the ban on bringing legal action against noble landowners as long as they were away on "the call of duty and in the service of the realm."[28]

Feuds among the nobility blurred the distinction between times of war and times of peace (hence also between military and civilian); however, such feuds did serve to reinforce the traditional medieval distinction between combatants (*bellatores*) and non-combatants (*oratores* and *laboratores*). They symbolically highlighted the difference between the estates, and in concrete terms led to the self-perpetuation of the feudal system. Peasants were often a target in these feuds and their subsequent need for protection was served by the feuding nobles. In return for this protection, the peasants recompensed the nobility by paying dues and offering obedience and gratitude.

Nonetheless, the distinctions between combatants and non-combatants in private feuds were not entirely clear cut. Often the peasants – who were otherwise an estate of non-warriors – took part in noble feuds on the side of their lord. In 1459 Philip Axelsen Thott, the royal bailiff on the island of Langeland, was accused of inciting the commoners of the island to attack his enemy Erik Eriksen Løvenbalk. The feud between Philip Axelsen and Erik Eriksen emanated from a private inheritance dispute, and the accusation against Philip Axelsen (which he denied) was, more precisely, an accusation that he had abused the militia system to mobilize the peasants. This case is, indeed, one of the most spectacular incidences of the militarization of peasants in a feud among the Danish nobility in the late Middle Ages, but there are a number of other examples of a similar nature.[29]

A feud between the Bishop of Roskilde, Niels Skave, and the Cistercian monastery of Sorø from 1489 to 1493 contains examples of both purport-

27 Vilhelm Lütken, *Bidrag til Langelands Historie,* Rudkøbing 1909, 549 (letter 5/2 1457)," Erik Reitzel-Nielsen and Ole Fenger, eds., *Danske Domme 1375–1662. De private domssamlinger* (Copenhagen: Det Danske Sprog- og Litteraturselskab, C. A. Reitzels Boghandel, 1978–1988), 48: 549.

28 Jeppe Büchert Netterstrøm, *At forsvare til rette. Værnsforholdet og bøndernes retslige stilling i Danmarks senmiddelalder 1400–1513* (Kerteminde: Landbohistorisk Selskab, 2003), 29. Netterstrøm, "Fejde og magt," 48, note 132.

29 Netterstrøm, *At forsvare til rette,* 94–95. Netterstrøm, "Fejde og magt," 39, 299–300.

edly innocent peasants who were brutally attacked by the feuding lord's henchmen, and peasants who played an active role in the service of their lord.[30] The feud arose from a principle dispute about the right of the bishop to visit and inspect the monastery, which, especially from 1488, claimed the right of the Cistercian order to exemption from the authority of the bishop. The reason (or pretext) for the escalation of the feud was a more local one. Since ancient times, Sorø monastery had owned all the land and property in the village of Stenmagle, with the exception of the presbytery. Since the presbytery had burned down a long time ago, the abbot had allowed the priest to move into one of the monastery's holdings in the village, for which the changing priests from then on paid rent to the monastery for many years. In 1489, a new priest was sent to the village. He refused to pay rent and thus challenged the monastery's proprietary right to the holding. The priest sought the support of his superior, the bishop, who was more than willing to offer help. At the beginning of April, the abbot requested that the priest leave but the priest refused and on 8 May the prior of the monastery and two monks turned up in Stenmagle to evict the priest.

According to the lawyer of the bishop and the priest before the papal supreme court in Rome, to which the case was later referred, the prior then resorted to violence – with the assistance of the village peasants. The priest was forcefully driven out of his home, beaten with sticks and whips, and the peasants ransacked and damaged his property, leaving him poor and homeless. The lawyer of the monastery insisted, however, that the peasants had behaved in a friendly manner to the priest, helping him to move at his own behest, which seems a less credible version of events. The bishop reacted by excommunicating the peasants. However, the abbot immediately rescinded the excommunication and the peasants continued their opposition to the

30 Johs. Lindbæk, "Biskop Niels Skave i Roskilde og Sorø kloster," *Historisk Tidsskrift* 8, no. 1 (1907–08): 254–83. Troels Dahlerup, *De fire stænder, 1400–1500* (Copenhagen: Gyldendal and Politikens Forlag, 1989), 281–88. Per Ingesman, *Provisioner og processer. Den romerske rota og dens behandling af danske sager i middelalderen* (Aarhus: Aarhus Universitetsforlag, 2003), 295–317. Also based on various sources including a transcript (in the Royal Danish Library) under Thomas Bartholin of part of the case for the papal supreme court (Roman Rota), transcribed and kindly lent to me by Professor Per Ingesman, Aarhus University. Per Ingesman is planning to publish this as well as other sources concerning Danish cases dealt with by the Rota in the Middle Ages.

priest, who still preached in the church. The peasants went to the church despite being excommunicated and sometimes stood by the door of the church to prevent the priest from entering.

The bishop then had the peasants outlawed at the regional court of Zealand. He thus obtained the right to punish the outlawed peasants and to use force to reinstall the priest in his residence. In September, the bishop dispatched eighty armed men, led by several of his noble vassals, to Stenmagle. They attacked the former presbytery, where one of the bailiffs of the monastery was now residing with large stocks of corn, money and goods which had been claimed in dues on behalf of the monastery. The bailiff and his wife and children were driven out, derided and mistreated and all their property and the monastery's dues were looted or destroyed. The peasants of the village who did not manage to flee were attacked by the bishop's men and abducted. According to the abbot's procurator, the prisoners were "imprisoned in narrow dungeons where they could hardly breathe, fettered and chained in a cruel, inhumane way and were moreover subjected to terrible torture, so that they lost the strength in their arms, hands and feet and other limbs, which became stiff and useless."[31]

This account – which the bishop's procurator did not deny but rather confirmed – plays upon the stereotype of the poor, weak and innocent peasant who is a victim of the almighty power of the feuding lord. The use of the word "inhumane" (*inhumaniter*)[32] in this context is interesting. The fact was, however, that the peasants in Stenmagle were not innocent in either a legal or moral respect. With their attack on the priest, they had made themselves party to the feud that the monastery had engaged in with the bishop of Roskilde. And the procurator of the bishop of Roskilde was able to bring into play the stereotype of the poor, pious priest who was assaulted by lawless, violent laymen. Both the stereotype of the poor, defenceless priest and the stereotype of the innocent, oppressed peasants stem from the ideals of the medieval peace movement. It is, by the way, striking that the bishop found it necessary to dispatch so many armed men

31 Lindbæk, "Biskop Niels Skave," 269.
32 Bartholin (see note 30 above), 670.

to Stenmagle; apparently, he anticipated considerable armed resistance by the village dwellers.[33]

The medieval ideological identification of nobles with combatants and peasants with non-combatants was thus relativized by the fact that the peasants participated in their lords' feuds, even though propaganda exploited traditional distinctions and stereotypes, and the participation of the peasants in the feuds of the nobility was at the will of the nobles and thus well within the framework of the feudal structure. The theoretical distinction was also relativized by the fact that peasants and burghers engaged in feuds on their own account and seem to have insisted on their right to do so as much as the nobles. It appears that feuds between peasant kins, and apparently also between common townsmen, were a widespread phenomenon in the late Middle Ages in Denmark. These feuds did not militarize peasants in the same way as the wars of the monarchy did and they did not have the same major social implications as feuds among the nobility. Nonetheless, the fact that members of an armed peasantry often found themselves embroiled in lengthy and bloody feuds[34] played a role in blurring the distinction between noble combatants and commoner non-combatants (and between war and peace).

The major peasant revolts of the late Middle Ages very much served to relativize the attempt to distinguish between a military and a civilian sector in Danish society. In the years 1438–41 and 1534, major peasant revolts wreaked havoc in most parts of the Danish realm, and in 1525 an equally extensive and serious uprising took place in Scania. Furthermore, there were a series of menacing peasant uprisings in Jutland in the 1520s and in 1531. In Sweden during the time of the union there was at least as many revolts, which must have affected the perception of military and civilian in Denmark as well. In times of rebellion, the peasants followed a fixed

33 In 1682 there were twenty-nine peasants and ten smallholders in the town, see Henrik Pedersen, *De danske Landbrug. Fremstillet paa Grundlag af Forarbejderne til Christian V.s Matrikel* (Copenhagen: Gyldendal, 1928), 27. See above reference. The number of peasants was presumably about the same in the late Middle Ages, while the smallholders probably came later. There were also household servants and adult sons of peasants living at home. Altogether, between forty and sixty adult men were living in the village in 1489.

34 Jeppe Büchert Netterstrøm, "Bondefejder i Danmark 1450–1650," in *Feider og fred i nordisk middelalder*, ed. Erik Opsahl (Oslo: Unipub, 2007), 35–72.

practice, which was implemented according to a familiar structure commonly used when social unrest was vented in the form of organized mass violence against the landowners, the church and the Crown. The peasants used power techniques that had otherwise been created (or usurped) by the state to control the peasants and mobilize them militarily. For example, the peasants used the warning system employed in times of national defence (burning beacons, messengers) and held muster at the district courts and regional courts, which under normal circumstances functioned as courts of judgement dominated by the upper classes. The peasants set up their own court martial, which condemned deserters from the revolt to death by hanging from their own beams, in emulation of the death sentences passed by the Crown on peasants who deserted the militia.

During their revolts, the peasants managed to raise efficient armies capable of causing extensive damage to the property of the king, the clergy and the nobility. In quite a few large-scale battles, the peasants defeated the troops of the upper classes. As a rule, the peasants' revolts were joined by individual members of the nobility, who were no doubt able to contribute considerable military expertise. However, in general terms, each of the peasant revolts led to the suspension for a period of time of the role of the nobility as the warrior class, and inhibited significantly, in both concrete and symbolic terms, the efforts of the Crown to attain an effective monopoly on military power. On the other hand, peasant revolts were a relatively rare occurrence and were ultimately quelled each time they occurred. The legal settlement and restoration of social order after a revolt by the peasantry led to the restitution and accentuation of the distinction between the military and the civilian by the ruling classes.[35]

Peasants and townspeople seem to have believed that they had the right to revolt, which naturally clashed with the principles of law of the authorities. However, towards the end of the Middle Ages, the nobility in Denmark did actually acquire the right to revolt against a tyrannical monarch. From 1483, this right to revolt was written into the coronation charters and it was made use of on several occasions by the nobility in Denmark, Nor-

35 See Anders Bøgh, Jørgen Würtz Sørensen and Lars Tvede-Jensen, eds., *Til kamp for friheden. Sociale oprør i nordisk middelalder* (Aalborg: Bogsmedjen, 1988) for articles on peasant uprisings in Denmark and Scandinavia.

way and Sweden – such as, for example, when the Danish nobility deposed King Christian II in 1523.[36] The right of the nobility to turn to arms against the king did, of course, undermine development towards a modern state. The fact that the right to revolt was the prerogative of the aristocracy and was ruled out for the lower estates reinforced the traditional view among the nobility of which groups in society had the right to conduct war.

To summarize, it can be said that there was a gap between theory and practice when it came to the distinction between military and civilian in Denmark in the late Middle Ages. The conglomerate of pacifist ideologies and ideologies legitimizing the estates, which together made up a normative differentiation between combatants and non-combatants throughout medieval Europe, was also present in Denmark in this period. In practice, this normative differentiation was modified in many different ways. Denmark hardly differed in this respect from the rest of Europe, where peasants and civilians were also used militarily and where in many places social upheaval and feuds reigned among the nobility as well as among the townsmen and peasants. The reason for what seems to be an increased belligerence among Danish peasants in the late Middle Ages was the improvement in their economic and social situation during the late medieval population crisis, which was more of a crisis for landowners than for the peasants. Uprisings and feuding among the peasants contributed to erasing the traditional distinction between *bellatores* and *laboratores*. The conscription of peasants and townsmen to the major wars of the monarchy had the same effect, but this was almost a modern trait presaging the future, unlike their participation in private feuds. The peasants' internal feuds impeded the emergence of a modern state with a monopoly on the use of force, and even though participation by peasants in the feuds of the nobility in its way relativized the distinction between warring nobles and peaceful peasants, it nonetheless took place within the framework of the feudal system, dominated as it was by the warring nobility.

36 Jens Peter Sørensen, "Oprørsretten som politisk instrument i kampen mellem kongemagt og aristokrati 1476–1505," in *Profiler i nordisk senmiddelalder og renaissance. Festskrift til Poul Enemark*, ed. Svend E. Green-Pedersen, Jens William Jensen and Knud Prange (Aarhus: Arusia – Historiske Skrifter, 1983), 77–82.

The nobility was still the warrior estate, both in fact as well as in name, and towards the end of the Middle Ages was presumably the social force that did the most to preserve the traditional distinction between combatants and non-combatants. They did this by continually translating the norms into reality: for example, in the wars of the monarchy, in the uprisings against the Crown, in the quelling of peasant rebellions, and in their feuds. The feuds of the nobility stand out as a phenomenon that greatly inhibited development towards the modern distinction between military and civilian. Noble feuds distorted the experience of a distinct contrast between times of war and times of peace. At the same time they inhibited the development of the state, which was later a prerequisite for the modern distinction.

Military and Civilian after the Reformation

The Protestant Reformation was implemented in Denmark by King Christian III (1534–59) in 1536. He had been victorious in the major civil war, Grevens Fejde (1534–36), that was fought essentially over the succession to the throne but also involved major social revolts. The Reformation, and Christian III's victory in *Grevens Fejde*, served to consolidate the Danish monarchy. The Catholic Church vanished as a factor of political and military power and church property (approximately one third of all property in Denmark) was confiscated by the Crown, vastly increasing the Crown's revenue. In the sixteenth century, a number of reforms were carried out in the fief system which limited the autonomous power of noble bailiffs on royal fiefdoms. Lutheran theology, generally, ascribed almost unrestricted power to the monarch. However, Denmark did not become an absolute monarchy until 1660. During the so-called "reign of the aristocracy" (1536–1660), the king had to share power with the nobility, whose privileges (such as exclusive entitlement to certain offices, protection of property and exemption from tax together with authority over peasants) grew significantly in formal terms compared to the Middle Ages. The king ruled over the realm in conjunction with the council of the realm (*rigsrådet*), where only secular noblemen had a seat. The privileges of the nobility as well as their constitutional rights were, as in the Middle Ages, legitimized by their military service, which continued to be identical with service in the cavalry. Society was thus still divided into estates defined along the lines of combatant and non-combatant. The military importance of the noble cavalrymen, however, rapidly declined from the sixteenth to seventeenth centuries, and likewise their institutional status on a par with the Crown was more formal than real. The expansion of the privileges of the nobility must be seen rather as a countermeasure to the growing power of the Crown than a sign of actual growth of noble power.

In reality, the "reign of the aristocracy" represented an alliance between the Crown and the high nobility, with the former clearly in the dominant position. The dominant position of the king compared to the nobility can be seen, among other things, by the fact that the right of the nobility to revolt was removed from the coronation charters. The nobility formally retained their right to feud, which features in all coronation charters up to the absolute monarchy; however, in practice the nobility ceased to conduct major feuds against each other after the Reformation. During the "reign of the aristocracy," there was a general shift towards a state monopoly on violence. In 1537 the death penalty was introduced for townsmen and peasants who committed manslaughter, which marked the end of the right of peasants to conduct blood feuds. In the case of homicide committed by members of the nobility, the milder provisions of the provincial laws on manslaughter applied right up to the law of the absolute monarchy, the Danish Law of 1683. In practice, however, there were tougher penalties for murder and violent crimes committed by the nobility after the Reformation, especially from the 1580s. It is significant for the state formation process during this period that there was never again a major rebellion by the peasantry in Denmark following Grevens Fejde.[37]

The fact that large-scale feuds among the nobility, rebellions among the peasantry, and feuds among townsmen and peasants died out after the Reformation no doubt sharpened the distinction between war and peace as compared to the late Middle Ages. War became the war of the king and the monarchy. Peace was no longer the absence of noble feuds, but rather the absence of wars of the realm. At the same time, the noble cavalry ser-

37 Netterstrøm, "Den danske stat."

vice was increasingly subject to state rule, not least due to the growing tactical demands of the period. Thus the nobles who fought in the service of the Crown became more disciplined and the noble cavalry was transformed from an army of medieval knights into a modern cavalry. Townsmen and peasants continued to be conscripted to military service in the same proto-modern way as in the late Middle Ages, and on a similar scale. They too were subjected in the sixteenth and seventeenth centuries to the discipline that was necessary to create up to date infantry formations.

These circumstances must have led to a sharper contrast between what one might call a military situation and a civilian situation. In peacetime there really was peace and most of society was more clearly a civil society. When there was war, or the threat of war, parts of the population were militarized at the behest of the state. Those who were militarized must have experienced the transition to a "military situation" as a bigger leap than in the medieval society of violence, also because the military had become more "military" than before owing to tighter discipline. The difference between militarized and non-militarized persons must have seemed more clear-cut than previously.

The Danish terminology of war and feud reflects this development. As mentioned, there was originally hardly any difference between the Danish terms for public war and private feud. In the sixteenth and seventeenth centuries, a linguistic shift took place. This linguistic shift was not the consequence of a clear allocation of the terms to either the domain of public war or the domain of private feuds. It was not, as one might have expected, that the word *feyde* was used increasingly to denote a private feud as opposed to *krig* and *orlog*, which exclusively meant public war – as is the case in modern Danish. Well into the seventeenth century, *feyde* was in fact one of the most common terms denoting wars waged by the Danish monarchy against other states.[38] At the same time, *feyde* was used less and less to denote a private feud simply because private feuds were more or less dying out. After the Reformation, the word *feyde* – in the sense of a private feud – was gradually only used as a morpheme in its own negation, namely as part

38 See, for example, the burial sermon for Herluf Trolle (*feide*=krig) in Gustav Ludvig Wad, ed., *Breve til og fra Herluf Trolle og Birgitte Gjøe* (Copenhagen: V. Thaning & Appel, 1893), 1: xiii–xxvi.

of the term *orfeyde* (non-feud), a term that was still in use in connection with trials for manslaughter.[39] Thus, this linguistic shift of the sixteenth and seventeenth centuries consisted in the word *feyde* gradually coming to mean a public war, whereas private conflicts were increasingly described using words with vaguer reference to legitimizing factors, such as the right to private feud. The connotation of the modern Danish word *fejde* as being a private conflict is thus a result of a more recent linguistic development.

One consequence of the Danish Reformation was, of course, that Denmark adopted Lutheran theology and social ideology. Thus it makes sense for us in this context to examine Martin Luther's view of war, soldiers and civilians.[40] Luther did not develop a revolutionary new theory of just war. With regard to this, he seems more or less to have followed the ideals of the Middle Ages. Luther was purportedly a strong opponent of offensive war; however, on closer inspection, he seems rather to follow medieval thinking, namely that an offensive war is permissible if the insult is sufficiently grave. The deciding factor seems to be the question of who originally provokes the conflict – for example, an attack can be construed as a type of self-defence. In his treatment of the question as to what extent a soldier may exercise his duty without committing a sin, we see the unfolding of Luther's underlying authoritarian view. Soldiers are fundamentally guilt-free because they have a duty to subordinate themselves to the orders of the prince. However, soldiers may not derive satisfaction from war or battle, or plunder out of greed. There are clear parallels here with medieval thinking; Luther is continuing the more authoritarian interpretations of *bellum justum*, which can already be found in the high Middle Ages and became prevalent in the late Middle Ages (see above). Luther thus believes that the monarch – and only the monarch – may conduct a just war. Noblemen, townspeople or others below the princely/royal level may never do this. Rebellion against

39 Netterstrøm, "Bondefejder," 67.

40 For the following discussion of the view held by Luther and other sixteenth-century thinkers on just war, see: Steffen Kjeldgaard-Pedersen, "Om synet på krig og oprør i 1500-tallets Europa – især hos Luther," in *Retfærdig krig. Om legitimeringer af krig og voldsudøvelse i historien*, ed. Carsten Selch Jensen (Odense: Syddansk Universitetsforlag, 2006), 113–65. See also Heinz Duchhardt, "War and International Law in Europe, Sixteenth to Eighteenth Centuries," in *War and Competition between States*, ed. Philippe Contamine (Oxford: Clarendon Press, 2000), 279–99.

public authority is under no circumstances legitimate, whereas the quelling of rebellion by a monarch is always legitimate. The prince has been chosen by God and all are subject to his authority, even if he is a tyrant. Even if war is not good, the people must obey and accept it as God's punishment for the sins of mankind.

The ultimate logic of Luther's radically authoritarian perspective is that the wars of rulers will always be seen as just wars; the crucial factor is merely whether the war is being waged by a prince or monarch. Luther did not go quite as far as this, but this viewpoint became gradually more and more prevalent among the war theoreticians of the sixteenth and seventeenth centuries. The solution to the paradox inherent in medieval thinking on *bellum justum* – namely that both sides in a war may claim at any time that they are conducting a legitimate war against an enemy for reasons of justice and peace – is to ascribe legitimacy to all warring parties as long as they are sovereign states. Thus, the medieval view that a just war must have a just intention gradually diminished. This clearly predicted an absolutist point of view.

In the question of the relationship between military and civilian Luther's authoritarian viewpoint with its emphasis on the position of the prince must be the most important factor. For Luther, military action may stem only from the power of the prince, thus implying a sharp distinction between military and civilian. Luther does not seem to be concerned in any detail with how civilians should be treated in war; however, his attitude to this question can be deduced precisely from his basic authoritarian viewpoint. Luther's explanation of the guiltlessness of the soldier – and the perception of war as God's punishment for human sin – tends to give soldiers *carte blanche* to treat civilians ruthlessly. However, this is counteracted by the fact that Luther makes certain moral demands on soldiers. It is counteracted even more by the responsibility which Luther places with the monarch, who has a duty to ensure that his soldiers are God-fearing and do not commit sin. Brutal killing and atrocities carried out in war are considered by Luther to be sinful actions, all the more so in the case of killing and atrocities carried out on civilians. This can be seen from Luther's scepticism towards offensive war, from the premise of soldiers' moral qualms described by Luther and from the fact that Luther generally did not abolish the notion of a just war. Thus, it is the prince who has responsibility for the conduct of the soldiers and who has the duty to restrain them from committing sin by attacking the civilian population. As we have seen earlier, these ideas – which favoured the secular power of the monarch, and at the same time placed the chief responsibility for soldiers' conduct on his shoulders – can already be found among some of the thinkers of the Middle Ages. The new aspect in Lutheranism (with regard to this subject) was that the thinking had become more one-directional and consistent than in the Middle Ages, where the diversity of ideas had given rise to a broader spectrum of possible perceptions. The most important ideological consequence of Luther's thinking on war thus seems to be a more unequivocal, secular-authoritarian theory of war than what came before it.

Lutheran theology and social ideology were clearly among the driving forces behind the various measures taken in Denmark immediately after the Reformation – such as the abolition of the right of the nobility to revolt, and of the right of townspeople and peasants to engage in feuds as well as the *de facto* abolition of noble feuds. The constitutional and symbolic elevation of the status of the king and his appropriation of church property were, of course, also consequences of the Reformation ideology. We should add that Lutheranism was not the only current of thinking in sixteenth-century Europe which attributed greater importance to the power of the monarch. A number of secular thinkers shared this tendency, above all Machiavelli, whose theory of war is an extreme version of the authoritarian and power-based approach. Machiavelli does not lay down any stipulations with regard to the treatment of non-combatants by combatants. His works do not contain any theories about the issue of a just war; any war which is advantageous to the king is a good war – all other considerations are immaterial.[41]

In the next section, we will look at the question of military and civilian in Denmark by looking more closely at the first major war fought by Denmark after the Reformation. How was military distinguished from civilian during the Seven Years' War from 1563 to 1570? What norms existed for the treatment of civilians by the military? Is there any indication of a sig-

41 Kjeldgaard-Pedersen, "Om synet på krig," 120–22.

nificant new development compared with the late Middle Ages, a development towards more modern concepts? Are there signs of a Lutheran influence? The next section examines these questions on the basis of selected events and sources, and does not pretend to be an exhaustive study.

Military and Civilian during the Seven Years' War, 1563–1570

The year 1523 saw the dissolution of the Kalmar Union with the election of Gustav Vasa to the Swedish throne, and over the following two hundred years the Danish-Norwegian monarchy and the Swedish-Finnish monarchy were arch enemies. The first of a long series of wars between the two states was the Nordic Seven Years' War from 1563 to 1570. The war grew out of a conflict over power in the Baltic and the Sound, which was fostered by an emotional conflict over heraldic symbols on the coats of arms of both realms. When Denmark declared war on Sweden in 1563, it demanded the restitution of the Nordic three-state union to be ruled over by the Danish King Frederik II (1559–88). A land war was waged in Scania, southern Sweden, and eastern Norway. There were conquests and lengthy sieges of important Swedish castles as well as several major battles between large armies; however, for long periods the war was more or less quiet. The military actions often consisted of quick raids and the plundering and burning of enemy rural areas. Both kingdoms had their fleets at sea and on several occasions there was a major naval battle. Eventually, when Denmark's coffers were empty, Frederik II was forced to the negotiation table. The war ended with a limited victory for Denmark. With the Peace of Stettin in 1570, Denmark received a number of moderate Swedish territorial concessions in the Baltic and compensation for the return of a conquered Swedish castle.[42]

In the following, we will look more closely at some specific aspects of the relationship between military and civilian during the Seven Years' War. We will start with the ordinance of war proclaimed in 1564, which was applicable to the Danish army. Subsequently, we will focus on a collection

42 Frede P. Jensen, *Danmarks konflikt med Sverige 1563–1570* (Copenhagen: Den danske historiske Forening, 1982).

of texts written by and about a high noble who fought in the war, Admiral Herluf Trolle. Finally, we will look at the Swedish massacre of the people of the Danish town of Rønneby in the eastern Danish province of Blekinge.

In December 1564, Frederik II issued an ordinance of war that applied to all Danish land forces involved in the war against Sweden, both mercenary forces and conscripted Danish townsmen and peasants (but not noble cavalrymen). The ordinance, the aim of which was to discipline the soldiers' conduct in a number of areas, was an elaboration of the so-called Articles of War and Articles of the Navy from the time of Christian III, and Frederik II's first years as regent. War and naval articles were a widespread European phenomenon linked to the military revolution and the growth of national armies and fleets. Other European states had already issued articles of war in the late Middle Ages;[43] in Denmark, however, this only took place after the Reformation.

The ordinance of war issued by Frederik II contains fifty-three clauses or "articles."[44] The provisions consist of prohibitions and commands, which in many cases carry the death penalty, often explicitly without the possibility of pardon. Any form of mutiny, desertion, neglect of guard duty, conspiracy, treason or spying for the enemy carries the death penalty. Also for what seem to be less serious offences, the Articles prescribe severe penalties: Soldiers shall at all times ensure that they carry their weapons on their person. If not they shall be punished by death (§13); a soldier who wilfully throws away his armour or weapons "shall be hanged forthwith without trial" (§14); if a soldier forgets the watchword he has been given to move around the camp and perform guard duty, he shall pay with his life (§37). The articles of war also seek to restrict drinking and gambling. For instance, if a soldier is inebriated while on guard duty, he shall be immediately incarcerated and subsequently punished as seen fit by the commander in chief (§33); if a soldier loses his armour or weapon in a wager, he shall be

43 Contamine, *War in the Middle Ages*, 290.

44 Published in V. A. Secher, *Corpus Constitutionum Daniæ. Forordninger, Recesser og andre Kongelige Breve Danmarks Lovgivning vedkommende 1558–1660* (Copenhagen: Selskabet for Udgivelse af Kilder til Dansk Historie, 1887), 1: 260–74. In the following, references to the articles of the ordinance will be given in the main text.

punished with death (§31); blasphemy and cursing "with the holy word of God" carry the death penalty "without mercy" (§3).

The war ordinance also acts against internal brawls and duels between the soldiers. Duels involving "deadly" weapons (guns, or long pointed weapons or striking weapons) are punishable by death. If a soldier harbours "an old hatred or grudge" towards another, he shall lay the hostility aside as long as there is battle. Duels are, however, permitted in certain circumstances, provided that they are fought using light swords, knives or bare hands. Should a brawl, duel or dispute start, bystanders shall intervene and urge the parties three times to "take peace." If they refuse to cease their fighting (or a dispute develops into a duel or brawl), the parties shall not necessarily be punished for this if the brawl is fought using permissible means. However, if one party is harmed or killed after the bystanders have tried to forge peace, he shall accept the consequences. If one strikes the other after "peace has been taken," he shall be punished with his life without mercy. The same applies to one party striking another party who is down or "defenceless" (i.e. unarmed) (§§19–21). Thus the ordinance dictates a form of state monopoly on violence applicable during the campaign. Interestingly, however, the provisions intending to limit private hostilities and conflicts are less extreme than many of the other provisions in the ordinance. The rules seem to be a little less harsh for a *landsknægt* (i.e. mercenary, cf. German *Landsknecht*). The ordinance appears to allow a *landsknægt* to fight another *landsknægt* in a duel once without being penalized. Only one time, however. If the two men fight a second time they are liable to punishment by death (§22).

The ordinance treats a much wider range of military offences than previous legislation (see above), and it establishes an actual military jurisdiction. Every warrior shall swear allegiance to the king and to his superiors in the military hierarchy. As long as he is enlisted, he is subject under oath to the provisions of the ordinance, which is much harsher than the laws applicable during times of peace and for civilians. Offences are judged by the commander in chief, who determines both the question of guilt and in some cases metes out the punishment according to his judgement (e.g. §33 and §37). During combat or patrols, any man in command has the authority to punish rank-and-file soldiers for violating discipline (§25). The ordinance also operates with a type of military police in the form of the provost and his men (§18), and the military has its own executioners to carry out the punishments. Any attempt to wrong the executioner or hinder him in exercising his duty also carries the death penalty (§30). If the provost arrests anyone for an offence, the other men may not resist the provost, obstruct him, gang up against him or defend the detainee. The penalty for this is death, although with the possibility of pardon (§42). If a man helps the accused to escape from the provost, he shall suffer the same punishment as the escapee (§43). In the same way, the ordinance provides special legal protection to a commander who during battle or patrol disciplines a subordinate. Anyone who subsequently attacks or conspires against the commander to wreak revenge shall be punished with death (§25).

The war ordinance not only prescribes an entire apparatus of military police and judges who shall impose discipline from above, it also orders soldiers to enforce the rules among each other. Thus soldiers shall aid the provost by carrying out arrests (§42), and if the provost himself is not in the vicinity, they shall themselves arrest a soldier who has committed "plainly outrageous acts" such as murder or theft (§43). If a soldier hears of someone plotting treason, he has a duty to inform the provost (§18). If a soldier urges his fellow men to flee during a battle, the soldier next to him shall strike him or stab him with his weapon. If the man dies of his wounds, the soldier who inflicted them shall not be punished for murder. On the contrary, he shall have "earned considerable gratitude" (§ 15). A similar provision applies to the case of a soldier leaving his place in the marching or battle order. In this case, the commander as well as the rank-and-file soldiers have a duty to drive him back to his place, and if he resists, he may be killed with impunity (§25).[45] Finally, as mentioned above, bystanders have a duty to intervene in internal disputes and fights (§21). Similar commands to aid the authorities in penalizing and enforcing discipline were not found in the civil laws.

The war ordinance contains an entire article stipulating how soldiers should treat civilians, to which we will, of course, devote special attention. "Soldiers shall, on pain of death without mercy, spare those women who

45 See also §48.

prepare for childbirth or women who lie in birth bed, virgins, young girls, old people, preachers and other clergymen, and subject them neither to violation nor assault" (§6). This provision is intended to protect civilians in Sweden against violent assault by the Danish army. All the named persons are protected against physical assault and young girls and visibly pregnant women are protected against rape. Notably, civilian men are not protected unless they belong to the category of "old people"; in other words, not only adult men but also young boys appear to be legitimate targets in Denmark's war against Sweden. The same applies to adult women, unless they are pregnant or old. Thus, the ordinance differs from most medieval rules pertaining to warfare, which protect all women and children irrespective of their social status and, in many instances, all men belonging to the lower estates.

The subsequent article forbids soldiers from looting or damaging churches on enemy territory. Instead, soldiers shall honour, protect and shield the churches and maintain "Christian custom and order as in ancient times" (§7). This article could perhaps be interpreted as being symptomatic of typical Protestant fear of God, but it would be more apt to focus on its continuity from the earlier Catholic era with its special protection of the clergy and the church (cf. the wording of the article).

A number of the articles in the ordinance concern plundering of the enemy by Danish soldiers. The provisions apply to looting of both military and civilian persons. Soldiers may plunder if they have conquered a fortified town, a castle or a naval vessel. The same applies when they have won a battle and, in this instance, their right to plunder extends to villages near the battlefield. However, the plundering shall take place under the orders of the commander in accordance with a certain structure and captured ammunition shall always be handed over to the king (§§10, 26, 47 and 48). Should the army, after agreement with the Swedish commander, occupy a castle, a ship or a fortified town for a certain period of time (a normal procedure in wars of the era), it is forbidden to plunder. In conjunction with this provision, soldiers are enjoined to act "peacefully" towards enemies (soldiers as well as civilians, it seems) who have received mercy and acknowledge the Danish king as their lord and master. This injunction must also have been applicable beyond the specific context in which it is named (§9). Soldiers may under no circumstances plunder in the king's own land or in any way "inflict any harm or violence on Our subjects." If the soldiers require supplies or similar goods while on Danish territory, they shall pay for them (§40).

Two provisions further concern burning enemy territory and extortion (i.e. blackmailing the enemy's peasants by threatening to burn their possessions and crops). An arsonist must have the permission of the commander since burning the enemy's fields and towns can destroy possible supplies for the Danish army (§27). Equally, only the commander may give permission to burn or otherwise destroy mills, forges and ploughs (§29).

At first glance, the provisions concerning plundering and burning could well be interpreted as the wish to show consideration for the Swedish civilian population, and in particular the rules pertaining to the peasantry could be seen to be reminiscent of medieval ideals about peace and sparing of members of the lower estates of society. In reality, however, they are motivated purely by military and fiscal concerns. The rules on burning arise from considerations concerning supplies and arms to the troops. The objective of the rules on plundering is to avoid disagreement among the Danish soldiers about sharing the booty and to prevent them from commencing their acts of plundering before the battle has been concluded (§48). The injunction to keep the peace with the Swedes who have surrendered and will be shown mercy is a logical consequence of their acceptance of being subjects of the Danish king, and/or of the fact that they should be protected under a local ceasefire out of political considerations. Finally, the prohibition of plundering and "assaulting" Danish subjects is motivated chiefly by the wish to secure property and sources of state taxation.

The war ordinance of 1564 issued by Frederik II includes both divergences from as well as a continuation of the concept of military and civilian. Both directly and indirectly, a sharp line is drawn between military and civilian persons. This applies in the case of the Danish military vis-à-vis Swedish civilians, as well as the Danish military vis-à-vis Danish civilians. This distinction is created by war between two sovereign kingdoms. The ordinance is issued by the king alone and a state-like apparatus of officials is to enforce the rules among the soldiers. In relation to earlier times, this does not constitute a clear-cut break, since, as we saw earlier, a more modern distinction was already emerging in the late Middle Ages, precisely in connection with the "major" wars of the monarchy. What is new is the extent and intensity to which the war is made a matter of state. The ordinance contains an unusually large number of provisions and exceptionally harsh punishments for violation of them, and it establishes a clearly organized and extensive military jurisdiction. It imposes the requirement, unprecedented in Danish law, that every man must help to ensure discipline, and contains a number of specific rules governing the relationship of the military with the civilian population, which had never before been enshrined in law.

The provisions on how soldiers were to treat civilians are rooted in the medieval distinction between combatants and non-combatants. However, they differ in that they present all male civilians (except for the elderly) as legitimate targets. The medieval norm of exempting working peasants and townsmen that emerged from the peace movements and ideology of estates is thus not contained in the ordinance. As mentioned, a number of medieval treatises on just war permitted assault on adult men, but, as far as is known, none of them permitted assault on boys. Even more radical is the fact that the ordinance indirectly sanctions the rape, murder or otherwise violent assault of adult women (except for the elderly or pregnant). Neither is the intention of the regulation of plundering and burning by Danish soldiers to protect either male or female *laboratores*, but is driven, rather, by an explicit military, fiscal and political rationale. This shift in the rules for legitimate war targets can be seen as a "modern" trait, despite the fact that it in a certain sense was a step backwards in the progress towards the present-day humane laws of war. The "modern" (or rather *early* modern) trait was that warfare was freeing itself from the ideological boundaries of the Middle Ages. The capability of the state to wage war in optimal conditions was gradually becoming the ultimate key consideration. It may be a rather daring assertion, but the minimization of the population groups who were to be spared in war according to the ordinance of 1564 seems to be based on purely military logic. The Danish king reserves the right to allow his soldiers to kill civilian men and women to reduce the enemy's tax revenue and recruitment potential, and possibly also to terrorize the civilian population and give the soldiers unimpeded access to plundering. And to incite his own troops, the king allows them to have their way with the Swedish women.

The Danish Articles of War and Articles of the Navy from the first half of the seventeenth century, which either reiterated or expanded upon the ordinance of 1564, have been interpreted as expressing Lutheran ideology and piety.[46] This interpretation applies to a certain extent to the ordinance of 1564. However, it is important to note that, in many respects, the 1564 ordinance is firmly anchored in medieval thinking and practice. Many of the specific provisions, which might be seen as a sign of Lutheran thinking, in reality echo ideas, norms and rules that were already prevalent (or at least in circulation) in the Middle Ages. The very issuing of an extensive military ordinance was inspired by practice in foreign countries prior to the Reformation. Thus it was not unequivocally a Protestant or Lutheran phenomenon.

On the other hand, there can be no doubt that Lutheran ideology was a key factor leading to the issuing of such military ordinances in Denmark after the Reformation. The new ideology gave the secular ruler unprecedented power, and at the same time charged him with the religious and moral responsibility for the conduct of the soldiers. Denmark's post-Reformation war ordinances reflect both sets of thinking. These Lutheran traits cannot, however, be deduced from any specifically Lutheran prohibition or command contained in the individual provisions. On this level, the ordinances often reproduce pre-Reformation norms. The Lutheran character of the war ordinances should be sought at a higher, more general level: it is to be found in the king's might and right to issue such novel and far-reaching ordinances in the first place, and it can be seen in the fact that he can and must subject his soldiers to cruel discipline. Furthermore, the minimization of moral restrictions on warfare by the state, which has been noted here, is possibly directly linked to Lutheran thinking. All the medieval restrictions on warfare could be claimed to be what the protestants would call Catholic/scholastic "inventions." It is worth noting that in this respect the ordinance of 1564 does not show much evidence of these being supplanted

46 Hans Henrik Appel, "Krigshåndværk, gudfrygtighed og den militære disciplin," in *Mentalitet og historie. Om fortidige forestillingsverdener*, ed. Charlotte Appel, Peter Henningsen and Nils Hybel (Ebeltoft: Skipperskovshoved, 2002), 152–58.

by Lutheran morals. There is certainly no clear evidence in the ordinance of 1564 of a return to the Bible, particularly to the Old Testament, which Luther advocated and which left its mark on civil legislation in Denmark after the Reformation. For example, there is a very lenient approach to the prohibition in killing of Mosaic Law. In this case the ordinance draws, rather, on the Augustinian principle that killing can be legitimized in a just war.

The definite Lutheran trait of the ordinance of 1564 is, thus, its authoritarian stamp, which can be seen as deriving from Lutheran teaching on the dominance of the "worldly authority" in earthly matters. However, far from all of the ordinance can be explained from the angle of Lutheran theology. If we look at it from a materialist point of view, rather than from the view of the history of ideas, it stands out as a product of the evolution of the state in the sixteenth century, which was linked to military development. Only by looking at the ordinance through this lens can we understand the state-military rationale running through it. It is also only by recognizing the dominance of this rationale that we can truly understand why the ordinance minimizes consideration for the Swedish civilian population, why plundering is permitted, why a Danish conscript can be sentenced to death for losing his armour in a gamble or falling asleep while on guard duty, and why a military jurisdiction exists at all. Considered from this angle, the function of Lutheran theology was primarily to give the king legitimacy and the possibility to choose from among the existing ideas, norms and rules (both Reformatory and non-Reformatory) those which were most beneficial to the Crown and to give them a clear authoritarian slant.

We will now look at the issue of the military and the civilian in Denmark during the post-Reformation period in the light of an aristocrat who fought in the Seven Years' War, namely Herluf Trolle. Trolle belonged to the high nobility and the inner circle of Frederik II; he was a member of the council of the realm and a royal bailiff and was thus in charge of a number of royal castles. During the Seven Years' War, he was appointed admiral and thus commander-in-chief of the Danish fleet. From 1563 he was fully occupied with his military office until he was wounded in battle in June 1565 off the island of Femern. He died of his injuries a few weeks later in Copenhagen.

A large number of letters written to the king, to fellow noblemen and to his wife Birgitte Gøye have survived. In the period between 1563 and 1565 many of these letters concern the war with Sweden.

We will start, however, with the sermon given at Herluf Trolle's burial.[47] Trolle's burial sermon was written by the prominent professor of theology Niels Hemmingsen, and the text very much bears his hallmark, although Trolle and his family no doubt had significant influence on its making and his family would have approved the sermon in its final version before it was read at the funeral. Hemmingsen was definitely aware that a prominent part of his congregation was of noble pedigree and the sermon's Lutheran discourse is accompanied by a noticeable aristocratic ethos.

It is therefore unsurprising that the sermon's treatment of the question of military and civilian is reminiscent of the medieval ideology of estates, with emphasis on the special status of the nobility. This is very clear from the following passages, which concern Hemmingsen's personal meeting with Trolle before he embarked on his last campaign in June 1565. Hemmingsen tries to persuade Trolle to stay at home, reasoning that he has risked his life in war for two years and thus does not have a duty to put himself in peril again. Trolle's answer to this is: "If I lose my life, I will regain my life. Do you know why we are called noble lords [*herremænd*], why we wear gold chains, have earthly goods and wish to stand above the others and be held in higher esteem? It is because it is our privilege, when our king and ruler, country and realm should need us, to fend off the enemies of the land, to protect our fathers' realm with all power and fortune so that our subjects may live in peace and tranquility: for life is at once sweet and bitter and the one shall not be had without the other."[48]

Trolle thus justifies his departure for battle by citing his duty as a noble lord and in doing so also justifies the privileges, special status and wealth of the nobility. The objective of going to war is to defend the commoners so they may live in peace. The distinction between combatants and non-combatants is thus between the warring nobles and the peaceful, labouring commoners. However, Trolle as well as Hemmingsen and his congregation

47 Wad, *Breve,* 1: xiii–xxvi.
48 Ibid., xxii.

at the funeral were aware that huge numbers of commoners fought in the war with Sweden. We know from conscription lists, for example, that in the war year 1564, almost 2,500 soldiers and mariners were conscripted to the navy from Danish towns.[49] Trolle's burial sermon does not conceal this fact. A central element of the quoted passage, therefore, is the words "with all power and fortune." Both the nobility and the commoners serve the realm in times of war, but whereas the military services of the commoners are limited in terms of time and money, the military services of the nobility are unlimited. This reasoning very much echoes the justification for the exemption of the nobility from taxes set forth in the Law of Jutland of 1241 (see above).

The ideology of the estates is omnipresent in the burial sermon, which endeavours to portray a consistently positive image of Trolle and the social order he represents. He is presented as the ideal lord who has "loving relations" with people of all stations, both nobles and commoners, rich and poor, townsmen and peasants, men and women, young and old. "He gave to each of the estates ordained by God their due honour, looking upon them each as a valuable limb of Christ." For his kindness towards people of all estates, Trolle is rewarded with the affection of the people, "clerics, townspeople and peasants revered him no less than like a father in all respects."[50]

Following the sermon, Trolle was loyal to the king in times of peace as well as in times of war. In times of peace he exercised his office as a royal bailiff according to the law. He did not invent new taxes to hinder the "poor subjects" (townspeople and peasants), and administered justice in the jurisdictions entrusted to him with a gentle hand. When Trolle was compelled

49 Fonnesberg-Schmidt, "Købstædernes militære ydelser før 1570." In 1563–64, peasants were conscripted from military levy districts in numbers of 15, 10, 6 or 5 men (cf. district sizes of the late Middle Ages, given above). A large part hereof manned the fleet which was under Herluf Trolle's command. After 1565, the conscription of peasants to personal war services drastically decreased and instead the military levy districts financed mercenaries. See Cecil W. Lebahn, "De danske nationale troppers deltagelse i syvårskrigen 1563–70," *Jyske Samlinger* 3 (1954–56): 243–60, 253–59.

50 Wad, *Breve*, 1: xx.

to sentence a subject to death or to punish a subject for a crime, he exercised his duty with inner sorrow.[51]

In war (*feide*), the manly demeanour of Trolle showed that he bore his sword justly.[52] He was loved by all the men on his admiral's ship, "to whom he was like a father of flesh and blood." When he was wounded in the battle of Femern, he refused to receive medical help before the other wounded had been tended to: "He stood with blood streaming from his wounds, yet he wished for the wounds of the poor soldiers and mariners to be dressed first." Trolle sacrifices himself for the common soldiers, which in the eyes of Hemmingsen was fatal ("that was indeed a dangerous adjournment").[53] Thus, ultimately, he truly did sacrifice his life so that his subjects (concretely the injured men) could "live in peace and tranquility." Trolle's words about the gold chains worn by lords and nobles serving in battle thus turn into a self-fulfilling prophecy. The special duty of the noble lord to risk his life for his king and subjects is seen as part of his destiny, in the same way as the privileges of the nobility are hereditary and the division of society into estates is God's will.

The burial sermon for Trolle deviates significantly from the war ordinance of 1564 in its definition of military and civilian. The sermon reflects the thinking of the nobility of the late Middle Ages, coupled with Lutheranism, loyalty to the king and patriotism. The distinction between military and civilian is more or less identical to the distinction between the nobility and the commoners, whereas the war ordinance draws a line between men who are militarized by the state and men who are not, more or less without heed to their estate. This difference between the burial sermon and the war ordinance can only partially be explained by the fact that the war ordinance was only applicable to rank-and-file soldiers. The burial sermon for Trolle does, however, depart from the thinking of the late Middle Ages in that it makes a clear distinction between war and peace. Or more precisely between feud and peace, as *feide* is the word used to mean the wars of the state (see above).

51 Ibid., xx–xxi.
52 Ibid., xxi.
53 Ibid., xxii–xxiii.

Let us now turn to Trolle's letters from the Seven Years' War and see what they tell us about the distinction between military and civilian. To begin with we can ascertain that the noble discourse is not quite as strong in his private letters as in the official burial sermon. When he talks of the military men of the fleet, Trolle distinguishes primarily between officers ("good men") and the rank-and-file, not between nobles and commoners. Officers were not necessarily from the nobility and the ordinary men of the fleet were largely conscripted members of the lesser estates. In many instances, Trolle not only praises officers to the king, but also the common men.[54] There are virtually no fundamental views expressed about nobles being more proficient or more committed warriors than the common men. Nonetheless, peasants are often described as less skilled warriors than mercenaries and nobles. In a letter to his fellow noble Mogens Gyldenstjerne, he reassures him, for example, with the fact that an imminent Swedish deployment consists for the most part of troops conscripted from the peasantry.[55] In another letter to Gyldenstjerne, who was one of the closest advisors to Frederik II, Trolle does, however, propose a fantastic plan to colonize Sweden with peasants from Jutland. According to Trolle, there are excessive numbers of peasants and smallholders in Jutland who could be armed and deployed in Sweden. Here, the peasants could be given permission to retain whatever property they capture. "It would be a veritable army of Huns!" he exclaims fervently. Even though the plan never came to fruition, it shows that Trolle believed in the military potential of the Danish peasantry. The proposal does, however, envisage the peasant colonists after their conquest living in peace and paying levies to the Danish Crown and the nobility. Interestingly, the plan also included the ethnic cleansing of Swedish peasants.[56]

54 Ibid., 135 and 146.

55 Ibid., 122.

56 Ibid., 274: "In Jutland there are so many people, and there are so many places, [where] two or three persons possess a farm with two or three additional sub-tenants, who have only very little. Now I do not know if this has any purpose or would bring any advancement, but these people, those of them who are skilful, could be summoned from all over Denmark and armed and dispatched to Sweden. Any land they conquered, they could retain; it would be a veritable army of Huns. If the enterprise was successful, as much good would be had of a Jutland peasant in Sweden as of a Swedish peasant."

In many of his letters, Trolle justifies the waging of war along the lines of the justification given in his burial sermon. This justification is put forward when Trolle expresses his hopes for a victory in war; thus, he tells the king that he will pray to God for a victory, "for the sake of God and the peace and tranquility of his Majesty's subjects."[57] In another letter, Trolle thanks Gyldenstjerne for the supplies he has sent and expresses his hope that God will let the Danish fleet perform in battle "such that God's will be done and the poor wretches be given peace and recompense for all their troubles."[58] The poor wretches are the peasants from whom Gyldenstjerne has demanded levies to be able to furnish supplies to the fleet. Thus, not only the official burial sermon but also the private letters express the aristocratic ideology about the nobleman waging war so that the peasants, who are liable to taxes, can live in peace.

A number of letters directly concern the relationship between soldiers and civilians in the Seven Years' War. Here Trolle distinguishes clearly between the two groups and he talks about what he perceives as being applicable laws of war. The letters concern Trolle's attitude to the Swedish population on Øland as well as his reaction to Swedish attacks on civilian merchants.

At the end of June 1564, the admiral and the Danish fleet were stationed off the coast of the Swedish island of Øland. From here, Trolle wrote an open letter to the "peasants and commoners" of the island, explaining that the Swedish King Erik XIV had provoked the war and had compelled Frederik II to attack Sweden. The Danish king had gathered a large army and navy and was about to ravage Sweden, causing great harm and ruin to many innocent Swedes. As the king wished the people of Sweden no ill, but preferred to keep them according to their old laws and customs, Trolle now offered to pardon all those inhabitants of Øland who surrendered to the Danish king. He would await the answer of the people of Øland before attacking the island. If they accepted, Trolle would, on behalf of the king, defend the inhabitants of the island and keep them according to their old laws and customs, which Swedish kings had suppressed in the last forty

57 Ibid., 251.
58 Ibid., 252.

years (i.e. since the coronation of Gustav Vasa). If Øland spurned the offer, Trolle's fleet would attack the island. The admiral concluded the letter by explaining to the peasants of Øland why Denmark would be victorious. It would be impossible for Sweden to resist Denmark's power with the help of God as God would not be against the Danish king, who had not initiated the war, but on the contrary would punish the Swedish king for his wrongdoing.[59]

Three months later, at the end of September, Trolle and the Danish fleet attacked Øland. In a letter to the king, he subsequently described how troops had "burned" on the island for five days without encountering any significant resistance.[60] The same day as the Danish soldiers left the island and the Danish fleet set sail to Bornholm, Trolle wrote once again to the common peasants of Øland. In his letter, the admiral justified the ravaging done by the Danish soldiers. He found the burning regrettable, but the people of Øland only had themselves to blame for they had ignored his warning letter and furthermore participated in "pillaging and burning" in Blekinge. Trolle concluded by declaring that he intended in the future to treat the inhabitants of Øland as foe.

Trolle's letters to the people of Øland reveal how important it still was to legitimize acts of warfare. His justifications are clearly sought in the medieval ideals of *bellum justum*. Furthermore, the letters play on the discourse of the merciful, protective and just lord, which is also echoed in his burial sermon. The letters to the people of Øland are in this respect very much inspired by letters which Frederik II himself sent out to the people of Sweden during the war.[61] Trolle's insistence that the war between Denmark and Sweden was a just war was thus representative of the official Danish legitimization of the war.

This propagandist and idealistic justification of warfare is contrasted by the private letters sent by Trolle to Frederik II concerning Øland. At the same time as Trolle sent the first open letter to Øland, he privately disclosed to the king that he was reluctant to dispatch troops onto Øland as

59 Ibid., 169–73.
60 Ibid., 277–82.
61 Ibid., 170–71, note 5.

he did not have sufficient men.[62] The first letter to Øland should thus be seen as a calculated attempt to buy time and induce the people of Øland to surrender without a struggle as well as part of a larger propaganda war, rather than the chivalric offer of peace it purports to be. After the ransacking of Øland, Trolle again wrote a private letter to the king and reported on the situation on the island. The report is a sober account of the Danish advance, the flight of civilians[63] and the weak resistance from the Swedish troops, and includes exact dates and records of which parishes had been burned down.[64] However, the letter does not contain the slightest hint of justification of any acts of warfare, unlike Trolle's almost concurrent valedictory letter to the people of Øland. This simply confirms the unsurprising fact that the motivation behind the campaign against Øland was purely military and that the open letters to the islanders were sent for tactical and propaganda reasons only.

In mid-July 1564, the Swedish fleet captured a large merchant fleet from Lübeck off the coast of Bornholm. As Lübeck was Denmark's ally, the Swedes stormed the ships and, according to sources, massacred the crew. News of the massacre reached Trolle as he was in council with officers from Lübeck on board a vessel of the combined Danish-Lübeck war fleet, far away from Bornholm. In a letter to Frederik II, Trolle recounts how he and the officers of Lübeck immediately pledged to wreak revenge.[65] A few days later, Trolle wrote a caustic letter to the Swedish king, in which he informed him about the assault on the merchant vessels from Lübeck and continued thus: "However, your Royal Highness' troops have behaved so tyrannically and inhumanely towards the poor people after they were captured, which is not the custom in war and unheard of in any other nation. His Royal Highness must surely know that God will punish the act in time and will give his Royal Highness and all the people of Sweden a bad name and a bad reputation amongst all nations"). In this way Trolle refers to an unwritten law of war ("the custom in war"), which is respected by

62 Ibid., 165–66.

63 "They also drove from the path beasts and cattle, women and children so that no human being was to be met."

64 Ibid., 277–82.

65 Ibid., 213–14.

an international community of peoples/states (cf. his reference to "nation" and "all nations"). According to this "custom in war," prisoners must not be assaulted or killed. This is in keeping with the Danish war ordinance of 1564, which prohibits assault on enemies who have been "pardoned," and with the pledge by Trolle to the people of Øland that he will pardon all those who surrender to the Danish king.

The letter to the Swedish king continues with an appeal to the king to prohibit his soldiers from treating prisoners so inhumanely in the future. Trolle intends, on his part, to ensure that the Swedes no longer take any Danish soldiers captive, which is certainly a declaration of intent to fight to the last man as long as it is unclear how the Swedes will treat their prisoners in the future. The admiral and his subordinates will avenge the Swedish attack by treating Swedish captives in the same way in the future as Swedes treated the crew on the merchant ship from Lübeck. This applies to all newly captured Swedish "soldiers, subjects and allies, of higher and lesser standing, regardless of where we encounter them, at sea or on land." In other words, to both soldiers and civilians. With this warning, Trolle feels that he is excused "if Christian blood is spilled after this day." Trolle lists a number of examples showing that Denmark has hitherto treated Swedish captive soldiers "in keeping with the custom in war" and reminds the Swedish king that Denmark has a large number of Swedish captives, including in the fleet under Trolle's command. He promises that the Swedes who have been taken captive up to that point will be treated "in keeping with the custom in war" and he will wait for a reply from the Swedish king, the implication being that if the Swedish king does not guarantee the safety of Danish prisoners in the future, the Swedish prisoners will suffer.[66]

Trolle's letter to the Swedish king is reminiscent in many ways – in style, structure and argumentation – of a feud letter from a late medieval noble feud. The difference is, of course, that the nobleman Herluf Trolle is acting in his official function and not in a private capacity. The letter was not immediately sent to the Swedish king, but instead to the Danish king for his approval. Frederik II ratified it in the beginning of August, but it

66 Ibid., 227–28.

is uncertain whether the letter was ever sent to Erik XIV.[67] Even though Trolle wrote the letter in his capacity as a military officer, it is for the most part phrased as if he is acting on his own account, almost from motives of personal vengeance. Another interesting aspect of the letter is that it operates on the basis that the war between Sweden and Denmark can be waged on different levels of escalation. With their massacre, the Swedes have violated the rules applicable to the level of war waged hitherto and thus Trolle feels justified in escalating the conflict. If this should lead to him breaking with the general "custom in war," it will be the fault of the Swedish king. This form of legitimization is, of course, rooted in the idea of just war. The notion that war can be conducted on different levels of escalation also derived from the Middle Ages (see above).

As was the case with Trolle's letters to Øland, the idealistic propaganda in the letter to Erik XIV concealed a more complex reality. In a private letter to the king, Trolle wrote that it was the admiral of the Lübeck fleet who had persuaded him to write to Erik XIV to urge him to treat his prisoners correctly, which Trolle considered inappropriate. Trolle himself would have found it more fitting to send a letter stating that they would "pay them back in the same measure," in other words a letter without any conciliatory tone or request to de-escalate the war.[68] Trolle's promise to Erik XIV to await his reply and until then treat his Swedish prisoners well was thus a consequence of reticence on the part of the Lübeck admiral, which, judging from other letters written by Trolle in the same period, had to do with the generally low morale among the Lübeck forces. Thus, behind the letter to Erik XIV there was no genuine noble intention to open up to negotiations or provide an honest warning of hostile actions; neither did it contain any honest feelings of revenge on the part of Trolle.[69] The background was

67 Ibid., 234–35, note 2.

68 Ibid., 234–35.

69 Ibid., 232–35. It is difficult to imagine Herluf Trolle being any more personally affected by the massacre than the Lübeck admiral, who was obviously not particularly vengeful as he proposed to adopt a more cautious approach to Sweden than Trolle. In the aforementioned private letter from Trolle to the king, there are no traces of any emotional attitude either. Ibid., 236–38. The same is true of Trolle's account to the king of a military engagement with the Swedish fleet a few weeks later, in which he does not describe the Danish victory in any way as retaliation for the massacre. Trolle's conspiring with the Lübeck officer to avenge the massacre (see above) should thus be seen as a calculated attempt by

rather the political consideration for Denmark's allies combined with a need to legitimize the escalation, which Trolle evidently wished, of the war.

We shall now leave Trolle and conclude our examination of the relationship between military and civilian during the Seven Years' War by looking at another bloody incident in the war, namely the massacre of the people of Rønneby led by the Swedish army. The incident took place during a Swedish onslaught on the Danish province of Blekinge bordering on southern Sweden in the summer of 1564. The commander of the campaign had received instructions from the king as to how the Swedish troops were to behave towards the Danish peasants and townspeople. They were to start by treating them well and persuading them to swear allegiance to the Swedish king. If this tactic proved successful, the plan was to deport any unreliable Danes to Sweden later on and to replace them with loyal Swedish subjects, in other words to carry out a form of ethnic cleansing. Should the Danes refuse to submit to the authority of the Swedish king, they should be punished harshly and every last man and woman slaughtered.[70] With these instructions, the Swedish army marched into Blekinge in August. The troops in the castle of Lykå quickly surrendered, and in the local courts/assemblies (*herredsting*) the peasants of Blekinge swore allegiance to Erik XIV. The townspeople in Rønneby, counting on reinforcements from Danish troops in the area, twice refused Swedish demands to surrender. However, the reinforcements never arrived, and on the 4th of September, the Swedish troops stormed Rønneby and quickly penetrated its weak defences. When all resistance had been overcome, the troops massacred a large number of the town's inhabitants. Shortly after, the Swedish army withdrew from Blekinge because of the threat of a major Danish attack on southern Sweden. The plan to colonize Blekinge with loyal Swedish subjects was thus abandoned.[71]

Around 1570, a historical account of the massacre on Rønneby was written by the Danish side,[72] which in its anti-Swedish version of events

the Danish admiral to raise the morale of the Lübeck forces, and the undertones of private feud and personal vendetta in the letter to Erik XIV were presumably owing to the same motivation, as well as the need for legitimization.

70 Lars-Olof Larsson, *Arvet efter Gustav Vasa* (Stockholm: Prisma, 2005), 94.

71 Ibid., 96–100.

72 Holger Rørdam, ed., "Den nordiske Syvaarskrigs Historie som det synes sammenskreven

draws on the prevailing norms for the treatment of non-combatants by combatants. It reports how the Swedish soldiers ruthlessly began to kill the townspeople immediately after conquering the town. The Swedes "committed such a big manslaughter on both men and women, girls and young children alike and spared none, neither young nor old, neither the priest, who was slain right in the doorway of his church. And they murdered the women as they fled through the streets carrying their infants and they snatched the new-born babies from women in their birth beds, cast them upon the fire and killed the women." The German mercenaries who took part in the invasion on the Swedish side were appalled at the conduct of the Swedish soldiers and went straight to the commander to protest. The otherwise hardened German mercenaries brought to the attention of the commander that "they had been in many wars with both heathens and Christians yet never had they seen such un-Christian slaughter as this." The Swedish soldiers were then given orders to spare the women and children. Instead they plundered the town and burned it to the ground and almost all the male citizens were killed, with the exception of a few who were taken to Sweden and later killed and hung from stakes outside the Swedish town of Kalmar. The corpses of the many Danes who were killed in the burning town of Rønneby were left unburied by the Swedes or were thrown onto the fire.

After the ransacking and burning of the town, all surviving women, girls and young children were taken to the Swedish field camp. When rumours circulated that the captives were to be executed, some members of the Swedish council of the realm interceded and pleaded with King Erik, who was present at the camp. The prisoners were pardoned and the king ordered his soldiers to refrain from rape. Instead the women and children were to be taken to Sweden as slaves for the rest of their lives. They were now divided into two groups, each of which was to be supervised by a provost. One group consisted of girls and young women, the other of the old and weak. The first group was sent off to Sweden, "but on the way the Swedish cavalrymen took most of the girls and young women up onto

1570 af Mester Jon Tursen efter samtidige Optegnelser af Axel Gyldenstjerne," *Monumenta Historiæ Danicæ*, 2:2, 199–445. Ibid., 2:2, 292–98.

their horses, as they pleased, and carried them off for where they wanted, according to their own will, and some of the children of the women they threw into the fields and left them there lying." When the provost of the other group saw this and heard, at the same time, how the women and children in his own group were starving and thirsty, he let them flee into the forest, "about which King Erik was greatly vexed and wanted, later, to execute the provost."

The description is, of course, very biased in its account of the brutality of the Swedish soldiers and the malice of King Erik, which is contrasted by the more humane attitude of the German foot soldiers, the Swedish councillors and the provost. Every time the civilians are shown mercy, it is their (the German soldiers', the councilors' and the provost's) doing, not that of the Swedish king or the majority of the Swedish soldiers. The leitmotif of the account is the Swedes' repeated disregard for ideals and rules regarding the treatment of the civilian population. The war crimes are measured according to the same scale as the ones we know from the moral code of the Middle Ages as well as the post-Reformation period. The worst crime is murder and other assaults on infants, children, pregnant women and priests. The abduction and rape of women is considered a slightly less serious crime. Mass killing of male citizens is strongly condemned, although not as strongly, however, as other crimes. The report indicates that the Swedes were (nonetheless) acting according to the same scale.

Of course, the norms expressed here are rooted in the medieval concepts of *Pax Dei* and *bellum justum*, although the population of Rønneby is not described as completely defenceless and innocent. For example, we are told that the townspeople together with a modest garrison of Danish soldiers[73] averted three attacks by the Swedes and that the fourth attack, which led to the capitulation of the town, pre-empted a planned attack on the Swedish camp. During the decisive attack on Rønneby, five hundred Swedish soldiers are purported to have been killed, which the ungodly Swedes did not manage to bury but instead threw into the river, "so that one could not see the water for dead bodies." The narrator's need to emphasize the civil

73 These men were conscripted peasants from other parts of Denmark. See Lebahn, "De danske nationale," 255.

courage and patriotism of the inhabitants of Rønneby is thus given higher priority than the potential portrayal of them as innocent, working, common subjects. The medieval ideology of estates, according to which certain social groups must be protected in times of war, is evident only in the report on the murder of the priest in the church doorway, which could equally be a reference to medieval *Pax Dei* or protestant fear of God.

While it is not surprising that the Danish portrayal of events squeezes as much as possible out of the Swedish assault and possibly even more, it is highly unusual that a Swedish account paints a detailed picture of the massacre and describes it in positive terms. A few weeks after the massacre, Erik XIV dispatched a victory bulletin addressed to the entire Swedish people, in which the attack is described as a great military triumph for the Swedish army, led by the warrior king Erik. In bloody language it recounts how the Danish soldiers were coerced to flee, after which the Swedes killed six hundred citizens of Rønneby who were defending the town, "so that the water in the river was red with the blood from the dead bodies, as well as those slain in the town. And the enemy was so terrified that they only offered little resistance, but the soldiers stabbed them like a herd of wild boar, and no one was spared, but all armed men were killed so that in the town more than two thousand men were killed and some women and children whom the powerless Finns killed."[74]

The aim of the victory bulletin issued by Erik XIV was to raise morale among the Swedish population and army. Notably the report emphasizes how defenceless the citizens of Rønneby were (the bulletin puts Swedish losses at only thirty men), instead of highlighting their resistance, which would have emphasized the courage of the Swedish soldiers and the prowess of Erik XIV as commander-in-chief. The author obviously does not expect to upset the target group of the bulletin but rather make it rejoice over the superiority of the Swedish forces. However, there are limits to how far the bulletin goes in its enthusiasm about the massacre. It is underscored that the victims of the Swedish soldiers were armed men, and it is the Finnish soldiers who kill the women and children. They do this apparently

74 English translation of quotation from Larsson, *Arvet efter*, 97, and Jensen, *Danmarks konflikt*, 98.

out of frustration at being cheated of their war booty by the Swedes (which is presumably why the Finns are described as "powerless"). All in all, the slaughter of women and children is toned down considerably compared with the Danish report. However, it is nonetheless interesting to note that the Swedish account does not completely omit to mention these murders. Clearly, it was believed that the Swedish army and public would celebrate them.

Lars-Olof Larsson, whose account of the sequence of events and the Swedish victory bulletin provides the basis for the present account, believes that posterity has exaggerated the unique character of the massacre of Rønneby. According to Larsson, these types of massacres were quite normal. He writes about it being "an ancient, in itself logical, practice; a stormed city was liable to the victor. The events do not, strictly speaking, reveal anything about exceptional cruelty from either Erik XIV or the Swedish troops; a stormed city was always struck by a bloody inferno." According to Larsson, the reason why posterity has come to consider the massacre as exceptional is, firstly, the wording of king Erik's bulletin, which Larsson admits is highly unusual in its celebration of Swedish atrocities, and, secondly, the fact that posterity's opinion of Erik XIV was generally formed by his enemies.[75] However, it is doubtful whether Larsson is right in his assertion that the obliteration of the whole population of a town during an attack was a normal or even ancient practice. Larsson's documentation (Swedish massacres in Varberg 1565 and Narva 1581) is certainly inadequate and is an indication, rather, that large-scale massacres of civilians were on the increase in the second half of the sixteenth century. However that may be, the victory bulletin of Erik XIV was quite unusual and Larsson points this out as well. Presenting the slaughter of the entire population of a town, including women and children, as a heroic deed would have been more or less inconceivable in the Middle Ages.[76] Thus the bulletin seems to testify to a shift in norms with regard to the treatment of civilians. The same can be said of the instructions issued by Erik XIV before the Blekinge campaign and similar instructions issued before other Swedish campaigns

75 Larsson, *Arvet efter*, 99.

76 However, this applies only to wars between Christians, not the holy wars waged by Christians (*bellum sacrum*) against heathens, i.e. the crusades.

during the Seven Years' War. This article has ascertained a similar shift in norms during the Seven Years' War on the Danish side, namely in the war ordinance of 1564 and in the proposal by Herluf Trolle to colonize Sweden with Danish peasants. An interesting possibility for future research could be to examine war practice in the late Middle Ages and the early modern period to establish whether this shift in norms was related to a real change in the treatment of civilians in connection with the development of the military and the state in the sixteenth century.

Conclusion

We have investigated here the distinction between military and civilian in fifteenth- and sixteenth-century Denmark. The investigation took medieval Europe as its point of departure and went on to show that a certain distinction between combatants and non-combatants that was widespread in most of Western Christendom also existed in Denmark from the thirteenth century onwards. This distinction was built on several different cultural elements, of which this article has focused on three that are considered to be especially important: the division of society into estates, the peace movements and the idea of just war. From this fusion of different elements emerged a distinction between a class of landowning warriors on the one side, and two to three classes of non-combatants on the other, for whom the warrior class had to show special consideration. In this context, various norms and rules evolved concerning the treatment of non-combatants. The important difference between medieval and present-day distinctions between combatants and non-combatants is that the medieval distinction was not based on what one might call a state monopoly on definition (i.e. definition of the military-civilian divide) or by any notion of universal human rights regardless of social status, gender, age, etc.

In the late Middle Ages in Denmark, the theoretical distinction between noble warriors and commoner non-combatants was relativized by phenomena such as feuds and uprisings amongst the peasantry. It was also relativized by the fact that common townspeople and peasants to a considerable degree served in the king's wars. While feuds and uprisings obstructed the efforts of the state to concentrate power and in certain respects (in particular in the case of feuds and uprisings among the nobility) helped to preserve the feudal social order with its particular dichotomy between combatant and non-combatant, the participation of the peasantry in wars of the monarchy was a proto-modern trait.

As to the question of whether the Reformation and the military development of the sixteenth century brought about a departure from medieval norms and practices, we can detect a certain continuity precisely in the case of the wars of the monarchy against foreign powers. During Denmark's first major war after the Reformation, the late medieval war organization was used as a basis. For example the conscription of townsmen and peasants was conducted in much the same way. The proto-modern characteristics in late medieval war organization did, however, intensify to a degree which makes it reasonable to talk of a departure. The war ordinance issued by Frederik II in 1564 consists of a hitherto unprecedented set of rules to discipline common soldiers and establishes a definite military jurisdiction. We can also assume that more peasants were conscripted to military service than ever before. At the same time, the noble cavalry of the Middle Ages was gradually losing its military importance and the Crown became altogether more powerful. Herluf Trolle's burial sermon, with its pronounced trait of medieval ideology of estates, can be seen as a conscious attempt to legitimize the privileges of the aristocracy at a time when the special military status of this social estate and its political power over the king was gradually being undermined. Trolle was in reality more of a public military official than a medieval lord and the aristocratic ideology of estates also, revealingly, plays less of a role in his private letters from the Seven Years' War than in his publicized burial sermon. All of these circumstances contributed to the gradual development of a more modern distinction between military and civilian. To an increasing extent, it was the state centred on a strong Crown which defined the distinction between military and civilian.

However, the changes that were taking place were not only in connection with the wars of the monarchy against foreign powers. At least equally important for the establishment of a clear and more modern distinction between military and civilian (and between war and peace) was the fact that the feuds and uprisings of the late Middle Ages ceased after the Reformation. Here we can see an unmistakable new direction of development.

With regard to the treatment of civilians by the military this article has demonstrated if not exactly a sharp turn then certainly a significant shift in norms. Both the Rønneby massacre and the account by the Swedish king, as well as the Danish war ordinance of 1564 (and Herluf Trolle's proposal to colonize areas of Sweden with Danish peasants and carry out ethnic cleansing), testify to the fact that the warring state was in the process of liberating itself from medieval constraints to pursue a more pure military rationale.

We may ask whether this shift in norms was due more to ideology or to material aspects. This article has argued from a materialist viewpoint. The shift, it is suggested, was caused by military development and centralization of the state. The most significant impact of Luther's theology and social ideology was the general allocation of more symbolic power and legitimacy to the secular rulers. Luther was not the author of a completely new theory of war with new rules for the treatment of civilians. In this respect he rather continued medieval thinking, selecting the most authoritarian components and assembling them into a coherent authoritarian ideology that could be exploited by the growing state.

In the second half of the sixteenth century, on the one hand, a distinction was emerging between the military and the civilian which is quite similar to the modern distinction. On the other hand, the ideal of the protective treatment of non-combatants was declining. Even though this ideal was still present, the Seven Years' War in this respect marks a "step backwards" in relation to the Middle Ages. Seen from this angle, present-day war law and its rules concerning the extensive regard for all civilians is the result of the state distinction between the military and the civilian being coupled with humanist ideals at a later stage. As recent research has shown, this process towards modern humanitarian laws of war reached a crucial stage already during the seventeenth century, not least due to a new military rationale which perceived the safeguard of non-combatants as a strategic and tactical advantage, and was further solidified during the eighteenth century with the introduction of a new, universal, egalitarian view of mankind that was alien to the medieval mindset.[77]

Translated by Nancy E. Ake Aaen

77 Geoffrey Parker, "Early Modern Europe," in *The Laws of War: Constraints on Warfare in the Western World*, ed. Michael Howard (New Haven: Yale University Press, 1994), 40–58. Gunther Rothenberg, "The Age of Napoleon," in ibid., 86–97. Jeppe Büchert Netterstrøm, "Soldater og civile i danske krigsartikler fra 1500- og 1600-tallet," *Temp – tidsskrift for historie* 4 (2012), 12–36.

References

Angermann, Norbert et al., eds. *Lexicon des Mittelalters*. 9 vols. Munich: Artemis & Winkler Verlag, 1978–1999.

Angermeier, Heinz. *Königtum und Landfriede im deutschen Spätmittelalter*. Munich: C. H. Beck Verlag, 1966.

Appel, Hans Henrik. "Krigshåndværk, gudfrygtighed og den militære disciplin." In *Mentalitet og historie. Om fortidige forestillingsverdener*, edited by Charlotte Appel, Peter Henningsen and Nils Hybel, 152–58. Ebeltoft: Skipperskovshoved, 2002.

Bøgh, Anders, Jørgen Würtz Sørensen and Lars Tvede-Jensen, eds. *Til kamp for friheden. Sociale oprør i nordisk middelalder*. Aalborg: Bogsmedjen, 1988.

Brunner, Otto, Werner Conze and Reinhart Koselleck. *Geschichtliche Grundbegriffe* 4 (1978): 2–3, 7.

Christensen, Aksel E. *Ret og magt i dansk middelalder*. Copenhagen: Gyldendal, 1978.

Christensen, Harry. "Rosenkrantz og Gyldenstjerne 1466–1469. Et forsøg." In *Profiler i nordisk middelalder og renaissance. Festskrift til Poul Enemark*, edited by Svend E. Green-Pedersen, Jens Villiam Jensen and Knud Prange, 29–48. Aarhus: Arusia – Historiske Skrifter, 1983.

Christensen, William. *Dansk Statsforvaltning i det 15. århundrede*. Copenhagen: Det Kongelige Danske Videnskabernes Selskab, G.E.C. Gads Forlag, 1903.

Contamine, Philippe. *War in the Middle Ages*. Translated by Michael Jones. New York: Blackwell Publications, 1984.

Dahlerup, Troels. *De fire stænder, 1400–1500*. Copenhagen: Gyldendal and Politikens Forlag, 1989.

Duby, Georges. *The Three Orders: Feudal Society Imagined* [1978]. Translated by Arthur Goldhammer. Chicago: University of Chicago Press, 1980.

Duchhardt, Heinz. "War and International Law in Europe, Sixteenth to Eighteenth Centuries." In *War and Competition between States*, edited by Philippe Contamine, 279–99. Oxford: Clarendon Press, 2000.

Fenger, Ole. *Fejde og mandebod. Studier over slægtsansvaret i germansk og gammeldansk ret*. Copenhagen: Juristforbundets Forlag, 1971.

Fonnesberg-Schmidt, Iben. "Købstædernes militære ydelser før 1570." In *Renæssancens befæstede byer*, edited by Søren Bitsch Christensen, 99–144. Aarhus: Dansk Center for Byhistorie and Aarhus Universitetsforlag, 2011.

Ingesman, Per. *Provisioner og processer. Den romerske rota og dens behandling af danske sager i middelalderen*. Aarhus: Aarhus Universitetsforlag, 2003.

Jensen, Carsten Selch. "'Gud vil det' – om retfærdige og hellige krige i middelalderen." In *Retfærdig krig. Om legitimeringer af krig og voldsudøvelse i historien*, edited by Carsten Selch Jensen, 86–109. Odense: Syddansk Universitetsforlag, 2006.

Jensen, Frede P. *Danmarks konflikt med Sverige 1563–1570*. Copenhagen: Den danske historiske Forening, 1982.

Kjeldgaard-Pedersen, Steffen. "Om synet på krig og oprør i 1500-tallets Europa – især hos Luther." In *Retfærdig krig. Om legitimeringer af krig og voldsudøvelse i historien*, edited by Carsten Selch Jensen, 113–65. Odense: Syddansk Universitetsforlag, 2006.

Kroman, Erik and Stig Iuul, eds. *Danmarks Gamle Love paa Nutidsdansk*. 3 vols. Copenhagen: Det danske Sprog- og Litteraturselskab, 1945–1948.

Larsson, Lars-Olof. *Arvet efter Gustav Vasa: en berättelse om fyra kungar och ett rike*. Stockholm: Prisma, 2005.

Lebahn, Cecil W. "De danske nationale troppers deltagelse i syvårskrigen 1563–70." *Jyske Samlinger* 3 (1954–1956): 243–60.

Lindbæk, Johs. "Biskop Niels Skave i Roskilde og Sorø kloster." *Historisk Tidsskrift* 8, no. 1 (1907–1908): 254–83.

Lütken, Vilhelm. *Bidrag til Langelands Historie*. Rudkøbing, 1909.

Netterstrøm, Jeppe Büchert. *At forsvare til rette. Værnsforholdet og bøndernes retslige stilling i Danmarks senmiddelalder 1400–1513*. Kerteminde: Landbohistorisk Selskab, 2003.

———. "Bondefejder i Danmark 1450–1650." In *Feider og fred i nordisk middelalder*, edited by Erik Opsahl, 35–72. Oslo: Unipub, 2007.

———. "Den danske stat og voldsmonopolet 1400–1660." *Den jyske Historiker*, no. 116 (2007): 88–119.

———. *Fejde og magt i senmiddelalderen. Rosenkrantzernes fejder med biskop Jens Iversen og Lage Brok 1454–1475*. Aarhus: Landbohistorisk Selskab, 2012.

———. "Soldater og civile i danske krigsartikler fra 1500- og 1600-tallet." *Temp – tidsskrift for historie* 4 (2012): 12–36.

Olesen, Jens E. *Unionskrige og stændersamfund. Bidrag til Nordens historie i Kristian I's regeringstid, 1450–1481.* Aarhus: Universitetsforlaget i Aarhus, 1983.

———. "Senmiddelalderens danske stændersamfund." In *Konge, kirke og samfund. De to øvrighedsmagter i dansk senmiddelalder*, edited by Agnes S. Arnorsdóttir, Per Ingesman and Bjørn Poulsen, 13–36 Aarhus: Aarhus Universitetsforlag, 2007.

Ordbog til det ældre danske Sprog (1300–1700), edited by Otto Kalkar. Copenhagen: Thieles Bogtrykkeri, 1881–1917. http://www.hist.uib.no/kalkar/.

Parker, Geoffrey. "Early Modern Europe." In *The Laws of War: Constraints on Warfare in the Western World*, edited by Michael Howard, 40–58. New Haven: Yale University Press, 1994.

Pedersen, Henrik. *De danske Landbrug. Fremstillet paa Grundlag af Forarbejderne til Christian V.s Matrikel.* Copenhagen: Gyldendal, 1928.

Poulsen, Bjørn. "Med harnisk og hest. Om adel, krig og vold i dansk senmiddelalder." In *Riget, magten og æren. Den danske adel 1350–1660*, edited by Per Ingesman and Jens Villiam Jensen, 44–77. Aarhus: Aarhus Universitetsforlag, 2001.

———. "Forholdet mellem land og by i dansk middelalder." *Historisk Tidsskrift* 109, no. 1 (2009): 1–19.

Poulsen, Bjørn and Gunner Lind. "Den danske adel og den militære revolution." In *Riget, magten og æren. Den danske adel 1350–1660*, edited by Per Ingesman and Jens Villiam Jensen, 576–603. Aarhus: Aarhus Universitetsforlag, 2001.

Reinle, Christine. *Bauernfehden. Studien zur Fehdeführung Nichtadliger im Spätmittelalterlichen römisch-deutschen Reich, besonders in den bayerischen Herzogtümern.* Stuttgart: Franz Steiner Verlag, 2003.

Reitzel-Nielsen, Erik and Ole Fenger, eds. *Danske Domme 1375–1662. De private domssamlinger* 48: 549. Copenhagen: Det danske Sprog- og Litteraturselskab, C.A. Reitzels Boghandel, 1978–1988.

Rørdam, Holger, ed. "Den nordiske Syvaarskrigs Historie som det synes sammenskreven 1570 af Mester Jon Tursen efter samtidige Optegnelser af Axel Gyldenstjerne." In *Monumenta Historiæ Danicæ*, 2:2, ed. Holger Rørdam, 199–445. Copenhagen: G.E.C. Gads Forlag, 1875.

———. "Om stormen på Rønneby." In *Monumenta Historiæ Danicæ*, 2:2, edited by Holger Rørdam, 292–98. Copenhagen: G.E.C. Gads Forlag, 1875.

Rothenberg, Gunther. “The Age of Napoleon.” In *The Laws of War: Constraints on Warfare in the Western World*, edited by Michael Howard, 86–97. New Haven: Yale University Press, 1994.

Secher, V. A., ed. *Corpus Constitutionum Daniæ. Forordninger, Recesser og andre Kongelige Breve Danmarks Lovgivning vedkommende 1558–1660*. 6 vols. Copenhagen: Selskabet for Udgivelse af Kilder til Dansk Historie, 1887.

Sørensen, Jens Peter. “Oprørsretten som politisk instrument i kampen mellem kongemagt og aristokrati 1476–1505.” In *Profiler i nordisk senmiddelalder og renaissance. Festskrift til Poul Enemark,* edited by Svend E. Green-Pedersen, Jens Villiam Jensen and Knud Prange, 77–92. Aarhus: Arusia – Historiske Skrifter, 1983.

Ulsig, Erik. “Landboer og bryder, skat og landgilde. De danske fæstebønder og deres afgifter i det 12. og 13. århundrede.” In *Middelalder, metode og medier. Festskrift til Niels Skyum-Nielsen*, edited by Karsten Fledelius, Niels Lund and Herluf Nielsen, 137–165. Copenhagen: Museum Tusculanums Forlag, 1981.

Wad, Gustav Ludvig, ed. *Breve til og fra Herluf Trolle og Birgitte Gjøe*. 2 vols. Copenhagen: V. Thaning & Appel, 1893.

War Observed at a Distance
Media Coverage and Attitudes to War in Denmark, 1939–1940

Palle Roslyng-Jensen

The events and consequences of war are usually described through the individual or collective experiences of soldiers or civilians. In this chapter I examine how war is observed at a distance by those who did not themselves have any direct experience of it. The particular focus of my attention is on Danish observers of three specific war events that took place between 1939 and 1940:

1. the outbreak of war between the European great powers, and the acts of war between Germany, the Soviet Union and Poland, in September 1939;
2. the Finnish Winter War – the Soviet attack on Finland on 30 November 1939 and the subsequent war between the two countries up until 12 March, 1940;
3. the war in Norway following the German attack on Norway and Denmark on 9 April 1940, to the capitulation of the Norwegian army and the retreat of British and French forces from the north of Norway in June 1940.

All three of these events took place close to Danish territory, were fought in a relatively short period of time and involved an attack without warning by a great power against one or several smaller states.

The observations of war in the period discussed here, 1939–1940, took place through the media and a number of personal diaries that reflected the observations and the attitudes of the diarists to the war events.[1] None

1 Palle Roslyng-Jensen, *Danskerne og besættelsen. Holdninger og meninger 1939–1945* (Copen-

of the diary writers were involved in or were part of any direct acts of war, and their "war experience" was exclusively through the media or through personal communication connected with media interpretation.

Analysis of the media's coverage of the war is based on a number of Copenhagen newspapers with different political affiliations and a different social composition in their readership. *Berlingske Tidende* was an independent non-socialist newspaper with middle-class readers and the main non-government newspaper in Copenhagen in the 1930s. *Politiken* was affiliated with the Social Liberal Party (Radikale Venstre), but had a significant number of readers who voted Social Democratic or Conservative. *Nationaltidende* was conservative and generally had a more nationalistic and anti-government attitude than *Berlingske Tidende. Socialdemokraten* was the official voice for the Social Democratic party, while *Aftenbladet* was politically independent with a majority of working-class readers. Finally, a pictorial magazine, *Billedbladet,* published by the *Berlingske Tidende* publishing house, represents the illustrated magazines that covered current affairs. *Politiken* and *Socialdemokraten* represented the political parties who were in government until the German occupation after 9 April 1940, where a broad-based government of national unity took over. It was headed by the Social Democratic party.[2]

The different conditions of the media in this period, and the varying involvement and engagement of the Danish public and their personal opinions towards the belligerent countries, affect the relationship between attitudes to war in the media and those of the civilian observers and sheds some light on the relationship between public and private opinions on war. This chapter is divided into two sections: the first presents the background for the media coverage of the war in 1939–1940, and the general media coverage in the three specific war events. The second section examines more closely the more extensive media and public conceptions and framings connected with war in 1939–1940.[3]

hagen: Gads Forlag, 2007), 13–21 on the characterization of the diaries used.

2 Jette D. Søllinge and Niels Thomsen, *De danske aviser 1634–1991*, 3 vols. (Odense: Odense Universitetsforlag, 1991), vol. 3.

3 For conceptions of war and metaphors concerning war, with regard to France, see Valerie Holman and Debra Kelly, eds., *France at War in the Twentieth Century* (New York: Berghahn Books, 2000), 10–14. These are mainly based on speeches, songs and state propa-

The Danish Media System and Foreign News before September 1939

The majority of the Danish public was quite well informed at the end of the 1930s about international current affairs. Most Danish families subscribed to a daily newspaper. Newspapers were chosen on the basis of political and social affiliation and, very often, a newspaper published in the local area was chosen if the family subscribed to only one newspaper. Newspapers in Copenhagen generally had more coverage of international affairs than the provincial papers and almost 20 per cent of families subscribed to two newspapers, usually a local paper and one from Copenhagen. More than 80 per cent of families owned a radio receiver and paid the obligatory radio licence to the State Broadcast. The News Service of the State Broadcast was independent from the State Broadcast, and its board was influenced by both the political parties and representatives of the printed newspapers, although the main interest of the latter was to avoid competition from the Radio News. According to contemporary listener surveys, approximately 90 per cent of the license holders listened to the Radio News at least once a day.[4]

Since January 1933 when the National Socialists came to power in Germany, the Danish Foreign Ministry had tried to avoid media criticism of Germany. The Danish policy of neutrality was from 1933 not even-handed with regard to the main powers, as threats against Danish sovereignty were perceived to emanate only from Germany. The question of the German demands for a revision of the border in the south of Jutland was a high priority, and the Danish Press avoided even mentioning the problem. On the other hand, discussions on Nazism, German policy concerning the Jews, and the deliberate German breach of the Treaty of Versailles often placed German politics on the public agenda. The German ambassador and press attaché regularly complained to the Foreign Ministry and its Press Bureau over specific articles, cartoons of Hitler, etc.

ganda as instruments in the metaphorical process. For the broader concept of "framing," see W. A. Gamson, *Talking Politics* (Cambridge: Cambridge University Press, 1992), 25.

4 Palle Roslyng-Jensen, "Nationale meningsfællesskaber. Danskernes reception af radionyheder om krig og krigsbegivenheder under 2. Verdenskrig," *Historisk Tidsskrift* 112 (2012): 62–91.

The Press Bureau of the Danish Foreign Ministry was established in 1919 and had close connections to the Danish legations in the capitals of the main powers, the leading newspapers and the press attachés of the great powers who were based in Copenhagen. In 1939, the leader of the Press Bureau was a former chairman of the Danish Association of Journalists, an obvious sign of its close contact with the editors and the press. The Press Bureau had regular meetings with representatives of the Danish press. At these meetings the foreign minister, Peter R. Munch from the Social Liberal Party, issued sincere warnings to the press. *Socialdemokraten*, especially, repeatedly transgressed what Munch saw as a prudent policy towards Germany. At meetings with the foreign press attachés, Munch confirmed as best he could that the Danish press adhered strongly to a strict and even-handed policy of neutrality.[5]

Foreign news in the Danish media came primarily from the international news agencies through the Danish news agency Ritzau (abbreviated RB). In 1938, Ritzau began to print (together with "Ritzau") in the heading of the specific articles the source for each telegram that came from the international agencies; and in January 1939, Munch specifically requested that the press include the declaration of the original source in their printed news – "RB/Reuters," or only "Reuters," for instance. The Press Bureau had close contact with Ritzau and was able to defer telegrams which the Press Bureau saw as especially harmful to the politics of neutrality, an arrangement that bordered on state censorship.[6]

The majority of foreign news on current affairs came from the leading national news agencies. Reuters in the UK, Havas in France and DNB in Germany were the three most used news agencies and all of them had close links to their respective governments. Reuters had an extensive global network of correspondents and Havas was especially well represented in Eastern Europe.[7] A few of the major newspapers had a direct subscription to the American news agencies AP and UP and subscribed to news reports from the largest English and American newspapers; for example, *Berling-*

5 Rasmus Kreth, *Pilestræde under pres. De Berlingske Blade 1933–45* (Copenhagen: Gyldendal, 1998), 40–42.

6 Ibid., 211.

7 Oliver Boyd-Barrett, *The International News Agencies* (London: Constable, 1980), 126–30.

ske Tidende received the reports from the Time News Service (*The Times*, London) and *Politiken* from the International News Service (*The New York Times*). Generally, the Danish international news had a strong bias towards sources from the leading Western powers. The largest Danish daily newspapers had correspondents in several European capitals, typically London, Paris and Berlin. In the case of larger crises or war events, "flying" correspondents were sent out to the crisis areas to provide supplements to the news telegrams with more personal commentary and descriptive reports.[8] All the major newspapers regularly featured articles on foreign policy, international and military affairs. The articles on military affairs were normally written by a Danish senior officer, who typically wrote one or two survey articles for each of the three military events.

Competition between the major newspapers in Copenhagen was strong, especially between the two largest newspapers, *Politiken* and *Berlingske Tidende*. Although the newspapers had different political affiliations, they were rather similiar in their prioritization of the content and on international affairs and war especially, but their broader framing was influenced by their political affiliation. In their seminal work on the Danish press, Niels Thomsen and Jette Søllinge provide an accurate general characterization of the political line of the major Danish daily newspapers towards Germany and the Western powers in the period right before the Second World War: "With very few exceptions – especially *Jyllands-Posten* – the Danish press in the thirties was supportive of the Western powers and against Nazism, but neutrality was most important, and therefore attitudes were expressed with caution, especially by papers supporting the government."[9]

The Media and War up until the Second World War

Very few Danes in the 1930s had personal experiences of war. The 1864 war over Schleswig-Holstein with Prussia and Austria-Hungary was the latest

8 Søllinge and Thomsen, *De danske aviser*, 3: 70–75.

9 Ibid., 3: 87, my translation. Kay Lundgreen-Nielsen, *Tro eller blændværk? Danmark og Den Spanske Borgerkrig 1936–1939. En undersøgelse af den danske presses og den danske regerings holdning* (Odense: Odense Universitetsforlag, 2001), 439–52.

military event on Danish soil. Denmark was neutral during the First World War, but close to five hundred Danish volunteers fought on the Republican side in the Spanish Civil War. In Denmark, therefore, observation of war was almost solely through the media, and several of the military conflicts of the 1930s were distant conflicts with limited media coverage. Conflicts in Europe, or involving major European powers, attracted most interest, especially the Spanish Civil War.

The Spanish Civil War was interpreted differently by the Danish daily newspapers according to their political affiliation, the Danish political agenda and the attitudes of the respective papers to fascism, Nazism and communism. There were frequent admonishments and recommendations from the Press Bureau to the newspapers that their reporting should support the Danish policy of neutrality and the policy of non-intervention in Spain, which Denmark strictly supported. Several Danish newspapers had correspondents in Spain and published reports from both the Republicans' side and Franco's.[10]

In August 1939, the international news in the Danish media had been dominated by the German demands, threats and accusations against Poland, by the French and English statements, and the abortive attempts at negotiations and the ensuing prospect of war. What happened, according to editor Svend Carstensen from Danish Radio News, was a complete parallel to the crises over Czechoslovakia one year earlier, "but none of us believed that the miracle would happen once again" – the miracle being the Munich agreement and the dismemberment of Czechoslovakia.[11]

In the weeks leading up to the German attack on Poland on 1 September 1939, newspapers sold in extra editions and the Radio News, in the preceding couple of days, had put out up to nineteen news broadcasts each day. Several diaries indicate that radio was the main media, and that people stayed at home with the radio receiver on.[12]

10 Lundgreen-Nielsen, *Tro eller blændværk?*, 439, 441, 443.

11 Svend Carstensen, *Syv Aar i Søgelyset* (Copenhagen: Steen Hasselbalchs Forlag, 1945), 18.

12 Ibid., 18ff.; Ernst Christiansen, Knud Rée and J. Rosenkjær, eds., *Statsradiofonien 1925–1950* (Copenhagen: Gyldendal, 1950), 163ff.; *Politiken* 1.9.1939; *Berlingske Tidende* 1.9.1939; Diary: Knud Gedde 31.8.1939; Diary: Vilhelm Bergstrøm: *En borger i Danmark under krigen* 1–2 (Copenhagen: Gads Forlag, 2005), 1: 56: 3.9.1939.

The Outbreak of War

News of the German attack on Poland on 1 September reached most of the population through the radio. In his diary, Knud Gedde described how he heard the German statement on a train ride from his home in North Zealand to Aalborg in North Jutland by radio transmission over loudspeakers on the ferry across Storebælt, and that it aroused intense anxiety and agitation amongst the passengers. During the day there were extra transmissions and news that German planes were bombing Polish towns. The demand for news was immense everywhere. In Copenhagen, mechanic Kaj Nielsen wrote in his diary on the 1st of September: "Heard the Radio News two times before going to work and two times after 5 p.m." The following day, he wrote down several citations from the Radio News. After having heard the decisive news, many Danes picked up their phone and passed on the news or exchanged opinions with friends and family. According to the newspapers there were 120,000 calls per hour in Copenhagen during the hours of the morning: four times the ordinary number of calls.[13]

The question of the French and British entrance into the war kept up the suspense over the following days, only to be relieved with their declarations of war on 3 and 4 of September. On Sunday, 3 September, the Danish radio transmitted the British Prime Minister Neville Chamberlain's speech, making it clear that the United Kingdom would be in a state of war the following day at 11 a.m. if Hitler did not withdraw German troops from Poland. The news was disseminated very quickly and nobody expected a German withdrawal. During the day on the 3rd of September, people in Copenhagen went out into the streets. Cinemas, theatres and restaurants filled with people and cars were taken for a drive for perhaps the last time after a possible ban on the use of private cars had been announced. A journalist from *Socialdemokraten* wrote that there were thousands of Copenhageners at a concert in the Copenhagen commons ("Fælledparken"), all of them in a serious mood, and patriotic songs were sung to loud applause. When the Social Democratic song "Denmark for the People" was played,

13 Knud Gedde, 30.8.1939, 1.9.1939; Bergstrøm, *En borger,* 1: 55, 3.9.1939; Diary: Kaj Nielsen, 1.9.1939, 2.9.1939; Kreth: *Pilestræde under pres*, 207; *Berlingske Tidende* 2.9.1939, 3.9.1939; *Politiken* 3.9.1939.

the applause rose to a gale according to the report: "[T]his song is developing into a new national anthem … a demonstration and homage to the peaceful Denmark ruled by and for the people."[14] At the Town Hall Square in Copenhagen, thousands of people followed the large news posters on the walls of the headquarters of the main newspapers.[15]

At the outbreak of war Denmark had declared itself neutral, and on 16 September the government issued a directive on press conditions to support this policy. The media was supervised by the Press Bureau of the Foreign Ministry, a control that was based on the experiences from the First World War. The press directive stated that information from one of the belligerent parties, which was disputed or which included elements of propaganda, should be counterbalanced by information from the opposite party, and it should be clearly stated from which country and which source the information came. It was not permitted to mention war events on Danish territory, any military preparations and movements of ships, and, in general, suggestions and statements which were inconsistent with Danish neutrality were forbidden. Finally, extreme reticence should be exerted with reference to foreign heads of state. Not many were in doubt that this was a warning against making attacks on Hitler.[16]

As war broke out, all the major newspapers planned to use extra resources to cover the war. *Politiken* wrote, on 3 September, that the war would be covered by a network of international correspondents from the International News Service as well as by *Politiken*'s own correspondents in Berlin, London and Paris, and that freelance correspondent Antoine Moller, who had covered the Spanish Civil War for the paper, had left the country for Poland, while Berlin was at present covered by the Swedish journalist Christer Jäderlund. Jäderlund was in Berlin for the Swedish paper *Stockholms-tidningen*, but by arrangement he also wrote for *Politiken*. How-

14 "Denmark for the People," a popular Social Democratic party song by Oskar Hansen, was also the name of the latest Social Democratic Party programme.

15 *Socialdemokraten* 4.9.1939; *Politiken* 3.9.1939, 5.9.1939; Bergstrøm, *En borger*, 1: 55, 3.9.1939.

16 Statsministeriet, fortroligt cirkulære til pressen 16.9.1939, in: Niels Alkil, ed., *Besættelsestidens Fakta. Dokumentarisk Haandbog med Henblik paa Lovene af 1945 om Landsskadelig Virksomhed m.v.*, 1–2, ed. Niels Alkil (Copenhagen: Sagførerraadet and J. H. Schultz Forlag, 1945–1946), 1: 3.

ever, Antoine Moller did not get to Poland. An article on Polish refugees at a Lithuanian border town was his only contribution.[17] Helge Knudsen was the correspondent in Berlin for *Berlingske Tidende* and he was supplemented by an extra correspondent in Germany who tried in vain to write articles covering the Western front from the German side. Two articles on public sentiments in Hamburg and Saarbrücken were his only contributions. *Socialdemokraten* and *Nationaltidende* had their own correspondents in Berlin, while *Aftenbladet* only had information from the international news agencies.[18]

War in Poland: The Media Coverage

Information in the newspapers on the initial military fighting in Poland was printed from both German and Polish sources. News of the alleged Polish attacks on "Volksdeutsche" in Poland, used by the Germans as *casus belli*, was included, while the immediate occasion for the attack, the alleged Polish attack on the German radio transmitter in Gleiwitz, was not given any notice in Danish newspapers.[19] German telegrams were generally given more space than the equivalent telegrams from the Polish side, and there were more details about the German military advance than the Polish military response. The broader articles from Berlin by the correspondents there were of special importance for the coverage. The printed news from Poland comprised telegrams from Havas, a few from Reuters, news from the Polish Press Agency through Ritzau, and news from the Polish radio. In most cases, the telegrams had a clear indication of the source, in compliance with the Press Directive.

The lack of journalistic reports from the front line and the lack of neutral war reporting was the main problem for the Danish newspapers. At an early stage during the German offensive in Poland, the German Foreign Office Press Bureau arranged a visit to the newly conquered areas in the Polish Corridor. Helge Knudsen and Christer Jäderlund took part in the excursion and their papers printed their reports. Two weeks later, *Berlingske*

17 *Politiken* 3.9.1939; the report from Lithuania appeared in *Politiken* on 16.9.1939.
18 *Berlingske Tidende*, 11.9.1939, 13.9.1939.
19 Michael Balfour, *Propaganda in War 1939–1945* (Routledge and Kegan Paul, 1979), 147.

Tidende received another report from Helge Knudsen from an arranged visit near the front line outside Warsaw. The German framing was obvious in the articles, which were the outcome of the tours arranged by the Germans in Polish territory. *Nationaltidende* and *Socialdemokraten* had no eyewitness reporting from Poland and *Aftenbladet* only featured interviews with Danish businessmen returning to Copenhagen from Poland.[20]

News of the Soviet attack on Polish military forces in the eastern part of Poland, from the 17th of September, was very limited. All papers had short news telegrams from Moscow from Havas and DNB, and on the 19th *Politiken* printed a broader Havas article from the Soviet occupation of Lvov (Lemberg), which had the appearance of an eyewitness report. Lvov had been conquered initially by German troops who retreated a few days later, leaving the town to the Soviet army. For an illustration, *Politiken* used a touristic photo from the centre of the town, a clear indication of the lack of photographic images from the current events. This telegram was the last news from Soviet-occupied Poland until the German attack on the Soviet Union in June 1941.

Photographs from the war in Poland were more German-dominated than the written telegrams and for the first two weeks they were almost exclusively from the German side of the front. In several newspapers, German planes and advancing troops featured on the front page. From the start of the outbreak of war, *Billedbladet* printed an extra weekly edition called "Last pictures," but the magazine had problems obtaining enough pictures if they were not to be completely dependent upon German propaganda. The first of these extra editions, from the 7th of September, had only German photos of the same kind as those that appeared in the newspapers. There were photos of the German military advance and of destroyed Polish cannons and tanks, and later there were some very militaristic-style German drawings of successful combat. The next editions had a few photos from the Polish side, but the 19 September edition only had photos of the Polish embassy in Paris. The captions to the pictures originating from the

20 Helge Knudsen, *Hitler bandt min pen* (Copenhagen: Gyldendal, 1945), 52–54; *Berlingske Tidende* 19.9.1939; *Politiken* 9.9.1939, 14.9.1939; Peter Longerich, *Propagandisten im Krieg. Die Presseabteilung des Auswärtigen Amtes unter Ribbentrop* (Munich: R. Oldenbourg Verlag, 1987), 279.

German side also had a general German bias. *Billedbladet* tried as best as it could to establish some neutrality in its coverage, but with two weekly editions and a steady supply of mostly German pictures it was difficult to achieve and the overall message in the magazine was of German military superiority, German effectiveness and sporadic Polish resistance and retreat. However, the pictures in both newspapers and *Billedbladet* also stressed the extensive destruction and the suffering of the civilian population in Poland as a result of Germany's air bombardments. According to some statements in the press, Warsaw was almost completely destroyed.[21]

In spite of dramatic headlines and telegrams from the war events, the overall political assessment of the war saw the development in Poland as secondary to the development on the Western front, where the main battles were expected to take place. The almost total lack of military clashes in the west at this stage was not in accordance with the professional expectations of the media, and, furthermore, as the newspapers could get no independent eyewitness reports from the battle scenes in Poland, a certain professional disappointment was discernible. The chief editor of *Ekstrabladet*, the tabloid newspaper from the Politiken publishing house, wrote to the chairman of the board of the publishing house, former Foreign Minister Erik Scavenius, almost with regret: "It is a strange war. No news, no great battle, only propaganda with telegrams and photographs."[22]

The will to keep up neutrality in the press coverage during September and October 1939 was clearly visible in all the newspapers, but the structural imbalance in the supply of news and photos meant that there was a clear preponderance of German-framed material in the Danish newspapers. This does not mean that their reception was orientated favourably towards Germany. In most of the diaries, a critical attitude to Germany and German warfare meant that the war in Poland was seen predominantly as a brutal but effective demonstration of German power.[23]

21 *Politiken* 13.1.1940 (Henrik V. Ringsted), *Politiken* 4.2.1940 (Christer Jäderlund), *Politiken* 10.2.1940 (DNB/RB), *Billedbladet* 12.10.1939, 24.10.1939, 14.11.1939.

22 Ole Cavling letter to Erik Scavenius 12.9.1939, *Ekstrabladet*, Korrespondance 1939, Dansk Mediemuseum.

23 Roslyng-Jensen, *Danskerne og besættelsesen*, 25–26.

War in Finland: The Media Coverage

After the Polish resistance came to an end at the end of September, the traditional war reports had to look for events elsewhere, in the air or at sea. There were plenty of political news and speculations, especially connected to the crises between, initially, the Soviet Union and the Baltic countries, and, a little later, between the Soviet Union and Finland. On the 30th of November, Soviet forces attacked Finland, and the Finnish Winter War dominated the war news for the next three and a half months.

This war created strong public sentiments of sympathy with Finland, and the Danish policy of neutrality in this case came under greater pressure from public opinion than over the war in Poland or the conflict between the great powers on the Western front. Various organizations collected money for Finland, and there were a huge amount of public meetings with demonstrations of solidarity. Danish volunteers for military war service in Finland were recruited. The Finnish Winter War did not imply the same threat to Danish neutrality as the conflict between the great powers or the war against Poland, where one of the issues was connected to the German surrender of territory at the Treaty of Versailles. Therefore the traditional Danish policy of neutrality, with special considerations towards Germany, changed to asymmetric neutrality during the Finnish Winter War. For Foreign Minister Peter R. Munch there were limits to the amount of support for Finland it would be prudent to demonstrate openly. He summoned the chief editors of the main newspapers to a meeting on 10 February 1940, and warned against unrestrained expressions of Nordic solidarity. This was generally without success, however, except in regard to *Politiken* as it was affiliated with the same political party that the foreign minister represented: the Social Liberal Party.[24]

The consequences and considerations for the press of the Danish policy of neutrality during the war in Finland were discussed several times between editors and board members in the Politiken publishing house. Board member and former prime minister Carl Theodor Zahle, opposed a poster from *Ekstrabladet* and a headline in *Politiken* which stated "that Sweden now

24 Danish Foreign Ministry Archives (UM), 110.D15, 2.12.1939.

gave unreserved and full support to Finland." Zahle's complaint was that none of the papers had mentioned that the support was within the limits of the Swedish policy of neutrality. At the same time, the chief editors gave assurances that there would be no reference in the papers to a public collection of money for Finland. Even the competition with *Berlingske Tidende* was suspended due to considerations about neutrality. *Berlingske Tidende* had a photographer in Finland during the war, while *Politiken* only sent one when the peace accord was signed, when the war events were over and public interest therefore had declined sharply.[25] *Nationaltidende* and *Berlingske Tidende* especially sought in every possible way to put pressure on the limits of the policy of Danish neutrality in the Finnish war. They published references to public collections for Finland and there was news on the recruitment of Danish volunteers for military service in Finland, which was actually prohibited according to Danish law.[26]

The vast majority of the news came from the Finnish side and was comprised of official Finnish political and military declarations, news from the Finnish news agency (Finska Notitsbyron) and the Western news agencies, especially Reuters. All the major Danish newspapers also had correspondents in Finland, most of whom had been posted a week before the war broke out as the political crisis became more acute. For a while, *Politiken* and *Berlingske Tidende* had an extra correspondent on the Finnish side of the front. Some of the correspondents in Finland consolidated their national reputation with their reportage from the front, typically those from the most national-orientated newspapers, for example Ebbe Munck from *Berlingske Tidende* and Peter de Hemmer Gudme from *Nationaltidende*.[27]

News from the Soviet side was extremely scarce; a few telegrams from the Soviet news agency Tass (through Ritzau), a few telegrams from Havas in Moscow, and *Berlingske Tidende* received news from the Moscow corre-

25 Politikens Hus, Møde hos Bestyrelsens Formand 16.1.1940, 8.2.1940, Politikens Hus 1938–1940, Dansk Mediemuseum; Bergstrøm, dagbog, 15.3.1940.

26 Jan Ahtola Nielsen, *I orkanens øje. Det danske Finlandskorps 1939–40* (Copenhagen: Gyldendal, 2006), 82–86.

27 UM, 110. 358. Pressebureauet, "Finnish Legation in Copenhagen: Approval of correspondents," 2.11.1939; Peter de Hemmer Gudme, *Finlands folk i kamp* (Copenhagen: Gyldendal, 1941); Janni Andreasen, *At vise flaget. Ebbe Munck – Krigskorrespondent – Modstandsmand – Hofchef* (Copenhagen: Høst & Søn, 2007), 144–48.

spondent of *The Times*, London. According to *Socialdemokraten*, the paper had applied to the Soviet embassy in Copenhagen for a visa for a correspondent to be on the Soviet side of the front. The visa was denied, which probably did not come as a surprise. Photographs only came from the Finnish side of the front.[28]

On the first day of the war, 31 November, Soviet planes bombed Helsinki and, as the international press and photographers were present in the city, there was extensive and detailed coverage of the attacks. The Finns won the propaganda war already on the first day. Danish newspapers printed news and descriptions stressing the civilian casualties and included photographs of destroyed residential buildings, with headlines such as "A day of horror in Helsingfors," or "The capital of Finland under bombardment." Generally, the reportage of the newspaper correspondents was more emotional than that of the correspondents from the News Agencies.[29] From the end of December, the news was dominated by Finnish military victories, extensive Soviet losses, and in most newspapers there were photographs of killed Soviet soldiers in the snow. News in January and the beginning of February followed the same lines and the Finns and the Soviet military had much the same role. Danish media users were generally under the impression that it would be possible for the Finns to defend themselves effectively against the Soviet attacks in the long run. In the beginning of January, headlines in the Danish papers were, for example: "Also Finnish offensive in the air," "Finnish soldiers are advancing into Russian territory" and "No Russian offensive at present."[30]

Among the less prominent subjects for the reportage were further Soviet air bombardments, Danish volunteers and the Danish mobile field hospital in Finland. At the end of February, the Soviet forces began an offensive which very soon broke the Finnish defences, and on 12 March the Finnish government sought and signed a peace accord. During the Soviet offensive, there was explicit news on the strength of the Soviet attack but, as press coverage at the same time stressed the courageous Finnish defence, the

28 *Socialdemokraten* 8.12.1939.

29 *Socialdemokraten* 1.12.1939 (Ove Nielsen), 26.12.1939; *Nationaltidende* 1.12.1939; *Berlingske Tidende* 1.12.1939 (Jørgen Bast); *Politiken* 1.12.1939.

30 *Socialdemokraten*, *Politiken* and *Berlingske Tidende* 5.1.1940, 6.1.1940, 8.1.1940.

most optimistic media users could maintain the hope that Finland might withstand the Soviet attack and, therefore, the final Finnish capitulation. The signing of the peace accord came as a surprise and disappointment for some.[31]

In general, the main newspapers gave a uniform description of the course of war and of the Finnish and Soviet soldiers; there was courage, perseverance and national solidarity on one side, and ruthlessness and senseless military compulsion on the other side. The broader framing of war was not uniform. *Socialdemokraten* had a clear ideological interpretation that the Soviet attack was not only directed in particular against the Finnish nation but was also against the Finnish working class. The headline on 12 January 1940 stated: "Soviet grenades against workers' homes" and "A clear-cut front against Soviet Nazism." All papers, except the communist paper, used the war in Finland to condemn the Danish Communist Party who supported the Soviet attack and warfare. *Socialdemokraten* and *Nationaltidende* gave the most vehement condemnations, and the denominations "red" and "communists" were used in the coverage of both the Soviets and the Danish communists.[32] In the coverage in *Politiken*, the main themes were the victims of the war, the senseless destruction and the importance of sustaining the neutrality of small states. The public enthusiasm for Finland should not lead the Danes to support an irresponsible policy led on by the British. Danish Prime Minister Stauning's statement that "[t]he solidarity with the Finnish people is stronger than ever before, but in this new conflict we are compelled to keep our policy of neutrality" was given a conspicuous place in both *Socialdemokraten* and *Politiken*.[33]

In the opposition papers, a direct comparison between the government's lack of will for defence and the neglect of the armed forces was drawn. The Finnish military struggle against the Red Army was proof that a small country's defence was useful and important and that military preparedness and a will to national defence were decisive for the ability of a small country

31 All the main Copenhagen papers, February–March 1940.

32 *Socialdemokraten* 22.12.1939, 23.12.1939, 4.1.1940, 12.1.1940, 15.1.1940; *Nationaltidende* 17.11.1939, 3.12.1939, 12.12.1939, 23.12.1939.

33 *Politiken* 6.12.1939, 7.1.1940, 22.1.1940, 23.1.1940, 26.2.1940; *Socialdemokraten* 6.12.1939.

to maintain its independence and sovereignty. The Danish political agenda was thus decisive for the interpretation of the Finnish Winter War.[34]

War in Norway: The Media Coverage

Immediately after the German occupation of Denmark on 9 April 1940, a more extensive control system of the Danish media was introduced. The State Radio had German controllers placed at the Broadcasting Headquarters and, in some cases, they exercised direct control. Ritzau was closely controlled by the Foreign Ministry Press Bureau. The newspapers, on the other hand, were subjected only to an indirect control system, based on a Foreign Ministry directive negotiated with the German occupation authorities. In several respects, this was an extension of the general lines of direction in the press directive from September 1939, only now the newspapers and Radio News had to manage in most cases without the use of any Allied sources. The Press Bureau of the Danish Foreign Ministry acted as supervisor and regularly issued rules for publication. A system for judging violations of the rules was established by representatives of the press and was organized by a tribunal consisting of leading editors from all the four main political groups of the press. The tribunal acted in conjunction with the Press Bureau and fined violations of the directions. The system was moderate compared with the direct censorship in other German-occupied countries, and to a large extent was based on self-censorship. Immediately, it was visible in the daily press that war news was now based mostly on DNB telegrams and official German military bulletins. The notification of the original sources in Ritzau telegrams was maintained both in Radio News and in the news in the daily papers, giving readers and listeners a chance to be aware of the change in sources.[35]

On the 9th of April, German troops landed in all major Norwegian ports and cities. The fighting continued in Norway for almost two months and included the intervention of Allied troops in the west and north of the country. The Danish public followed the events in Norway with immense

34 *Nationaltidende* 22–29.12.1939; *Berlingske Tidende* 22.12.1939, 29.12.1939, 2.1.1940.

35 L. Bindsløv Frederiksen, *Pressen under besættelsen. Hovedtræk af den danske dagspresses vilkår og virke i perioden 1940–45* (Aarhus: Universitetsforlaget i Aarhus, 1960), 13.

interest. The fighting there was connected with the military occupation of Denmark and at this early stage the result of the war in Norway was seen as influential for changes in the German occupation of Denmark. Some of the Danish observers followed events based on a strong feeling of Nordic solidarity, while others considered the fighting in Norway as a case of courageous national resistance in contrast to the almost immediate surrender of the Danish forces.

From the first day of the occupation, the media users harboured a clear distrust of the Danish media, seeing it as a mouthpiece for German messages, and in the first couple of days there was very little news from Norway. Therefore, after the 9th of April, other sources of news from Norway were sought: alternative sources at this stage were the Swedish Radio and the British Broadcasting Corporation (BBC). The BBC began reporting in Danish and Norwegian on 9 April, and according to the diaries, the shortwave broadcasts from London were found on their radio receivers early on by many Danes.[36]

In the Danish media, the war in Norway was almost exclusively seen through telegrams from DNB or other news agencies accepted by the occupation authorities. Swedish Radio used both German and Allied telegrams, but exercised a cautious policy of neutrality much like the policy exercised by the Danish media up until 9 April.[37] There were no Danish or Swedish correspondents in Norway who were able to publish their articles during the war, but there were German news agencies offering written and photographed descriptions of life in Norway, which, of course, emphasized their interpretation of the war. In *Aftenbladet*, a DNB report on the impressions of German soldiers from an occupied Norway was clearly German-biased, and at a later stage in the war *Billedbladet* featured reports on "The Germans in Norway" with many photographs of the German soldiers there, emphasizing peaceful scenes and contact with the local population. An article on "the tragedy of Narvik" in *Billedbladet,* on 18 June 1940, pointed to the meaningless destruction of the town by British forces.[38]

36 Roslyng-Jensen, *Danskerne og besættelsen*, 46.

37 Göran Elgemyr, *Får jeg be om en kommentar? Yttrandefriheten i svensk radio 1925–1960* (Stockholm: Stiftelsen Etermedierne i Sverige & Prisma, 2005), 207.

38 *Aftenbladet* 18.4.1940; *Billedbladet* 30.4.1940, 18.6.1940.

The one-sided background of the news and reporting meant that the Danish newspapers seem to have downsized their coverage of the war in Norway relatively early on, even though the diaries clearly indicate a huge public interest in the war. Already, on 15 April, *Aftenbladet* had as its main front-page story, "Ration cards for butter to people with low incomes," and the war in Norway was the third or fourth story in the paper. However, in most of the papers, Norway was on the front page every second or third day during the following weeks. In all of the newspapers, the message was that the German army was advancing steadily, the end result was clear and that the Norwegians were returning to work and normal conditions.[39]

To summarize: with regard to all the war events the media coverage depended on the available supply of news and photographs, which was extremely different in the three cases discussed above. In the case of Poland there was a structural preponderance of news from the German side. This was also the case regarding the war in Norway, although to a much higher degree with the exception of the broadcasts from London. The war in Finland had a strong Finnish bias in both sources and interpretation. The reception of news in all of these three cases was determined not only by the supply and content of the news but also depended on the engagement of the public and the position of the belligerent parties to the value system of the media and the media users.

Framings and Interpretations of War

War observation as seen through the media and the diaries discussed above provides evidence of how the three war events were interpreted, and how the nature of war and its effects were ascertained from a distance and how this was affected by different levels of public engagement. Research on later war events has concluded that private engagement was as decisive as public engagement. Research on war in the media after the Cold War stresses that war was to a significant degree seen as either a technical matter, a "spectator sport," where the victims of war are ignored, or a humanitarian endeavour.[40]

39 *Aftenbladet* 15.4.1940, *Aftenbladet* 16.4.–1.5.1940; *Politiken*, *Berlingske Tidende* and *Socialdemokraten,* ibid.

40 Nete Nørgaard Kristensen and Mark Ørsten, eds., *Krigen i medierne, medierne i krig*

This was based on a survey of public attitudes to the initial phase of the second Gulf war in 2004, where TV was the primary form of media for a majority of the population, while the conclusion does not apply to the wars observed in 1939–40, where newspapers and public service radio were the main media for a majority of the population. In the interpretation of public attitudes to these wars, the idea of the public sphere according to Jürgen Habermas has been chosen to establish a value system on the interpretation of war in the years 1939–40. Habermas divides his structure of interpretation in four layers: First a layer of formal, institutional authorized opinions and attitudes, and next layers of informal, personal opinions and attitudes comprising: a) group-experienced layers of taste, b) life experiences and attitudes based on personal experiences, c) cultural obtrusive matters.[41]

The following analysis is based on seven interpretations of attitudes to war and conflict in the years 1939–40. They comprise: distrust, personal fear, pity (on victims of war), fascination and suspense, war seen as a noble and heroic endeavour, questions of legality or humanism and war as a national sacrifice or purification. The three last forms of attitudes are closely connected to the formal and institutional opinions (often based on political and ideological affiliations), while the former four attitudes are generally based on the three mentioned layers of informal personal opinions or attitudes.

The diaries, and their writers who represent the receivers of the media, could also be divided, in this respect, into two different value systems

(Roskilde: Forlaget Samfundslitteratur, 2006), 16. Martin Shaw, *Civil Society and Media in Global Crises: Representing Distant Violence* (London: Pinter Publishers, 1996), 127–32. In Martin Shaw's investigation on attitudes and perceptions in Britain on the Gulf War 1990–91, differences in attitudes to war depended on whether the individual had some form of personal involvement, that is, if they had friends or families who were or had been soldiers. An investigation into the attitudes of the American population to the Vietnam War has a different conclusion: self-interest through the military service of friends or relatives did make the respondents pay more attention to the war, but had only weak effects on their attitudes to the war as a political issue. Richard R. Lau, Thad A. Brown and David O. Sears, "Self-Interest and Civilians' Attitudes Towards the Vietnam War," *Public Opinion Quarterly* 42, no. 4 (1978): 463–83. Among the observers in the three events of war discussed here, none had direct personal involvement, but for some observers national engagement or personal anxiety had an effect on their attitudes to the observed wars.

41 Jürgen Habermas, *Strukturwandel der Öffentlichkeit* (Neuwied und Berlin: Luchterhand, 1974), 288–94.

connected with war and occupation. One group placed great trust in the authorities, and had a general belief in law and order and an acceptance of the deep-rooted Danish policy of neutrality that was officially in force even after the German occupation, here named the "neutralists." The second group consisted of those who were critical of the authorities and very often extremely critical of the Social Democratic and Social Liberal government. Politically, they were often placed to the left or right of the government that was in power until the German occupation, and many tended to have a definite anti-German attitude and supported a stronger Danish defence, a group called the "activists."[42]

Distrust: The First Casualty of War is the Truth[43]

A consequence of the directives for neutrality in the media, that telegrams from both sides should be used, was that the personal interpretation of war was dependent to a significant degree on the attitudes of the observer of the belligerent parties and their political systems. This was the case during the war in Poland, where activist observers with strong nationalistic or democratic ideals sought as long as possible to maintain an optimistic perception of the development of the war, and gave no space to the existence of military problems or setbacks for the German military. To claim that there were outright German defeats during the war was not possible, even with the most optimistic telegrams from Poland.

An example of this kind of interpretation can be seen in the diaries of Knud Gedde, who several times used the expression "according to German information," "as stated," "if the German declarations of victories are correct." On 5 September, he wrote: "The Germans are claiming constant military progress in Poland; the truth is probably that the Germans have succeeded in isolating 120,000 Polish soldiers in the upper part of the Polish Corridor." Contrasting information was written down and he supported an interpretation in which the German information was exaggerated. On

42 Roslyng-Jensen, *Danskerne og besættelsen*, 325–26.

43 The phrase "The first casualty of the war is the truth," was first used by Senator Hiram Johnson in 1917. See Philip Knightly, *The First Casualty: From the Crimea to Vietnam: The War Correspondent as Hero, Propagandist, and Myth Maker* (London: Pan Books, 1989).

9 September, Gedde was still able to find hope in the Polish and French statements, which contrasted with the German statements. However, a couple of days later, Gedde had to admit that the Polish forces had suffered severe defeats and that Warsaw was threatened by German forces. Other diary writers with much the same attitude to the war repeated newspaper headlines in their diaries with indications of regret. In contrast, a number of the diarists deplored war in general, but kept a strictly neutral attitude to the belligerent parties and did not show any open distrust towards the messages in the media.[44]

There were no public or personal expressions of distrust in the media coverage of the war in Finland, although news from the Soviet side was almost completely absent. The public engagement on the Finnish side was strong and the presence of news telegrams from different news agencies and reports from well-known Danish correspondents created a feeling of trust among the media users. The main newspapers interpreted the war from different perspectives, but they were uniformly engaged on the Finnish side and strongly condemned the Soviet attack and all aspects of Soviet warfare.[45]

With the German occupation of Denmark, an extensive attitude of distrust not only in the news but to the media itself became predominant. Personal attitudes to the war in Norway did not correspond with the image of the war as seen in the Danish media. General distrust, rumours, personal exchanges of information, and news from the British broadcasting service were prevalent and created a gulf between the official and controlled content of the media and personal opinions of the war in Norway.[46] Edle Beyer wrote on 13 April: "It is very unpleasant that the press and radio are now uniform, we hear and we read only about the victories of the Germans and news from other countries which is favourable to the Germans." Roar Skovmand wrote much the same in his diary: "I listened to the radio from London – really quite another message than the Danish-German one."

44 Diarists: Knud Gedde 4.9.–6.9.1939, 9.9.1939 and Valdemar Anthon 10.9.1939 had the same basic attitude. Elise Jensen 4.9.1939 and Aage Danielsen September 1939 [no dates in the diary] had more neutral attitudes to Germany and Poland.

45 Roslyng-Jensen, *Danskerne og besættelsen*, 26–27.

46 Ibid., 48–49.

Marie Prytz, in her diary, did not trust the media at all: "According to the newspaper and the radio, the Germans are advancing in Norway, but Leif [her son] says that I should not believe one word of it."[47]

There were false rumours of huge naval battles in Norwegian waters and of battles in Norway, and personal communication replaced news in the media. Anna Hoffmann wrote on 26 April: "There must have been a large naval battle for many dead corpses have been washed ashore on our coast"; and on 11 May: "We are under censorship, but a lady came home and said that large provincial towns [in Norway] were completely demolished by bombing." In April and May, several other diarists were giving more credence to personal messages and less to the news from their daily newspaper and the Danish State Radio. They would rather believe in a personal message, even if it was second or third hand, than the media news which was controlled by the occupation power.[48] The result was an immediate decline in the circulation of all the main papers, especially of *Politiken*, as well as a decline in listeners to the Danish radio news and an increase in listeners to the broadcasts from the BBC. Many listened to both Danish radio news and the BBC with a comparative attitude. Marie Prytz wrote in her diary on 27 April: "Listened to radio from London – undeniably another message than in the Danish-German [radio on the war in Norway]."[49]

The public engagement in the plight of the Norwegians was no less than with the Finns, but the war in Norway was connected intimately with the background and prospects of the German occupation of Denmark. In the early stage, reactions were divided between those who kept some sense of neutrality and those with a strong anti-German attitude, although both parties had a strong feeling of solidarity with the Norwegians. On 29 April, expressing solidarity with the Norwegians and neutrality in the conflict between the great powers, Anna Hoffmann, wrote: "The war in Norway has now lasted a week longer than the war in Poland … poor Norwegians between two great powers." Marie Prytz had a clear anti-German attitude; after a story on the Norwegian resistance to German soldiers based on an oral source, she concluded: "Does Denmark have heroes like that?" The

47 Diarists: Edle Beyer 13.4.1940; Roar Skovmand 11.4.1940; Marie Prytz 18.4.1940.

48 Roslyng-Jensen, *Danskerne og besættelsen*, 34–35.

49 Ibid., 45–46; Marie Prytz 27.4.1940.

obvious answer was no, and her attitudes were based not on the media but on a general national framing.[50]

The question of trust in the media and its messages was therefore, in this case, much more a question of group experiences: attitudes to the belligerent parties and the personal and national interpretation of the issues connected more with the war than with the content of war coverage and the distribution of sources in the media.

Bombs and Personal Fear

The chief editor of *Ekstrabladet*, Ole Cavling, noted in his diary on 16 March: "Maybe those of us who remember the World War (1914–18) have to experience horrors even worse than last time … I don't reckon that there will be an air bombardment of Copenhagen, but terrible things could happen because we are at the entrance to the Baltic Sea."[51] There were no experiences with air bombardments in Denmark but a marked fear of bombing was prevalent however in the 1930s. This was a common phenomenon in the whole of Europe and led to civil defence precautions in many countries. In 1933, the Danish Red Cross published a pamphlet on air and gas attacks on the population and the Ministry of Interior Affairs had appointed a commission, the Gas Commission, which had parliamentary support for the first Danish law on civil defence against air attacks in 1935 and the creation of the "State Civilian Air Defence Agency" in 1938. In 1938–39, the Civilian Air Defence authorized the acquisition of a large stock of gas masks, the construction of air shelters, preparation for blackout in the cities and mobile squads to assist in case of bomb damage. All this was covered in the press and in the radio and through many activities, public meetings, posters and pamphlets all over the country. These activities were extended during the occupation and consisted of the organization of civil air defence

50 Diarists Anna Hoffmann 29.4.1940; Marie Prytz 4.5.1940; Roslyng-Jensen, *Danskerne og besættelsen*, 51; Kreth, *Pilestræde under pres*, 222.

51 Diarist Ole Cavling 16.3.1939, and 28.3.1939 expresses the same basic attitude; also Valdemar Anthon 10.9.1939 compares the situation in September 1939 with the early stage of the First World War.

in factories, house wardens in residential areas and recruiting conscripts and volunteers for Civil Defence detachments.[52]

Foreign Minister Peter R. Munch held a meeting with representatives of the press a few days before war broke out and his main message was that it was the duty of the press to "keep the mood calm." At the same time, the readers of *Socialdemokraten* had their minds set at rest with the headline: "Everything is ready to protect the population against air attacks." Several other newspapers had equivalent reassuring messages that the authorities had made all necessary arrangements, and on 13 September the minister of interior affairs stated, "There is no need for fear in neutral Denmark," after schools had arranged evacuation exercises in case of air attack warnings and leading educators had said that "schoolchildren became anxious."[53]

The first news from the Polish side on the war in Poland consisted to a large degree of information on air attacks on Polish cities and especially on Warsaw. The newspapers on 2 September featured headlines such as: "Six air attacks on Warsaw," "The Germans use gas," "Many Polish women and children were killed," and "1500 killed by air attack." The German news consisted of a telegram: "Many Polish military airfields have been destroyed," and a photograph: "Street in German town after bombardment from Polish war planes" with no indication of the actual town that this referred to. For the next two weeks, the air bombardments of Warsaw were a dominant theme in the press: "A rain of bombs on Warsaw," "Warsaw in flames," etc. But it was not until 12 September that the first photographs from Warsaw appeared. *Politiken* printed a picture of a large burning building and people fleeing.[54] Articles from correspondents in Paris and London had fear of air bombardments and gas attacks as a prominent topic. From

52 *Statens civile Luftværn 1938–1949*, 3 vols. (Copenhagen: Civilforsvarsstyrelsen, 1949); Robert Mackay, *Half the Battle: Civilian Morale in Britain during the Second World War* (Manchester: Manchester University Press, 2002), 20–23.

53 Kreth, *Pilestræde under pres*, 207; *Socialdemokraten* 2.9.1939, 14.9.1939; "How Do Children and Young People React to War?" *Nationaltidende* 1.9.1939; *Politiken* 14.1.1940. UM 109, 26.8.1939.

54 *Berlingske Tidende* 3.9.1939; *Socialdemokraten* 3.9.1939; *Aftenbladet* 2.9.1939, 3.9.1939; *Politiken* 12.9.1939.

London, the news was: "People are wearing gas masks in the street" and "Paris expects German air bombardments any moment."[55]

The fear of air attacks in Denmark became a reality almost at once. On 4 September at 4.40 p.m., just a few hours after the French and British declarations of war against Germany, four bombs were dropped on the city of Esbjerg. One hit a residential building; one person was killed and three wounded. The newspapers and the radio did not have any information on who had dropped the bombs or why. A headline said simply: "A war plane drops or loses four bombs on Esbjerg." The bombs had actually been dropped by a British plane that had lost orientation over the North Sea and thought it was attacking a German harbour city. The immediate consequence was speculation and rumours all over the country, and many saw their worst presentiments of the dangers of the coming war confirmed. The next day, the news of the bombs on Esbjerg completely relegated the events in Poland from the first pages of the papers. A Polish telegram saying "300 killed and 500 wounded by air attacks on two cities" was placed on page three.[56]

Diaries from that same day which referred to the events are completely dominated by the bombs on Esbjerg, the first bombs that had ever been dropped from the air on Danish territory, and the more timid observers expressed fear and personal anxiety. Diarist and reporter Vilhelm Bergstrøm wrote that his wife and several of her female friends broke down in tears expecting Danish cities to be bombed and complete neighbourhoods evacuated. Housekeeper and diary writer Elise Jensen very often saw the news through a framing based on general human compassion and personal fear, especially how her own family might be hit by war events. On 3 September, she wrote: "If only we could be kept out of the war."[57]

In contrast to the war in Poland, personal fear was not prevalent with regards to the war in Finland. The air bombardments and gas attacks in Finland were on the front pages of the newspapers on 3 November but

55 *Berlingske Tidende* 3.9.1939, 5.9.1939.

56 *Socialdemokraten* 5.9.1939; Claus Bundgaard Christensen, Joachim Lund, Niels Wium Olesen and Jakob Sørensen, eds., *Danmark besat. Krig og hverdag 1940–45* (Copenhagen: Høst & Søn, 2005), 67.

57 Elise Jensen 5.9.–6.9.1939; Bergstrøm, *En borger*, 1: 63–64, 5.9.1939; Hjalmar Gammelgaard 5.9.1939; Knud Gedde 5.9.1939.

this was mostly to stress the brutality of the Soviet warfare.[58] Observers of the war in Norway were more divided than observers of the Finnish war. Neutral observers were relieved that there had been almost no fighting in Denmark when they followed reports on the war in Norway. From 20 April 1940, there were air attacks carried out by the British Royal Air Force on German-occupied airfields in Denmark, so air sirens sounded in several cities and personal fear increased markedly. In the first few weeks, when there were still British soldiers in western Norway, a few even saw the British planes as a prelude to a British military invasion in Denmark. More activist observers saw any sign of allied military activity against the Germans as an advantage.[59] In general, fear of war was based on informal personal opinions but supported by formal, institutional warnings and official preparations for protection against air raids.

Personal and National Pity with the Victims of War

In general, observers of the war in Poland felt pity for the Polish civilian population who were being hit by the bombing and having to flee their homes and towns. War and its effects in general played a role in the national sense of pity by giving rise to a feeling of solidarity with the civilians affected by war, but also by creating a sense of shared values with a population who were the victims of German aggression and ruthless attacks. In spite of the considerations of neutrality for the press, the news of the events and suffering in Warsaw supported these sentiments.

The bombarding and shelling of Warsaw, "the burning capital," was a predominant subject in the press coverage of the war in Poland. After 28 September, when the city capitulated, *Nationaltidende* wrote: "The city is now mostly reduced to rubble. Nine hospitals were destroyed by bombs and shells." The inhabitants of Warsaw, and Poland, were the victims and any mention of the German military was connected with industrial and non-human metaphors such as "the German war machine," "ruthless German advance." Elise Jensen wrote on 18 September: "Poor Poland, they are

58 *Socialdemokraten* and *Nationaltidende* 3.12.1939: Both newspapers use the same headline: "The Russians are using poisonous gas."

59 Palle Roslyng-Jensen, *Danskerne og besættelsen*, 52–53.

now, for I don't know how many times, divided and ruined and the population is on the run before the enemy."[60]

On 26 September, the war in the air was once again on the front pages with typical headlines coming from both sides, headlines Elise Jensen wrote down in her diary: "Yesterday French planes were bombing Friedrichshafen," and "A rain of bombs over Warsaw." With reference to the last article, her comment was: "Thousands of people killed. Horrible." Despite her generally neutral attitude, her sympathy was with the victims of the bombings in Warsaw, not with the victims of the bombings in Friedrichshafen.[61] Valdemar Anthon had voted for the Social Liberal party at the previous parliamentary election and he saw the war events from a generally critical interpretation of the military. In his diary entry for 10 September, with the German army deep into Polish territory, he expressed marked sympathy with the Poles and dissociation with the Germans, but at the same he evidenced that war was terrible: "We have to feel sympathy for all the innocent people hit directly by the horror of war … but for how long a time the murders will go on this time we do not have any well-founded opinion about … I am engulfed by a feeling of disgust by all the shrill announcements on the barbarism which the newspapers are full of, but still I am not able to resist the daily craving to seek news from the battle sites in the morning papers."[62]

The reporting from the Finnish war stressed the bombing of civilians and photos appeared regularly of burning houses, a destroyed hospital, or refugees leaving places of battle or bombardment.[63] Entries in the diaries shared the condemnation of the Soviet warfare, and no difference between those who leaned either towards neutrality or more towards activism is discernible in this case. "The infamy of red pilots" was written in one; "many innocent victims in Helsingfors and other cities" in another. A diarist with an extensive reading of different papers wrote: "The horrors in Finland are increasing … the whole world is indignant, except of course Germany, where they are only reproducing the Russian official news." Compared

60 *Nationaltidende* 28.9.1939; *Aftenbladet* 28.9.1939; Elise Jensen 18.9.1939.
61 Elise Jensen 3.9.1939, 18.9.1939. Also: Kaj Nielsen 17.9.1939, 26.9.1939.
62 Valdemar Anthon 10.9.1940.
63 All newspapers 1.12.1939, 22.12.1939: "Soviet bombs against Finnish hospital."

with opinions on the war events in Poland, the anger and condemnation was much stronger in opinions on the Finnish war. Engagement and a feeling of Nordic solidarity in the Danish public had without doubt some influence, but the character of the press coverage must also be part of the explanation.[64]

As the Danish newspaper coverage of the war in Norway depended mostly on German or German-controlled sources, it is obvious that an open voice in the newspapers against the German warfare in Norway and strong expressions of sympathy with the Norwegian defence and Norwegian casualties were not possible. The relative lack of expressions of sympathy with the Norwegians was probably one of the reasons why Danish radio listeners turned at such an early date to the news in Danish from the BBC. The Swedish radio was extremely careful not to allow open voices of sympathy with the Norwegians and condemnation of the Germans, and therefore it was not a satisfactory medium for the activists seeking confirmation and expression of their attitudes.[65]

Fascination and Suspense

War in the trenches became a symbol of senseless slaughter of human life, during and after the First World War while war in the air often became a symbol of modernity, personal heroism and individual combat. After the war the fascination of air war (and to some degree war at sea) was transmitted to the public in novels, newspapers and other media and was present in newspaper reportage from the war in Poland in September 1939.[66]

In the first reports from Warsaw, *Aftenbladet* printed a headline to a telegram from Reuters dated 2 September: "Exciting air battles over the centre of town." In another paper, there was a more neutral and descriptive headline: "Air battles over the streets of Warsaw. Eye witness report from

64 Ole Cavling 1.12.1939; Kaj Nielsen 1.12.1939; Hjalmar Gammelgaard 1.12.1939; Bergstrøm, *En borger*, 2.12.1939; Valdemar Anthon 30.1.1940; Christian Reinhard 15.1.1940.

65 Roar Skovmand 11.4.1940; Marie Prytz 21.4.1940; Elgemyr, *Får jeg be*, 207–8.

66 Linda R. Robertson, *The Dream of Civilized Warfare: World War I Flying Aces and the American Imagination* (Minneapolis: University of Minnesota Press, 2003).

the German air attacks." In these reports the focus was not on the victims or any destruction, but on the excitement and the drama of the battle.[67]

In *Socialdemokraten* and in *Politiken*, any interpretation that could be connected with a sense of excitement was completely absent. A poem by the Social Democratic party poet and activist Oskar Hansen on the front page on 2 September gave a clear indication of a general opposition and dissociation to war: "The first fallen soldiers, destinies have been trampled down. The war has begun," and headlines, photographs and editorials stressed the destruction of war and loss of life, not battle scenes or advancing German soldiers as other newspapers did. On 11 September, a large photograph on the front page was captioned with the text "The destruction of war," and another photograph on 16 September with the text "Cities in ruins."[68]

Later in November and December 1939, the sinking of the German warship *Graf Spee* in the South Atlantic brought the engaging and dramatic news that Ole Cavling from *Ekstrabladet* in his diary had deplored were missing after the war in Poland was over in late September. Dramatic news were rare from the Western front, although on 18 December *Nationaltidende* had a report from its correspondent in Paris on a dogfight between German and French planes: "The real face of the Western Front. War like a fight with Red Indians and white men, and more exciting than novels by Cooper." The editors of *Politiken* and *Socialdemokraten* would have found this wording too bellicose.[69] Excitement with war in regard to Finland was not found in the general framing of the newspapers, or among the diarists, only with Finnish victories, as the two belligerent parties were not placed in the same category morally. Any sense of thrill in relation to the news from Norway was not present at all; the strong engagement on the side of Finland and Norway led instead to political and moral interpretations. In the structure of interpretation by Habermas this kind of attitude could be placed in different forms of personal experiences but clearly supported by authorized opinions connected to political and ideological divisions.

67 *Aftenbladet* 2.9.1939, 3.9.1939, 5.9.1939.

68 *Socialdemokraten* 2.9.1939, 11.9.1939, 16.9.1939.

69 Ole Cavling diary October (no date) 1939; *Ekstrabladet* 14.11.1939–21.11.1939; *Nationaltidende* 3.12.1939.

A Noble War and Heroism

Attitudes to war stressing heroism, soldierly virtues and chivalry did occur in the Danish media but only in German telegrams, German reports or German photographs that were printed in Danish newspapers. On 3 September, a German submarine sank the British passenger liner *Athenia* in the Atlantic with the loss of more than a hundred lives, including many Americans. The sinking was a serious matter for the German propaganda machine. Over the following days, several press reports and messages were distributed from the German side with the aim of creating an impression of noble and morally correct warfare on behalf of the Germans.[70] On 6 September, a DNB story was presented under the heading: "Foes – but noble adversaries" on the chivalrous behaviour of a German air force pilot and an English ship's captain in an encounter in the Atlantic. And in a later DNB telegram it was claimed, quite falsely, that the captain of the German submarine had behaved chivalrously towards the crew of the *Athenia*, a telegram which several Danish newspapers published. A later telegram also contained the story of another German submarine captain saving the lives of the crew from a torpedoed freighter.

The rising anger in the Danish population over the continued German sinking of Danish merchant vessels and the significant loss of the lives of Danish seamen was clearly visible in the diaries, and Germany's ruthless naval warfare was condemned. Valdemar Anthon expressed disgust with war in general and German warfare in particular, and during the Finnish war he placed the Germans and the Soviets in the same category: "The blameless sailors ... had been murdered in cold blood by these ruthless executioners (German submarines and planes), who like the Russian pilots prefer being heroes against non-armed civilians instead of the more risky attacks on the armed forces of the enemy." There are, however, examples of a more neutral attitude on this issue, that attacks on merchant ships were part of the conditions of modern warfare, regrettable but nevertheless a fact.[71] Probably very few Danes accepted the German stories of gallant

70 Balfour, *Propaganda in War*, 157–58.
71 Valdemar Anthon 31.1.1940; Hjalmar Gammelgaard 8.9.1939.

pilots and noble submarine captains. The sinking of Danish freighters was always put on the front page of the newspapers, but without specifying how the ship was sunk. Few Danes were in any doubt as to which side the perpetrators belonged.[72]

Initially, the German messages on the war in Poland did not have stories about noble warfare or respect for the rules of war. On the contrary, the DNB telegrams contained details of Polish attacks by guerillas (*Freischütze*) on German soldiers from behind. It was the Poles, therefore, who were breaking the rules of law and the German army was responding righteously with the harshest possible means. At a later stage, the German propaganda machine published Polish photographs of a fortress at Westerplatte at the entrance to the harbour in Danzig, which had been given prominence in the Allied news telegrams. The Polish photographs were used to emphasize chivalrous German military behaviour. After the German forces had conquered the fortress, "the courageous commander" of the Polish forces was rewarded by German officers "for his soldierly endeavour by presenting him with honourable conditions for the surrender of him and his men." A complete pictorial report of Polish officers in a German prisoner of war camp was published three weeks later, and it stressed how correctly and chivalrously they were being treated.[73]

In the media reporting from the Finnish war brave and noble acts by the fighting soldiers were described but of course only on the Finnish side. In *Billedbladet* a reportage on the military exploits of the famous cross country skier Pekka Niemi accentuated the deeds of an individual Finnish soldier. In several articles in the press, it was stressed that the Finns kept the rules of war, and showed mercy towards the enemy. In *Billedbladet*, on 16 January, a whole photographic report was presented with the headline: "Russian officers in captivity are treated with humane care in Finland."[74]

72 *Berlingske Tidende* 6.9.1939; *Socialdemokraten* and other newspapers 8.9.1939; *Berlingske Tidende* 8.12.1939: "A Noble German Captain of a Submarine"; *Billedbladet* 9.4.1940: "The Mercy of War. A German Torpedo Boat, which had sunk an English Destroyer, saves the Crew."

73 *Billedbladet* 26.9.1939.

74 *Billedbladet* 16.1.1940: "Pekka Niemi's patrol of death." *Billedbladet* 13.2.1940, 19.2.1940, 12.3.1940.

There was no framing based on any ideas of noble warfare or soldiering as a noble game in general. Not even in the Finnish and Norwegian cases. The diary writers and Danish journalists who wrote freely did not share the value system or institutional set of authorized opinions behind this view on war, no matter how politically and ideological diverse they were.

Legality and Humanity

Poland was almost a neighbouring state to Denmark, but culturally and politically distant. Not many Danes had travelled in Poland or knew Poland, so the reactions to what happened in Poland did not produce the kind of sentiments which events in Finland or Norway were met with and where support was almost self-evident. In the support for Poland, humanitarian, anti-German or legal arguments were mobilized.

Hjalmar Gammelgaard noted in his diary on 4 September that the Germans did not submit a declaration of war on Poland in contrast to France and Britain with their declarations of war on Germany on 3 September: "Several Polish cities were bombed from the air. War has begun without a declaration of war." Mechanic Kaj Nielsen wrote several months later about a discussion regarding the outbreak of war: "Card playing evening with friends. Fierce discussion about which of the two belligerent sides had begun the war. K. supported that the allies had declared war on Germany, but actually it was Germany who in a military sense began the war." It is obvious at this early stage of the war, as seen from Kaj Nielsen's diary, that the war had not yet been interpreted either nationally or politically. It was still just interested observers who were discussing openly who started the war, drawing on what they had read or heard in the media.

Diarist Knud Gedde was a conservative, a democrat and a traditional anti-German attitude can be found in his diary entry for 4 September: "In Danzig … a fierce bombardment from the German warship Schleswig-Holstein, which had come to Danzig on an official courtesy visit last week … On a visit with ammunition in the cannons, that is a typical example of the special German way of being courteous."[75] It is obvious that even

75 Hjalmar Gammelgaard 1.9.1939; Kaj Nielsen 20.12.1939; Knud Gedde 4.9.1939;

though the media coverage was dominated by German news telegrams, arguments could be found that made an interpretation of the outbreak of war possible that was in accordance with the observers' existing general attitudes.

In the Finnish war, the legality and humanity of the Finnish actions were taken for granted, and reports on the exclusion of the Soviet Union from the League of Nations confirmed this. The anti-Soviet and anti-communist feelings were prevalent with everyone except the Danish communists, but there was a division between those who interpreted the war from a humanistic attitude that excluded the fallen Soviet soldiers and those who included them. Elise Jensen wrote, on 9 December: "Poor unfortunate Finland. In these days they are asking the whole world for help"; and on 4 January: "It is terrible how the soldiers are suffering in Finland. The Russians are wounded and dying of the cold in their thousands." On 19 December, Aage Danielsen wrote: "The Finns have won a new battle to the many victories they have already won; more than 18,000 Russian soldiers died, it is terrible to think of." Other observers were only able to extend humanity to the Finnish side and looked at the Soviet losses as an encouraging sign of Finnish military progress.[76]

For the majority of Danes, the arguments against the German war in Norway were obvious. The arguments were not found in the Danish media or the Swedish radio, and the BBC functioned mostly as an emotional confirmation of anti-German attitudes. Johanne Rambusch wrote on 18 April: "London, radio 10.40 p.m. … it was in Danish and pure balsam for the soul after you had heard the Danish radio news at 10 p.m." And this is Valdemar Anthon on 20 June: "The words of the Danish speaker (on the BBC) gave me much doubt and encouragement with its correction of all the German boasting." But even here, the legalistic attitude of neutrality can be discerned, in spite of the German military occupation.[77]

Roslyng-Jensen, *Danskerne og besættelsen*, 25–26.

76 Bergstrøm, *En borger*, 8.12.1939; Ole Cavling 19.12.1939; Christian Reinhard 18.1.1940.

77 Johanne Rambusch 18.4.1940; Valdemar Anthon 20.6.1940; Anna Hofffmann 11.4.1940, 13.4.1940; Roslyng-Jensen, *Danskerne og besættelsen*, 60–62.

War and National Sacrifice

The discussion in the 1930s on the use and importance of a Danish military defence was to a high degree connected with a morally framed attitude about whether a national sacrifice – that is, to give one's life in support of the national sovereignty or national interests, even though prospects for military success were extremely modest – was important or not. From public debate in Britain and France on the appeasement policy, the catchword "Mourir pour Danzig?" or its equivalent was well known.[78] The strong anti-militaristic tradition in Denmark since the 1864 defeat meant that the discourse on the aimless sacrifice by a military defence against Germany was quite strong, but it did not exist openly in the reaction to the three war events in 1939–40 discussed here. It was, however, more visible and open in relation to the Danish acceptance of the German ultimatum to Denmark on 9 April.[79]

There are several examples of newspaper articles in the coverage of the Finnish war that stress courage and personal sacrifice in battle, that never describe this as futile. A report from 27 December says: "The first 'lotter' have fallen on their posts in the wasteland of Finland." The war reportage from Finland established the denomination "lotte" so strongly in Denmark that it was an inspiration for the establishment in 1940 of a women's corps of volunteers supporting Danish military and civil defence, "Danske Kvinders Beredskab," renamed in 1946 as "Danmarks Lottekorps."[80]

The emphasis on a heroic defence and on military endeavours that were in the strict strategic sense in vain, but which strengthened national sentiments and self-respect, is mostly found among conservative and nationally orientated observers, and not in, for example, *Politiken*, which was critical

78 The catchword was formed by French socialist Marcel Déat in a newspaper article against French military guarantees to Poland on 4 May 1939. The catchword was used in German propaganda directed against France and Britain. Déat later became a prominent ideological collaborationist in occupied France.

79 Roslyng-Jensen, *Danskerne og besættelsen*, 38. The Danish military defeat to Prussia and Austria in 1864 on the Schleswig-Holstein question.

80 *Nationaltidende* 27.12.1939; also see *Billedbladet* 19.3.1940: "Lotterne. The Sisters of Front Soldiers"; The denomination "Lotte" (Swedish "Lotta") derives from Finnish poet Johan Ludvig Runeberg in 1860 and Lotta voluntary women's unarmed military corps established after the First World War in both countries.

of a military defence. The conservative and national crime reporter at *Politiken*, Vilhelm Bergstrøm, wrote in his diary on 18 September, "Warsaw is defending itself in spite of all common sense. Well, in some way it is sensible enough. The capital gave a sacrifice in blood by which the fourth Poland will rise again like a Phoenix." And similarly, on 24 September: "The Poles do not say: what use is it for? They prove that they are a nation that will survive." He never voiced opinions such as those in the newspaper. The nationally minded diary keeper Christian Reinhard was so deeply disappointed over the Finnish-Soviet peace accord that the interpretation of a national sacrifice was not enough: "Finland yields although their army has not been defeated ... the fallen soldiers died in vain."[81]

No diarist wrote that the Norwegian resistance against the German army had been in vain, as such a judgement would be too closely connected to the situation in Denmark, and the difference between the two cases was obvious. The neutralists were at this stage too much in doubt as to how the situation in Denmark should be judged, and the nationally minded activists were almost envious of the military resistance offered by the Norwegians and did in no way see it as a futile sacrifice.[82]

In Conclusion. Attitudes to Wars at a Distance based on Institutional or Personal Interpretations

In the first two cases of war, in Poland and in Finland, the diaries provide evidence of a general trust in the news and reporting of the war, even though there was a state control system at work and the structural distribution of sources was not even-handed in relationship to the belligerent parties. The military occupation of Denmark created an immediate and prevalent distrust of the media, and especially towards the German news from the war in Norway. Coverage of the events in Poland, and the not very large-scale war events between the great powers (the phony war), were

81 Bergstrøm, *En borger*, 18.9.1940, 24.9.1940, "What use is it for?" is a citation from the Danish anti-militaristic politician Viggo Hørup on the building of the Copenhagen land fortress in the 1880s; Christian Reinhard 13.3.1940; Roslyng-Jensen, *Danskerne og besættelsen*, 26–28.

82 Roslyng-Jensen, *Danskerne og besættelsen*, 46–49.

transmitted within a framing influenced by the institutional Danish policy of neutrality, and yet, as in the Polish case, still with a structural imbalance of reporting and pictures. It did not mean that the German framing of the war was accepted by the diary writers, where both a neutral interpretation is discernible as well as an activist one and where anti-German opinions are clearly visible. The latter made interpretations of the war in general, and especially of German and later Soviet warfare, contrast openly with the war news and explanations coming from Germany.

Regarding the war in Finland, there was a clear accordance between media framing and media reception, as the well-known, double-sided neutral reporting was more or less suspended in this case. The combination of the one-sided media coverage of the war in Norway, and a strong personal distrust of the media in general, created an imbalance between media framing and media reception, and was instrumental in motivating many Danes to listen to British or Swedish radio news. The Danish media system, the control exercised over it and the predominant neutrality rules for presenting the war news meant that, generally, Danes were well trained in receiving and interpreting conflicting views, an experience which they could use expediently during the subsequent years under German occupation. The Finnish case was an exeption in this context, where institutional authorized opinions, media framing and a complete imbalance of sources created a reception and personal interpretation of the media which were almost without exception on the Finnish side.

References

Alkil, Niels, ed. *Besættelsestidens Fakta. Dokumentarisk Haandbog med Henblik paa Lovene af 1945 om Landsskadelig Virksomhed m.v.* 2 vols. Copenhagen: Sagførerraadet and J. H. Schultz Forlag, 1945–1946.

Andreasen, Janni. *At vise flaget. Ebbe Munck – Krigskorrespondent – Modstandsmand – Hofchef.* Copenhagen: Høst & Søn, 2007.

Balfour, Michael. *Propaganda in War 1939–1945: Organisations, Policies and Publics in Britain and Germany.* London: Routledge and Kegan Paul, 1979.

Bergstrøm, Vilhelm. *En borger i Danmark under krigen.* 2 vols. Copenhagen: Gads Forlag, 2005.

Boyd-Barrett, Oliver. *The International News Agencies.* London: Constable, 1980.

Carstensen, Svend. *Syv Aar i Søgelyset.* Copenhagen: Steen Hasselbalchs Forlag, 1945.

Christensen, Claus Bundgaard, Joachim Lund, Niels Wium Olesen and Jakob Sørensen, eds. *Danmark besat. Krig og hverdag 1940–45.* Copenhagen: Høst & Søn, 2005.

Christiansen, Ernst, Knud Rée and J. Rosenkjær, eds. *Statsradiofonien 1925–1950.* Copenhagen: Gyldendal, 1950.

Elgemyr, Göran. *Får jeg be om en kommentar? Yttrandefriheten i svensk radio 1925–1960.* Stockholm: Stiftelsen Etermedierne i Sverige & Prisma, 2005.

Frederiksen, L. Bindsløv. *Pressen under besættelsen. Hovedtræk af den danske dagspresses vilkår og virke i perioden 1940–45.* Aarhus: Universitetsforlaget i Aarhus, 1960.

Gamson, William A. *Talking Politics.* Cambridge: Cambridge University Press, 1992.

Gudme, Peter de Hemmer. *Finlands folk i kamp.* Copenhagen: Gyldendal, 1941.

Habermas, Jürgen. *Strukturwandel der Öffentlichkeit. Untersuchungen zu Einer Kategorie der bürgerlichen Gesellschaft.* 6th ed. Neuwied and Berlin: Luchterhand, 1974.

Holman, Valerie and Debra Kelly, eds. *France at War in the Twentieth Century: Propaganda, Myth and Metaphor.* New York: Berghahn Books, 2000.

Knightley, Philip. *The First Casualty: From the Crimea to Vietnam: The War Correspondent as Hero, Propagandist and Myth Maker*. London: Pan Books, 1989.

Knudsen, Helge. *Hitler bandt min pen*. Copenhagen: Gyldendal, 1945.

Kreth, Rasmus. *Pilestræde under pres. De Berlingske Blade 1933–45*. Copenhagen: Gyldendal, 1998.

Kristensen, Nete Nørgaard and Mark Ørsten, eds. *Krigen i medierne, medierne i krig*. Roskilde: Forlaget Samfundslitteratur, 2006.

Lau, Richard R., Thad A. Brown and David O. Sears. "Self-Interest and Civilians' Attitudes Towards the Vietnam War." *Public Opinion Quarterly* 42, no. 4 (1978): 463–83.

Longerich, Peter. *Propagandisten im Krieg. Die Presseabteilung des Auswärtigen Amtes unter Ribbentrop*. Munich: R. Oldenbourg Verlag, 1987.

Lundgreen-Nielsen, Kay. *Tro eller blændværk? Danmark og Den Spanske Borgerkrig 1936–1939. En undersøgelse af den danske presses og den danske regerings holdning*. Odense: Odense Universitetsforlag, 2001.

Mackay, Robert. *Half the Battle: Civilian Morale in Britain during the Second World War*. Manchester: Manchester University Press, 2002.

Nielsen, Jan Ahtola. *I orkanens øje. Det danske Finlandskorps 1939–40*. Copenhagen: Gyldendal, 2006.

Robertson, Linda R. *The Dream of Civilized Warfare: World War I Flying Aces and the American Imagination*. Minneapolis: University of Minnesota Press, 2003.

Roslyng-Jensen, Palle. *Danskerne og besættelsen. Holdninger og meninger 1939–1945*. Copenhagen: Gads Forlag, 2007.

———. "Nationale meningsfællesskaber. Danskernes reception af radionyheder om krig og krigsbegivenheder under 2. Verdenskrig." *Historisk Tidsskrift* 112 (2012): 62–91.

Shaw, Martin. *Civil Society and Media in Global Crises: Representing Distant Violence*. London: Pinter Publishers, 1996.

Søllinge, Jette D. and Niels Thomsen. *De danske aviser 1634–1991*. 3 vols. Odense: Dagspressens Fond, 1991.

Statens civile Luftværn 1938–1949. 3 vols. Stencileret. Copenhagen: Civilforsvarsstyrelsen, 1949.

NEWSPAPERS AND MAGAZINES

Aftenbladet
Billedbladet
Berlingske Tidende
Nationaltidende
Politiken
Socialdemokraten

DIARIES

Anthon, Valdemar
Bergstrøm, Vilhelm
Beyer, Edle
Cavling, Ole
Danielsen, Aage
Gammelgaard, Hjalmar
Gedde, Knud
Hoffman, Anna
Jensen, Elise
Nielsen, Kaj
Prytz, Marie
Rambusch, Johanne
Reinhard, Christian
Skovmand, Roar

ARCHIVES

Danish Media Museum, Odense.
  Ekstrabladets arkiv 1939.
  Politikens Hus 1938–1940.
Royal Archives (Rigsarkivet), Copenhagen.
  Udenrigsministeriets arkiv (UM).
  The Press Agency (Pressebureauet)

Wartime Violence against Civilians
Philosophical Reflections on War Rape

Robin May Schott

"They cut my hand. They thorn [sic] out all clothes and underwear that were on me. They got free reign to their desires on my body. I was screaming and fighting. J. hit me on my head with his leg. I had to suck their sexual organs, for all five of them. J. tried to rape me, but I was screaming and he hit me again. I fainted down.

When I became conscious again I saw that I was completely naked. Their sperm was in my mouth; they were squeezing my breasts, and when I fainted they raped me, all five of them... There were some other girls there, all at age of 12 to 15, and all of them were raped... There were some girls left without one breast as while they were sucking their breasts they used to bit off their nipples. Many of the girls were unconscious... Brothers and fathers were taken into look their sisters and daughters be raped... They then came with my son, who was all covered with blood, and ordered him to rape me. They were saying: 'You must rape your mother.' He answered: 'You can kill me, but I'll not do that.'"[1]

Much philosophical reflection on wartime violence takes place under the auspices of just war theory, which presupposes a categorical distinction between combatants and non-combatants. Just war theorists expend considerable energy exploring the question: when is violence against civilians a necessary strategy for waging just war? Michael Walzer, one of the pre-eminent just war theorists, reminds us of Napolean's claim "Soldiers

1 Mirsad Tokača, ed., *The Sin of Silence, The Risk of Speech* (Sarajevo: Commission for Gathering Facts on War Crimes in Bosnia and Herzegovina, 1999), excerpt from the statement No. 5019/95 – Banja Luka.

are made to be killed," and adds, "*no one else is made to be killed*."[2] Walzer adds that soldiers cannot rape and murder civilians because civilians have not surrendered their rights as soldiers have done.[3]

I will not here enter the substantial debate about the tenability of the combatant/civilian distinction, but I do align myself with the critics who claim that this distinction is ultimately untenable. This distinction does not empirically provide a meaningful measure of the dangers posed to civilians during wartime. For example, in World War Two, one database lists over 19 million total combatant deaths and over 17 million total civilian deaths.[4] In the Viet Nam war, there were an estimated 1.1 million Viet Cong guerillas and North Vietnamese soldiers who died, and an estimated two million civilian deaths in the North and South between 1954 and 1975.[5] In the recent war in Iraq, unnamed U.S. military officials have said that between 10,000 and 15,000 Iraqi soldiers were killed. Estimates of civilians killed since the U.S. invasion in 2003 ranges between 86,864 and 94,782. These deaths are due to coalition and insurgent military action, sectarian violence, and criminal violence resulting from the breakdown of law and order.[6] Such examples indicate that civilian casualties in military conflict are almost as high as combatant casualties, and often are significantly higher.

2 Michael Walzer, *Just and Unjust War: A Moral Argument with Historical Illustrations* (New York: Basic Books, 1977), 136. The following three paragraphs are drawn from my article, "Just War and the Problem of Evil," *Hypatia: A Journal of Feminist Philosophy: Special Issue on Just War* 23, no. 2 (April–June 2008): 128, 133.

3 It is unclear what Walzer would make of the status of women soldiers. Do they surrender their rights to their sexual dignity, or merely surrender their right not to be killed? Presumably the former would be treated under rules relating to the torture of enemy soldiers.

4 *The World War II Multimedia Database*, "Casualties in World War II" (accessed 18 May, 2005) http://www.worldwar2database.com/html/frame5.htm. The site lists total combatant casualties as 19,775,866 and total non-combatant casualties as 17,439,287.

5 *Wikipedia*, s.v. "Vietnam War" (accessed 18 May 2005) http://en.wikipedia.org/wiki/Vietnam_War.

6 Jerry Isaacs, "US Will Provide No Estimate of Iraqi War Casualties," *World Socialist Web Site*, 28 April, 2003 (accessed 19 May, 2005) http://www.wsws.org/articles/2003/apr2003/casu-a28.shtml. According to this report, the number may be considerably higher, and the U.S. assault has wiped out a large portion of the young generation of Iraqi men. For statistics on civilian casualties, see *Iraq Body Count* (accessed 8 September, 2008), http://www.iraqbodycount.net. The header on this site is a statement by General Tommy Franks, U.S. Central Command, "We don't do body counts." For information about this site, see also Wikipedia, s.v. "Iraq Body Count Project" (accessed 8 September, 2008) http://en.wikipedia.org/wiki/Iraq_Body_Count_project.

The combatant/non-combatant distinction is also problematic conceptually. As Sara Ruddick notes, it operates within a conceptual universe that is characterized by abstraction, dichotomy and unbounded definition.[7] Just war theorists typically give an account of war that is characterized by an abstraction from the experience of war. Although Walzer's text does include excerpts from soldiers and war journals, there is no account of the evils done to civilians, only the recognition that there are evils, some of which he claims are justifiable.[8] In such a universe, as Ruddick notes, one operates with a discourse that makes it "increasingly difficult to give *weight* to the varieties of loss and pain suffered by individual victims and conquerors, their communities, and their lands."[9] And the dichotomies of just war theory – which presuppose a clear distinction between combatants and civilians, between wartime and peace time (either in terms of a pre-war or post-war period), as well as a distinction between homefront and battlefront – do not apply to the experience of war in the twentieth century (e.g., World War Two, the Viet Nam war, the Palestinian Intifada, the wars in Bosnia, Kosovo, Rwanda and Sierra Leone). But surely it did not apply to the battle of Troy either. And even if the distinction between combatant and civilian were viable, as Robert Holmes points out, that is not the same as claiming that innocent lives will be protected.[10]

7 Sara Ruddick, "Notes Toward a Feminist Peace Politics," in *Gendering War Talk*, ed. Miriam Cooke and Angela Woollacott (Princeton: Princeton University Press, 1993), 115.

8 Jean Bethke Elshtain, also a prominent just war theorist, is herself critical of this tendency toward abstraction in narratives of war. Embracing feminist sensibilities, she calls for assessing policies in terms of their effect "on our most vital and fragile human relationships." She argues, "[J]ust war as politics embraces a standpoint: the standpoint of the child and the child's needs and it requires that one evaluate periods of 'peace' as well as times of 'war' with reference to minimal requirements of both justice and mercy." "Just War as Politics," in *But Was it Just? Reflections on the Morality of the Persian Gulf War* ed. Jean Bethke Elshtain, Stanley Hauerwas, Sari Nusseibeh, Michael Walzer and George Weigel (New York: Doubleday, 1992), 55.

9 Ruddick, "Notes Toward a Feminist Peace Politics," 116.

10 Robert Holmes argues, "The killing of *anyone* who has done no wrong relative to the war in question is, in the relevant sense, the killing of an innocent person. This suffices to show that the distinction between combatants and non-combatants, however deeply enshrined it is in various codes of war, and however common it is in discussions of more recent just war theorists, is neither equivalent to the distinction between innocents and non-innocents nor adequate for framing the central moral issue in the assessment of war." Robert Holmes, *On War and Morality* (Princeton: Princeton University Press, 1989), 186.

How, then, does one give weight to the varieties of loss and pain suffered by civilians during war-time violence? One path for an ethical narrative *of* war is to give weight to the role of the witness in wartime. The word for witness in ancient Greek is *martys*, derived from the word meaning to remember. The martyr, a word derived from *martys* is a witness.[11] The role of the witness has emerged in literary and philosophical discourse, especially after Auschwitz,[12] and Elie Wiesel writes, "If the Greeks invented tragedy, the Romans correspondence and the Renaissance the sonnet, our generation has invented a new literary genre: the testimony."[13] The witness – most usually a survivor of wartime violence, but also a bystander who gives testimony – generates a discourse of war that is not abstracted from their experience of war. This is apparent in the many memoirs written by survivors of Auschwitz, who testify to their powerlessness, humiliation and the meaninglessness of their suffering, such as spending entire days on their knees under order of the German officers, or becoming thoroughly drenched during roll-call, with no hope of getting dry when they returned to the barracks because of leaking roofs.[14] This discourse cannot be one that is filled with triumphant endings, since the pain continues long after the

11 Giorgio Agamben, *Remnants of Auschwitz: The Witness and the Archive*, trans. Daniel Heller-Roazen (New York: Zone Books, 1999), 26–28.

12 I follow the practice of many philosophers in using Auschwitz as a symbolic name which refers to the Nazi death camps. Although historians would criticize this practice for its lack of historical precision, philosophers such as Giorgio Agamben have chosen this term as an alternative to the problematic term "Holocaust," which has an anti-Semitic heritage. Ibid., 28ff.

13 François Hartog, "The Witness and the Historian," trans. Lesley Walker, in *Making Sense of Global History: The 19th International Congress of the Historical Sciences*, ed. Sølvi Sogner (Oslo: Universitetsforlaget, 2001), 320–37.

14 Olly Ritterband, *Ét Ord er et Skrig. Auschwitz 1944–45* (Copenhagen: Aschehoug, 1998), 54–56. Some of the prominent texts published by survivors of the Nazi death camps include Primo Levi's *If This Is a Man*, trans. Stuart Woolf (New York: Orion Press, 1959), which was written immediately after the war, but which first received an audience with its republication in Italy in 1957; and his book *The Drowned and the Saved*, trans. Raymond Rosenthal (New York: Vintage Books, 1989), first published in 1986; the Austrian-born survivor Jean Améry's book *At the Mind's Limit: Contemplations by a Survivor on Auschwitz and its Realities*, trans. Sidney Rosenfeld and Stella P. Rosenfeld (London: Granta Books, 1999), was published in German in 1966; and the French resistance fighter and survivor Charlotte Delbo published the first volume of her trilogy *Auschwitz and After* in French in 1965: *None of Us Will Return*, trans. John Githens (New York: Grove Press, 1968).

physical violence ceases. Jean Améry writes, "Whoever was tortured, stays tortured. Torture is ineradicably burned into him, even when no clinically objective traces can be detected."[15] Survivors' testimonies indicate that by giving testimony, survivors reconstitute their role as ethical subjects and thereby refuse to be victims of their own memory. The psychiatrist and child survivor Dori Laub writes, "The survivors did not only need to survive so that they could tell their story, they also needed to tell their story in order to survive."[16] The discourse of witnesses also makes evident that there are many more complex positions in war than the position of the warrior or the victim. Primo Levi, for example, introduces the concept of the "grey zone" to refer to groups such as the Sonderkommando who were themselves prisoners in the death camp, but who were charged with carrying out cremation detail. These individuals were both victims of the evils of the death camps, but also implicated in perpetuating similar evils on others who were victims like themselves.[17]

Based on the experience of these witnesses of wartime violence, witnessing has also emerged as an ethical concept in discussions of war and of human conflict. The ethical meaning of the term "witnessing" can be contrasted with its epistemological meaning, i.e. whether the witness gives true or false testimony (as in debates about false memory syndrome). Instead, the ethical meaning of witnessing raises the question: how is it possible to give witness to the most extreme forms of atrocities? As Levi noted, those who witnessed the most extreme atrocities did not live to tell the story. He wrote, "[W]e, the survivors, are not the true witnesses … those who saw the Gorgon, have not returned to tell about it or have returned mute… The destruction brought to an end, the job completed, was not told by anyone, just as no one ever returned to describe his own death… We speak in their stead, by proxy."[18] Hence, witnessing – where one speaks on behalf of another, or even on behalf of oneself – also points to what is missing in

15 Améry, *At the Mind's Limit*, 34.

16 Shoshana Felman and Dori Laub, *Testimony: Crisis of Witnessing in Literature, Psychoanalysis and History* (New York: Routledge, 1992), 78.

17 See Claudia Card's discussion of Levi's concept in "Groping Through Gray Zones," in *On Feminist Ethics and Politics*, ed. Claudia Card (Lawrence: University of Kansas Press, 1999), 9.

18 Levi, *The Drowned*, 83–84.

testimony. At the same time, it is the necessary incompleteness and inadequacy of witnessing which also gives weight to the varieties of pain and loss suffered by individuals and communities.

Survivors also bear witness to the experience of shame. One feels shame not only in witnessing one's own degradation, but in witnessing the degradation of another, whose fate one has escaped. Although shame was an important notion for the ancient Greeks, modern philosophers have moved away from this concept and focused instead on the notion of guilt. But as the British philosopher Bernard Williams has pointed out in his book *Shame and Necessity*, shame is an ethical emotion that expresses in a broad sense who one is and how one is related to others.

The Greek word for shame is *aidos*, and provides the root for the Greek word for genitals.[19] Shame is connected with nakedness, particularly in its sexual connotations. The basic experience of shame is to be seen naked by the wrong people in the wrong conditions. More generally, shame indicates exposure, vulnerability and powerlessness. One can feel shame in front of a public witness, but one can also feel shame by oneself in the face of one's own internal witness. Feeling shame at violating a particular social or moral norm of behaviour is only one aspect of shame. Levi describes shame as the impulse to flee from that which one can never escape. On the deepest level, what one seeks to flee is one's own unmaking as a subject. Agamben writes, "In shame, the subject thus has no other content than its own desubjectification; it becomes witness to its own disorder, one's own oblivion as a subject. This double movement, which is both subjectification and desubjectification, is shame."[20]

Giving weight to the experience of survivors not only focuses attention on the ethical concepts of witnessing and shame, but it also brings attention to aspects of wartime experience that often have been overlooked, and that should be subject to ethical reflection. In particular, it brings attention to the role of sexual violence in wartime. The explosion of ethnic and national violence that took place in the former Yugoslavia during the early 1990s has brought renewed attention to atrocities. We are reminded that

19 Bernard Williams, *Shame and Necessity* (Berkeley: University of California Press, 1993), 78.

20 Agamben, *Remnants of Auschwitz*, 106.

one can never say "never" again. The forms of violence in the concentration camps in Bosnia were not identical with what took place in Auschwitz; Elie Wiesel writes, "Omarska was not Auschwitz. Nothing, anywhere, can be compared to Auschwitz."[21] Yet the concentration camps in Bosnia-Herzegovina, like Auschwitz, did create both dead and living dead. They were also characterized by another phenomenon that was not widespread in the Nazi death camps: the systematic mass rape of women for the purposes of genocide.

War rape is not new in human history. We find references to it in Homer's *The Iliad*, as well as references to capturing women in war in the Hebrew bible. Not until the fourteenth century did European leaders announce standards of chivalry to forbid rape, though these rules were rarely enforced. The licence to rape was considered a major incentive for being a soldier. Not until the nineteenth century did humanitarian law protect non-combatants, including women. In the twentieth century, mass rape occurred during the Rape of Nanking, which refers both to the rape of 20,000–80,000 Chinese women by Japanese soldiers in 1937, and the killing orgy that took 350,000 lives in a few weeks. During World War Two, up to two million women were raped by soldiers in the Soviet army.[22] The French army allowed Moroccan soldiers to rape Italian women. And there was evidence of major Nazi sexual crimes against French women, though the Nuremburg tribunal did not mention rape in the final judgement.[23] Rape did take place in Auschwitz, though there has been a conspiracy of silence about it, and the victims of rape in the camps were psychologically the "sickest" after liberation.[24] In the 1990s, not only did war rape take place in Europe, but during the genocide in Rwanda when 500,000 to 800,000 Rwandans were massacred, the majority of them Tutsi, at least a quarter of a million women were raped. In the Congo today, every armed group has discovered that

21 Elie Wiesel, foreword to Rezak Hukanović, *The Tenth Circle of Hell: A Memoir of Life in the Death Camps of Bosnia*, trans. Claire Messud (London: Abacus, 1998), vii.

22 Antony Beevor, *Berlin: The Downfall, 1945* (New York: Viking, 2002).

23 The International Criminal Tribunal for Rwanda [ICTR], "Rape and Genocide in Rwanda: The ICTR's Akayesu Verdict," accessed 27 October 2003, http://homepages.uc.edu/thro/rwanda/RwandaRapeCase2.htm.

24 Henry Krystal, ed., *Massive Psychic Trauma* (New York: International Universities Press, 1968), 342.

rape is a cheaper weapon of war than bullets.[25] A Human Rights Watch specialist noted that women have had their lips and ears cut off and eyes gouged out after they were raped, so they cannot identify or testify against their attackers.

In terms of legal responses to these events, only after World War Two did the international community begin to prosecute rape as a crime. Article 27 of the Fourth Geneva Convention (1949) states: "Women shall be especially protected against any attack on their honour, in particular against rape, enforced prostitution, or any form of indecent assault." War rape has now been formulated as a crime against humanity in the new statutes for the permanent International Criminal Court. The statutes state that crimes against humanity include "rape, sexual slavery, enforced sexual violence of comparable gravity … when committed as part of a widespread or systematic attack directed against a civilian population, with knowledge of the attack."[26]

Rape is an act of violence and humiliation which destroys the victim's sense of self and her trust in the world and in ordinary human relations. The Danish psychologist Libby Tata Arcel, who for two and a half years led a psycho-social treatment programme in Zagreb for Bosnian torture and war victims, gives the following definition of rape:

> Forcible penetration or near-penetration (vaginal, rectal, oral) of a woman's body openings by body parts of or any instruments used by a person in official capacity during armed conflict or during peace with the purpose of manifesting aggression and causing physical and psychological damage. Rape includes cases where a woman is coerced to exchange sexual favours for certain entitlements for herself or her family (food, necessary papers, health services) or is coerced to sexual intercourse because she fears for her safety.[27]

25 Jan Goodwin, "Silence=Rape," *The Nation*, 8 March 2004, http://www.thenation.com/article/silencerape.

26 ICTR, "Rape and Genocide."

27 Libby Tata Arcel, "Gender-based Violence: Torture, Cruel, Inhuman, and Degrading Treatment of Women and Psychological Consequences," in *Philosophy on the Border*, ed. Robin May Schott and Kirsten Klercke (Copenhagen: Museum Tusculanum Press, 2007), 163–64. In her definition, Arcel emphasizes that rape is *sexual* violence, not merely

Arcel notes that there are other forms of sexual assault (e.g. forcing women to take part in unnatural sexual relations with family members or animals or other captives, inflicting pain or mutilation on the genitals or breasts, forced witnessing of rape, forced masturbation, sexual threats, molestation without penetration) which are equivalent to rape in a psychological sense. Estimates of the numbers of women raped during the war in the former Yugoslavia range from 20,000 to 50,000 and although the majority of victims were of childbearing age, victims also included young children (e.g. a four-year-old girl[28]) and women in their seventies. Although it is impossible to know how many women were impregnated because of rape, one small-scale study showed that 10 per cent of victims who sought help had become pregnant.[29]

According to the U.N. Commission of Experts, the war rapes in the former Yugoslavia follow five patterns of rape, regardless of the ethnicity of the perpetrators or the victims: 1) Sexual violence occurred before widespread fighting broke out in a particular region. 2) Sexual violence occurred during fighting, attacking a town and raping or assaulting women in their homes. 3) Sexual violence occurred in detention facilities: men were tortured or executed or sent off to work camps, while women were sent to separate camps; soldiers, camp guards, paramilitaries and civilians raped or sexually assaulted many of the women and frequently also murdered them; gang rapes occurred frequently and were accompanied by beatings and other forms of humiliation. 4) Sexual violence occurred in rape camps established in hotels, schools, restaurants, hospitals, factories, brothels, barns and auditoriums; frequently, Serbian captors told women that they would create "Chetnik babies"; women who became pregnant were detained until

violence, since it is an attack on the embodied sexuality of the woman. It is a crime that has lifelong consequences for a woman's sexuality, if the trauma is untreated. Moreover, she defines rape as a crime that has women as its primary victims, though men too can be raped. When men are victims of rape, they become feminized. This discussion is drawn from my chapter "Feminist Ethics of Conflict" in my book *Discovering Feminist Philosophy: Knowledge, Etnics, Politics* (Lanham: Rowman and Littlefield, 2003), 102–3, 110.

28 Kelly Dawn Askin, *War Crimes against Women: Prosecution in International War Crimes Tribunals* (The Hague: Kluwer Law International), 281.

29 Libby Tata Arcel, "Sexual Torture of Women as a Weapon of War: The Case of Bosnia-Herzegovina," in *War Violence, Trauma and the Coping Process*, ed. Libby Tata Arcel (Copenhagen: International Rehabilitation Council for Torture Victims, 1998), 191.

it was too late to get an abortion. 5) Sexual violence occurred in bordello camps, where women provided sex for men returning from the front lines; many of these women were killed.[30] All parties to the conflict have been guilty of these atrocities. Rape in detention was practised in camps run by Croats and Muslims. But Bosnian Serbs raped Muslim women as part of a consistent policy. Although the majority of victims were Bosnian women, this does not diminish the cruelty toward or suffering of Serbian women who were raped and tortured.

Although there is a long history of mass rape in wartime, in Bosnia war rape was used specifically as a weapon of ethnic extermination. As such, these atrocities were heir to the planned genocide that took place in Auschwitz, which left us, as Hannah Arendt wrote, with "a potentiality and an ever-present danger (that) is only too likely to stay with us from now on."[31] Viewing war rape from the family of concepts developed about survivors of the Nazi death camp also shows the importance in this context of the intertwined concepts of shame and witnessing. Despite Agamben's statement that "there is certainly nothing shameful in a human being who suffers on account of sexual violence" and that one can only speak of shame if one takes pleasure in his/her suffering,[32] shame is a crucial concept for understanding war rape. In shame, one becomes witness to one's own disintegration as a subject. In war rape, the victim also experiences this feeling of shame that engulfs her. Susan Brison's book *Aftermath: Violence and the Remaking of a Self* specifically focuses on the unmaking and remaking of the self following sexual trauma. The victim feels shame not because she is reduced to her minimal physical conditions, but because she witnesses this attempt to reduce her to a bloody, dirty thing, to an abject object that provokes disgust.

30 Todd Salzman, "'Rape Camps,' Forced Impregnation, and Ethnic Cleansing," in *War's Dirty Secret: Rape, Prostitution, and other Crimes against Women*, ed. Anne Llewellyn Barstow (Cleveland: The Pilgrim Press, 2000), 72–74. In male camps sexual assault took place as well, as in the instance of a prisoner being forced to bite off the genitals of another.

31 Hannah Arendt, *The Origins of Totalitarianism* (New York: Harcourt Brace Jovanovich, 1973), 478.

32 Agamben, *Remnants of Auschwitz*, 110.

The term "abject" refers to that which is disgusting and loathsome – the loathing of an item of food, of filth, of faeces. It is not the object's lack of cleanliness or healthfulness that causes abjection. As Julia Kristeva writes, the abject is that which disturbs identity, system and order[33] and is thus linked to Mary Douglas's definition of pollution as matter out of place. When a woman who is the victim of rape in wartime feels that she has become abject and disgusting, this feeling stems from the ways in which the things which organize her relation to her own body and her position in the community are out of place. In the physical act of rape, a woman's interior body parts have been opened by brutal force, leaving her exposed in her most intimate self. Thus, the border between the interior and the exterior world has been trespassed.[34] In the situation of forced pregnancy, the women often feel that a foreign body has lodged itself in their real body. Some women who were forcibly impregnated described themselves as on the brink of madness while pregnant, others committed suicide. Hence, women come to feel homeless in their own bodies.

Not only does sexual violation trespass the borders of the woman's body, but it challenges a woman's position in her family and community as well. In being raped, she has been defiled and dishonoured. Hence the father who gave his raped daughter a rope to hang herself with, and the husbands who divorced their raped wives. The woman's emotions of fear and shame themselves become an instrument of war carried into family relations. A woman's fear and shame may lead her to hide the rape(s), which contribute to her sense of isolation and alienation within her own family, and which prevent her from identifying and testifying against her aggressor. When a woman does reveal the rape(s), she risks further isolation, marginalization and exclusion both in her family and community. The position of women in the community is also undermined when violence takes place through the wanton violation of taboos, as it did in Bosnia-Herzegovina. Soldiers raped women old enough to be their mothers or grandmothers (seventy-year-old women were raped) and very young girls (e.g. a four-year-old girl), sons

33 Julia Kristeva, *Powers of Horror: An Essay on Abjection*, trans. Leon S. Roudiez (New York: Columbia University Press, 1982), 4.

34 See also Bülent Diken and Carsten Bagge Laustsen, "Becoming Abject: Rape as a Weapon of War," *Body Society* 11, no. 1 (2005): 111–28.

were forced to rape their mothers, and fathers were forced to rape their daughters. Not only did the war rapes violate the very taboos that structure human relations in a community, but they were used to destroy the sense of national, cultural and religious identity. When a Muslim woman was forcibly impregnated by a Serbian rapist, she was defiled by a foreigner. The baby was identified by the Serbian father, and the child became a foreign element in the community. Thus, the victim of war rape is unmade as a subject, as a member of a family, and as a member of a community. And her unmaking becomes a tool to destroy the community in which she plays such a vital role.

Moreover, the use of *enforced impregnation* as occurred in Bosnia leads to a radical transformation of the symbolic meaning of birth. When Hannah Arendt introduced the concept of natality as the central concept for understanding human community, it was the newness of each life that became a metaphor for the possibility of creating new values, new ideas and meaning in a publicly shared space. However, she was also aware of the fact that when new life occurs in a destructive environment – e.g. in an environment of totalitarian violence – it would reflect this destructive environment. When Arendt used the category of birth, she used it as a philosophical term that refers to the fundamental conditions of human existence. She was not interested in analyzing the social and political conditions that effect the ways in which human beings reproduce, as many feminist philosophers have done since. But enforced pregnancy in wartime does indeed affect fundamental conditions of human existence. One could suggest that war rape brings birth into a culture of death, in that it leads to the death of individual women. War rape also leads to social death, a concept introduced by Orlando Patterson in his discussion of slavery in the U.S. Social death refers to the social chaos which results from atrocities when social identities and relations become meaningless, and when it is impossible for members of a community to create meaningful lives for themselves.[35] Rape often leads to the exclusion of women from their families and communities

35 Claudia Card develops the notion of social death in relation to mass war rape. See "Genocide and Social Death," in *Feminist Philosophy and the Problem of Evil*, ed. Robin May Schott (Bloomington: Indiana University Press, 2007), 71–86. Card uses social death to analyze what is central to the harm of genocide.

and to the traumatization of children born in this context. By throwing the social identities of women into chaos, systematic rape in wartime disrupts the communities in which women play such an important role. War rape also leads to political death, in that it undermines the public world that is necessary to guarantee individuals' political rights, and it leads to irremediable harm to the concept of political rights as such.[36] In this context, birth no longer represents newness. Instead, birth becomes part of a biopolitics of death – which means that human biology itself becomes subject to political power, and this political power aims at creating death. The French theorist Michel Foucault introduces the term *thanatopolitics*, which derives from the Greek word *thanatos*, meaning death, and the word "politics," to refer to the way in which political power in the modern age becomes the power to let die. (Freud used the term Thanatos to refer to the death drive in his theory of the human psyche.) In the context of war rape, where political violence is used to force biological birth in the service of death, I will introduce the term *thanatonatality*.

Agamben uses the term thanatopolitics to describe the nature of power in Hitler's Germany, where the absolute power of the state over biology to create life co-existed with the absolute power of the state to make death.[37] During the wars in the former Yugoslavia, the Serbian military leaders exercised this same kind of power both to make life and to make death. But forced impregnation could only be used for the purpose of ethnic extermination because there had been a break in the cultural perception of the relation between birth and nationality. Previously natality meant that one was born into a specific community that was also a national, ethnic or religious community. And that is why the Nazis could not exterminate the Jews by making Jewish women pregnant. Only when the connection between birth and national community became weakened could forced impregnation become a strategy for genocide, and *thanatonatality* emerge as a new historical phenomenon.

36 For a fuller discussion of the distinction between social death and political death, see my "War Rape and the Political Concept of Evil," in *Evil, Political Violence, and Forgiveness: Essays in Honor of Claudia Card,* ed. Kathryn J. Norlock and Andrea Veltman (Lanham: Lexington Books, 2009). I introduce the notion of political evil to refer to the processes which undermine political rights and the concept of the political as such.

37 Agamben, *Remnants of Auschwitz*, 83.

Conclusion

Contemporary wartime experience shows the impossibility of maintaining a categorical distinction between combatants and non-combatants. This distinction is untenable in light of the effects of wartime violence on civilians – degradation, violent death, rape, traumatization, loss of livelihood, property rights and wealth. War rape in particular shows the untenability of the combatant/non-combatant distinction in that non-combatants themselves are turned into weapons of war to destroy their own community. This strategy is evident when women are forced to give birth to children conceived during war rape, and when the feeling of shame caused by rape becomes a hindrance to publicly reporting the rapes.

War rape should also command the attention of philosophers, who typically have viewed sexual violence in war as an expression of men's naturally aggressive sexuality which goes unchecked in the midst of the chaos of war. This attitude naturalizes violence, and makes it impossible to develop adequate ethical concepts in response to violence. What one needs is a kind of conceptual revolution, where one gives attention to that which has been ignored or excluded. Instead of focusing philosophical analysis of war primarily on just war theory, philosophers can give weight to the experience of survivors by analyzing the concepts of witnessing and shame in the context of both non-sexual and sexual atrocities.

In the case of war rape, the survivor faces different barriers than the survivor of Auschwitz. Although it is humanly necessary to bear witness in order to survive and to reconstruct one's identity, the social institutions of the family and of religion often make it forbidden to bear witness. The woman's own feeling of shame also becomes a barrier to bearing witness, at the same time as it reveals the depth of her pain. The shame experienced by the victim of rape reveals that she is a person who has witnessed the disintegration of herself as a subject, and that she has become homeless in her own family and her own community. Of particular contemporary importance is the philosophical question: how can one construct ethical relations in a community that consists of both perpetrators and victims of past violence? Experts from the fields of religion, law, psychology and philosophy today are apt to answer this question by turning to the concept of forgiveness. This strategy focuses on how to reintegrate perpetrators into society after conflict and how to normalize relations between victims and perpetrators. But a focus on survivors, including survivors of sexual atrocities, turns attention instead to reintegrating survivors into the communities that have marginalized them. Such an approach recognizes that it is necessary to transform relations that prevailed in societies prior to conflict, rather than to reintegrate them into pre-existing relations, since these very patterns of human relations have conspired in shaming survivors into silence. Such an approach to post-conflict relations will also help remove war rape, and the related historical phenomenon of *thanatonatality*, from the arsenal of weapons of war.

References

Agamben, Giorgio. *Remnants of Auschwitz: The Witness and the Archive.* Translated by Daniel Heller-Roazen. New York: Zone Books, 1999.

Améry, Jean. *At the Mind's Limit: Contemplations by a Survivor on Auschwitz and its Realities* [1966]. Translated by Sidney Rosenfeld and Stella P. Rosenfeld. London: Granta Books, 1999.

Arcel, Libby Tata. "Sexual Torture of Women as a Weapon of War – The Case of Bosnia-Herzegovina." In *War Violence, Trauma and the Coping Process*, edited by Libby Tata Arcel, 183–211. Copenhagen: International Rehabilitation Council for Torture Victims, 1998.

———. "Gender-based Violence: Torture, Cruel, Inhuman and Degrading Treatment of Women and Psychological Consequences." In *Philosophy on the Border*, edited by Robin May Schott and Kirsten Klercke, 155–94. Copenhagen: Museum Tusculanum Press, 2007.

Arendt, Hannah. *The Origins of Totalitarianism* [1951]. New York: Harcourt Brace Jovanovich, 1973.

Askin, Kelly Dawn. *War Crimes against Women: Prosecution in International War Crimes Tribunals.* The Hague: Kluwer Law International, 1997.

Beevor, Antony. *Berlin: The Downfall, 1945.* New York: Viking, 2002.

Card, Claudia. "Groping Through Gray Zones." In *On Feminist Ethics and Politics*, edited by Claudia Card, 3–26. Lawrence: University of Kansas Press, 1999.

———. "Genocide and Social Death." In *Feminist Philosophy and the Problem of Evil*, edited by Robin May Schott, 71–86. Bloomington: Indiana University Press, 2007.

Delbo, Charlotte. *None of Us Will Return.* Translated by John Githens. New York: Grove Press, 1968.

Diken, Bülent and Carsten Bagge Laustsen. "Becoming Abject: Rape as a Weapon of War." *Body Society* 11, no. 1 (2005): 111–28.

Elshtain, Jean Bethke. "Just War as Politics: What the Gulf War Told Us about Contemporary American Life." In *But Was it Just? Reflections on the Morality of the Persian Gulf War*, edited by Jean Bethke Elshtain, Stanley

Hauerwas, Sari Nusseibeh, Michael Walzer and George Weigel, 43–60. New York: Doubleday, 1992.

Felman, Shoshana and Dori Laub. *Testimony: Crises of Witnessing in Literature, Psychoanalysis, and History*. New York: Routledge, 1992.

Goodwin, Jan. "Silence=Rape." *The Nation*, 8 March 2004. http://www.thenation.com/article/silencerape.

Hartog, François. "The Witness and the Historian." Translated by Lesley Walker. In *Making Sense of Global History: The 19th International Congress of the Historical Sciences*, edited by Sølvi Sogner, 320–37. Oslo: Universitetsforlaget, 2001.

Holmes, Robert L. *On War and Morality*. Princeton: Princeton University Press, 1989.

International Criminal Tribunal for Rwanda. "Rape and Genocide in Rwanda: The ICTR's Akayesu Verdict." http://homepages.uc.edu/thro/rwanda/RwandaRapeCase2.htm (accessed 27 October 2003).

Iraq Body Count. www.iraqbodycount.net (accessed 8 September, 2008).

Isaacs, Jerry. "US Will Provide No Estimate of Iraqi War Casualties." *World Socialist Web Site*, 28 April 2003. http://www.wsws.org/articles/2003/apr2003/casu-a28.shtml (accessed 19 May 2005).

Kristeva, Julia. *Powers of Horror: An Essay on Abjection*. Translated by Leon S. Roudiez. New York: Columbia University Press, 1982.

Krystal, Henry, ed. *Massive Psychic Trauma*. New York: International Universities Press, 1968.

Levi, Primo. *If This Is a Man* [1947]. Translated by Stuart Woolf. New York: Orion Press, 1959.

———. *The Drowned and the Saved* [1986]. Translated by Raymond Rosenthal. New York: Vintage Books, 1989.

Ritterband, Olly. *Ét ord er et skrig. Auschwitz 1944–45*. Copenhagen: Aschehoug, 1998.

Ruddick, Sara. "Notes Toward a Feminist Peace Politics." In *Gendering War Talk*, edited by Miriam Cooke and Angela Woollacott, 109–27. Princeton: Princeton University Press, 1993.

Salzman, Todd. "'Rape Camps,' Forced Impregnation, and Ethnic Cleansing." In *War's Dirty Secret: Rape, Prostitution, and other Crimes against Women*, edited by Anne Llewellyn Barstow, 63–92. Cleveland: The Pilgrim Press, 2000.

Schott, Robin May. *Discovering Feminist Philosophy.* Lanham: Rowman and Littlefield, 2003.

———. "Just War and the Problem of Evil." *Hypatia: A Journal of Feminist Philosophy: Special Issue on Just War* 23, no. 2 (2008): 122–40.

———. "War Rape and the Political Concept of Evil." In *Evil, Political Violence, and Forgiveness: Essays in Honor of Claudia Card*, edited by Kathryn J. Norlock and Andrea Veltman, 77–96. Lanham: Lexington Books, 2009.

Tokača, Mirsad, ed. *The Sin of Silence: The Risk of Speech.* Collection of reports from the international conference on Violation of the Human Rights of Women in Bosnia and Herzegovina During the War 1992–1995, Sarajevo, 10–11 March, 1999. Sarajevo: Commission for Gathering Facts on War Crimes in Bosnia and Herzegovina, 1999.

Walzer, Michael. *Just and Unjust Wars.* New York: Basic Books, 1977.

Wiesel, Elie. Foreword in *The Tenth Circle of Hell: A Memoir of Life in the Death Camps in Bosnia*, v-ix, by Rezak Hukanović. Translated by Claire Messud. London: Abacus, 1998.

Wikipedia. s.v. "Iraq Body Count project." http://en.wikipedia.org/wiki/Iraq_Body_Count_project. (accessed 8 September 2008).

Wikipedia. s.v. "Vietnam War." http://en.wikipedia.org/wiki/Vietnam_War (accessed 18 May 2005).

Williams, Bernard. *Shame and Necessity.* Berkeley: University of California Press, 1993.

The World War II Multimedia Database. s.v. "Casualties in World War II." http://www.worldwar2database.com/html/frame5.htm (accessed 18 May 2005).

Demobilizing Civilians

Steffen Jensen and Finn Stepputat

Armed groups of civilians play, and have played, important roles in conflicts, and often they continue to do so after conflicts have formally ended. This much is becoming increasingly clear, as still more diverse groups enter war and conflict, such as paramilitary groups, militias, illegal combatants, etc. The existence of these groups questions commonsense understandings of armed conflict, as well as established ways of dealing with them during conflict and in relation to demobilization in the aftermath of conflict. A question therefore, and the one we explore here, is how can civilians be demobilized?

To "demobilize civilians" seems to be a contradiction in terms. Once mobilized, civilians are no longer civilians but combatants who are incorporated into military structures. Hence, civilians cannot be demobilized. However, this apparent contradiction is based on the generalized perception of a "military-civilian dichotomy," which is fundamental to common ideas of the modern state. Fundamental though it may be, the dichotomy does not correspond to the reality of "modern warfare," that is, the kind of warfare that involves guerilla tactics and counterinsurgency programmes, which characterize many, if not most, of the violent conflicts in the contemporary world.

Our aim here is twofold: firstly we wish to explore the field of Disarmament, Demobilization and Reintegration (DDR), which has become one of the preferred international post-conflict resolution instruments. We argue that the policies and practices of demobilization programmes often are structured by the civilian-military dichotomy and certain assumptions regarding community, the civilian and the military. Furthermore, we suggest that subjects of DDR programmes (the armed individuals) fall between different, sometimes competing, policy fields, for instance small arms control, programmes for vulnerable groups in war, community development, and security sector programmes. Secondly, we wish to explore the implications for groups of armed civilians, who fall between the military and civilian categories. We argue that their presence often reproduces or perpetuates particular forms of violence. Furthermore, what they want is seldom what the programmes offer, with the consequence that the groups of armed civilians negotiate or resist the programmes.[1] In our analysis, what these groups craved for was recognition from the state either in the form of development programmes, monetary compensation or actual enrollment into the state's security branches.

When we began working with the demobilization of armed civilians it was a relatively unknown or unconceptualized field. This is no longer the case. With the advent of the war on terror and the war in Iraq, we have been given an entirely new vocabulary, and reports of armed civilians, in the shape of illegal combatants and such like, have filled air waves and print media. They have even entered the more recent guidelines for DDR operations as a problem which is difficult to deal with.[2] However, the issue is far from new. As we argue elsewhere,[3] colonial conflict, wars of independence and more recently a diverse set of crime-fighting initiatives incorporate civilians in security operations across the global South. At the same time as there are remarkable similarities in how armed civilians are demobilized (see below), there is a need for context-specific analyses. Hence, after the review and discussion of the modes of demobilization, we analyze two separate case studies. The first one discusses the rural civil defence patrols of the Guatemalan civil war. The second details the demobilization and reintegration of former urban, ANC activists into South African society. Both these conflicts ended in the mid-1990s and both featured important

1 Henrik Vigh, *Navigating Terrains of War: Youth and Soldiering in Guinea Bissau* (New York: Berghahn Press, 2006).

2 United Nations Inter-Agency Working Group on Disarmament, Demobilization and Reintegration (UN IAWG DDR), *Integrated Disarmament, Demobilization and Reintegration Standards* (New York: United Nations, 2006); see note 4.

3 Lars Buur, Steffen Jensen and Finn Stepputat, eds., introduction to *The Security-Development Nexus: Expressions of Sovereignty and Securitization in Southern Africa* (Uppsala and Cape Town: Nordiska Afrikainstituten and HSRC Press, 2007), 9–33.

dimensions of civilian incorporation with subsequent demobilization. We conclude by considering some of the problems of developing policies and practices that target armed groups of civilians for demobilization.

International Action for Disarmament, Demobilization and Reintegration

During the 1990s, it was recognized that transitions from armed conflict to peace were seldom linear affairs. Rather, conflicts seemed to develop in cycles between periods of armed encounters and periods of relative peace, a neither-nor situation that seems to have characterized many regions of the world for decades. International agencies and others have applied different instruments and policies as means of controlling violence and preventing conflicts from sliding back into open warfare. Programmes for disarmament, demobilization and reintegration (DDR) have come to constitute one of the most important fields of policy and operation in international attempts to "break the conflict cycle," but, as we shall argue, these programmes have tended to ignore the participation of civilians in armed conflict.

While the demobilization of ex-combatants has a long history, the phenomenon entered a quantitatively and qualitatively different phase at the end of the Cold War. During the 1990s, the number of demobilized soldiers increased substantially.[4] Furthermore, most demobilization took place in developing countries. The international community entered this field because a lack of demobilization in unstable peace processes was seen to threaten development, stability and democratization.[5] The Secretary General of the UN stated in 2000 about the importance of DDR:

> In the civil conflicts of the post-cold-war era, a process of disarmament, demobilization and re-integration has repeatedly proved to be vital to stabilizing a post-conflict situation; to reducing the likelihood of

4 Natalie Pauwels, ed., *War Force to Work Force: Global Perspectives on Demobilization and Reintegration* (Baden-Baden: Nomos Verlagsgesellschaft, 2000), 9.

5 Chris Dolan and Jessica Schafer, *The Reintegration of Ex-Combatants in Mozambique: Manica and Zambezia Provinces* (Oxford: University of Oxford, 1997).

> renewed violence, either because of relapse into war or outbreaks of banditry; and to facilitating a society's transition from conflict to normalcy and development. Furthermore, the process of disarmament, demobilization and reintegration may have a symbolic and political importance beyond the sum of its parts. Even if full disarmament and demilitarization prove unachievable, a credible program of disarmament, demobilization and reintegration may nonetheless make a key contribution to strengthening confidence between former factions and enhancing the momentum toward stability.[6]

Cambodia, Nicaragua, Namibia, El Salvador, Angola, Somalia, Guatemala, Mozambique, Eritrea, South Africa, Liberia, Sierra Leone, Rwanda, Burundi, Haiti and Uganda are all examples where international agencies have been involved in the demobilization of ex-combatants. DDR programmes do not constitute a new field of knowledge and practice, but the changing contexts of the 1990s brought much new experience and many new challenges. On the basis of the experiences, a number of lessons learnt has been deduced to the extent that it makes sense to speak of a standardized and streamlined intervention mode. This mode works with presumably clear categories of beneficiaries and with the entire gamut of internationally sanctioned financial management systems, management information systems, and monitoring and evaluation systems. In short, DDR programmes have become routinized development interventions, as demonstrated by the publication of the UN's "Integrated DDR Standards."[7]

According to USAid's "Lessons Learned," the demobilization process, "though complicated by political issues, is usually straightforward, with a checklist of issues that staff need to address."[8] Conventionally, the DDR

6 United Nations Security Council, "The Role of the United Nations Peacekeeping in Disarmament, Demobilization and Reintegration. Report of the Secretary-General," S/2000/101 (11 February 2000), §3.

7 UN IAWG DDR, *Integrated Disarmament.*

8 Kimberly Mahling Clark, "Fostering a Farewell to Arms: Preliminary Lessons Learned in the Demobilization and Reintegration of Combatants. (PN-ABY-027)" (Washington, D.C.: Research and Reference Services, United States Agency for International Development, Center for Development Information and Evaluation, 1997).

process is divided into four phases:[9] assembly and disarmament, demobilization, reinsertion and reintegration. The process is seen as forming part of "a natural continuum" within the wider peace process. Where disarmament ends, demobilization begins, and where demobilization ends, reinsertion and reintegration begin. While this may be an oversimplification of what is actually a series of complex and overlapping stages, overall DDR programmes institutionalize the transition from military to civilian status: in the classical sense of rituals of transition, assembly and encampment is a kind of liminal phase between the military and the civil. Thus, the DDR process is a reversal of the mobilization process, whereby soldiers are recruited, put in a uniform, given a military identity, and sent off to their posts. Soldiers are stripped of uniform and guns (disarmament); they are discharged, registered as civilians and given livelihood skills and orientation of civilian life and human rights (demobilization) and they are shipped back to their respective communities with resources so as not to be a burden to their family, kin and neighbours (reintegration). In this way, DDR is an important process for maintaining the separation of the civilian and military fields.

However, challenges and dilemmas related to the civil-military dichotomy have faced DDR programmes. Firstly, it has proved very difficult univocally to distribute combatants into straightforward categories. Often programmes define a combatant as someone with a conventional weapon,

9 For further details, see ibid., United Nations Development Programme (UNDP), *Sharing New Ground in Post-Conflict Situations: The Role of UNDP in Support of Reintegration Programmes* (New York: UNDP, 2000); United Nations Security Council (UNSC), "The Role of the United Nations Peacekeeping in Disarmament, Demobilization and Reintegration. Report of the Secretary-General," S/2000/101, 11 February 2000; Nicole Ball, "Demobilizing and Reintegrating Soldiers: Lessons from Africa," in to Work Force Rebuilding Societies after Civil War: Critical Roles for International Assistance, edited by Krishna Kumar (Boulder and London: Lynne Rienner Publications, 1997); Pauwels, ed., *War Force*; DAC, *DAC Guidelines on Conflict, Peace and Development Co-operation* (Paris: OECD, 1997); Béatrice Pouligny, *The Politics and Anti-politics of Contemporary Disarmament, Demobilization and Reintegration Programs* (Paris: CERI, 2004); United Nations (UN), *Disarmament, Demobilization, Reintegration (DDR) and Stability in Africa* (conference report, Freetown, Sierra Leone, June 21–23, 2005) (United Nations: New York, 2005); United Nations UN IAWG DDR, *Integrated Disarmament*. We have also benefited from valuable comments and insights from Anton Baare and Jairo Munive Rincón.

but, for instance, civil patrols do not always have conventional weapons. Secondly, combatants are imagined as alienated from their communities and therefore in need of being resettled and reintegrated into their former communities, which are usually seen as unproblematic entities of homogeneous, victimized populations. Thirdly, most of the countries where DDR programmes have been carried out have faced enduring political, social and military tensions. Although the primary (national level) conflicts may have been solved, the social structures of the countries concerned are still influenced by violence. However, few commentators and reports deal with anything but the organized, military side of conflict. In recent years, the proliferation of small arms has been blamed for the high levels of violence in general and in post-conflict situations in particular. But the ways in which the distribution of small arms among civilians has been organized as part of insurgency or counterinsurgency campaigns has received little attention.

A review of armed conflicts and DDR programmes during the 1990s suggests that this phenomenon is very common. In Mozambique, for example, the government armed and organized communal villages in defence against the RENAMO insurgency, and according to an Interpol estimate, some 1.5 million AK47s were distributed during the war which have never been retrieved.[10] The Angolan government distributed a similar number of guns as part of its counterinsurgency campaign. In Guatemala, civilian patrols, which were organized and armed by the army, were responsible for a large share of the human rights abuses. In South Africa, both the ANC and the government organized the population in the townships for insurgency and counterinsurgency purposes. The Truth and Reconciliation Commission attributed by far the largest share of violence to forces such as vigilante groups and self-defence units, which did not formally take part in the armed conflict (see below). In Cambodia, although an estimated 250,000 militia soldiers outnumbered the otherwise huge army of 200,000 regular soldiers, the militias were never incorporated into any DDR programmes. In the Eritrean war of liberation, both the Ethiopian

10 Alex Vines, "Disarmament in Mozambique," *Journal of Southern African Studies* 24, no. 1 (1998): 192.

army and the Eritrean liberation army organized the population for military purposes, but there is no evidence of the fate of Ethiopian irregulars in post-conflict Eritrea. Finally, in Sierra Leone, civil defence forces have been involved in armed conflict with insurgent troops to such a degree that they have been officially incorporated into the DDR programme.[11]

With the possible exception of Sierra Leone, all these weapons and people have not been part of DDR programmes until very recently.[12] Rather, they have been targeted by other interventions – for instance, psycho-social intervention for children and other vulnerable groups and especially through small arms programmes, including for "mopping up," "swapping" or "buying back" small arms and light weapons in exchange for access to community development programmes, credit schemes and the like. Even less attention has been given to the "software" of armed civilians – that is, the conditions and forms under which people have been armed, even though these influence the possibilities of achieving the goal of disarmament programmes.

The software of disarmament and small arms control encompasses questions of livelihood, identity and organization. As implied in the reinsertion and reintegration involved in DDR programmes, it may be difficult for ex-combatants to give up their weapons if they have no alternative livelihood options. This is no different for armed civilians. Likewise, as revealed in the case studies below, identity and organization are important elements in the involvement of armed groups of civilians in violent conflict. Systematically organized by one or more of the parties to the conflict, the groups may have achieved some measure of independent existence during the conflict and its aftermath, and images of masculinity and community

11 Mats Utas, "Watermelon Politics in Sierra Leone: Hope Amidst Vote Buying and Remobilized Militias," *African Renaissance* 4, no. 3–4 (2007): 62–66; United Nations (UN), *Disarmament, Demobilization, Reintegration (DDR) and Stability in Africa*, Conference Report, Freetown, Sierra Leone, June 21–23, 2005 (New York: United Nations, 2005).

12 UN IAWG DDR, *Integrated Disarmament*, 2.30/6.4 mentions "non-signatory armed groups" such as "informal militias" and "criminal gangs" as groups that have been involved in conflict without being represented in peace agreements. The manual recommends that they are dealt with through some kind of framework agreement either by the UN or a mandated organization, which may qualify them for participation in DDR.

have implications for the possibilities of their demobilization, as is shown by the cases of Guatemala and South Africa.

The Military-Civilian Dichotomy

Implicit in the above analysis, we suggest that DDR programmes operate through a number of taken-for-granted assumptions about the nature of armed conflict, combatants, civilians and their communities, which are informed by the idea of a military-civilian dichotomy. Although we recognize the normative need to separate the military and civilian sectors for the purposes of establishing civilian control of the military and ensuring the protection of groups of people from the ravages of armed conflict, these assumptions need to be questioned from the level of empirical evidence. We begin with the combatant.

The modern soldier, or combatant, emerged in the nineteenth and twentieth centuries in the defence of the nation state. The organization of the armies mirrored the institutional innovations of the bureaucracy at large. Once in the army, a soldier ceased to be an individual and became the instrument of a national cause. The separation of the soldier from normal society constituted the basis for the military-civilian dichotomy. Combatants involved in the internal armed conflicts of the 1990s have been seen as imperfect copies of this ideal type of modern soldier: separated from civilian life, uniformed and armed, but without receiving sufficient training and equipment to fit the model. The modern combatant is also inserted into organizational structures that are considered to be weak and characterized by a lack of capacity, as well as often being deeply involved in the civilian economy and politics. This is particularly true of guerilla armies, but also of government forces, although to a lesser extent. This also has implications for the perception of the combatants to be demobilized, who are depicted by donor agencies as "semi-illiterate," "unskilled," "physically and psychologically handicapped by war," lacking "independent initiative and capability to cope with … civilian life," and having "an imperfect understanding of the state of the economy."[13]

13 Nicole Ball, "Demobilizing and Reintegrating Soldiers," 86.

However, is it reasonable to assume that warfare is always conducted by soldiers in uniform, that former soldiers are the only ones capable of employing violence in post-conflict situations, or that they are particularly inept at surviving post-conflict situations? Ample evidence from the history of internal armed conflicts suggests that this is not the case. Combatants are not only soldiers who have been alienated from the civilian population and their place of residence, put into a uniform, armed, and inserted into a military command structure. The civilian, whether armed or not, is at the heart of contemporary armed conflict, of "modern warfare."[14]

The fate of civilians, defined as those who do not fight wars, has been a concern of the international community since at least 1864, when the first Geneva Convention was adopted. Since then, a range of conventions has been adopted to regulate the conduct of war. Concerns for civilians re-emerged and took centre stage in the wake of the end of the Cold War as the principles of non-intervention came under attack.[15] This led to a number of international interventions to protect the civilian population against the excesses of internal armed conflict.[16] The interventions have often been framed in terms of the need to protect civilians. Implicitly, the interventions, and the range of policy papers, reports and programmes in which the civilians figure, are informed by the notion that they are not involved in armed conflict. Hence, the Danish Foreign Ministry asserted that "[c]ivilian populations have to a growing extent been involved in conflicts as hostages in power struggles between opposing parties that have led to suppression and ethnic cleansing."[17]

14 Roger Trinquier, *Modern Warfare: A French View of Counterinsurgency*, trans. Daniel Lee (New York: Frederick A. Praeger, 1964); John A. Nagl, foreword to *The U.S. Army/Marine Corps Counterinsurgency Field Manual: U.S. Army Field Manual no. 3–24 / Marine Corps Warfighting Publication no. 3–33.5*, by United States Dept. of the Army (Chicago: University of Chicago Press, 2007); John J. McCuen, *The Art of Counter-Revolutionary War* (London: Faber & Faber, 1966).

15 Georg Sørensen, "Sovereignty, Change and Continuity in a Fundamental Institution," *Political Studies* 47, no. 3 (1999): 590–604.

16 Roland Paris, "International Peacebuilding and the 'Mission Civilisatrice'," *Review of International Studies* 28, no 4 (2002): 637–56.

17 Danida, *Denmark's Development Policy: Analysis: Partnership 2000* (Copenhagen: Ministry of Foreign Affairs of Denmark, Danida, 2000), 105.

The report quoted goes on to assert that this has led to a growing level of misery and poverty within the civilian population. Poverty and misery are not the only byproducts of conflict: another is "the deliberate targeting of non-combatants."[18] The Secretary General's Report acknowledges that the "dividing line between civilians and combatants is frequently blurred."[19] But the separation is nonetheless maintained, since the report asserts that civilians only support combatants without being actively involved in the fighting. This analysis ignores the experience from a number of conflicts, where the most serious killings have been carried out by neighbours, not by "combatants"; Sierra Leone and Rwanda are but two examples of this.[20] Arguably, nowhere has the dilemma of distinguishing between combatants and civilians been greater than in relation to humanitarian intervention.

Humanitarian interventions – working uniquely with civilians – became increasingly criticized because, critics have asserted, it risked fuelling conflicts[21] because too little attention was given to identifying the *real* victims, the civilians. In societies that have been shattered by conflict and lack of resources, relief assistance is in itself a significant economic resource and becomes an object of strife between the conflicting parties. In this way, relief assistance can contribute to the prolongation of a conflict.[22] However, the hard-won lesson that humanitarian assistance is always caught up in politics is phrased in such a way as to depict civilians as a-political pawns with no interest or involvement in the conflict.[23]

18 United Nations Security Council (UNSC), "Report of the SG to the SC on the protection of civilians in armed conflict," S/1999/957 (1999): 2.

19 Ibid.

20 See Arjun Appadurai, "Dead Certainty: Ethnic Violence in the Era of Globalization," *Development and Change* 29, no. 4 (1998): 905–25.

21 Mary B. Anderson, *Do No Harm: How Aid Can Support Peace – Or War* (New York: Lynne Rienner Publishers, 1996).

22 For a succinct critique of this position, see Nicholas Stockton, "Accountability in Peacebuilding: The Case of the Democratic Republic of Congo," Paper presented at the FAU Conference, Gjerrild, Denmark, March, 2005. Stockton argues that the fear of fuelling conflicts caused more than three million Congolese people to perish in 1999 and 2000 of preventable disease and hunger.

23 See also UNSC, "The Role of the United Nations Peacekeeping"; Kees Kingma, "Demobilization and Reintegration – an Overview," in *Converting Defense Resources to Human Development: Proceedings from an International Conference, 9–11 November 1997* (Bonn: BICC, 1997).

The civil-military dichotomy is also highly gendered. The Secretary General's report on the protection of civilians asserts that men "account for the largest numbers of combatants," whereas "women and children are disproportionably represented among civilians affected by conflict."[24] The statement feeds into stereotypical notions of men as perpetrators and women as victims. To give but one example, one article which attempts to measure the effects of conflict on the civilian population claims that women and men under sixteen and over fifty are victims, whereas other men are combatants.[25]

Also unproblematized notions of community and locality figure centrally in the usual assumptions about civilians and combatants. Civilians are assumed to live in a specific locality to which the combatants bring war and destruction. As a result communities are shattered by war, and most interventions aim at reconstructing communities. Ideas of the reconstruction and reconciliation of communities are informed by the notion that communities are coherent and homogeneous, and that it is due to outside influence – the coming of the conflict and the arrival of the combatants – that divisions are introduced. However, the community is seldom the unproblematic entity that it is presumed to be, as struggles over leadership, status, membership, rights and economic resources disrupt alliances and alienate factions and individuals. These local conflicts often take on new and sometimes violent forms when they are articulated and interpreted through the lens of a primary, national conflict. This also means that community members fight each other, often violently, because one part of the community is made up of combatants – like the civil patrols in Guatemala, for example, who were enrolled by the state to fight the insurrection in and around their own villages. These combatants did not come from afar and when the conflict ended, they often managed to supplant earlier forms of authority. This was also the case in South Africa, as we shall see later.[26]

24 UNSC (1999): 3.

25 David R. Meddings, "Civilians at War: A Review and Historical Overview of Involvement of Non-Combatant Populations in Conflict Situations," *Medicine, Conflict and Survival* 17, no. 1 (2001): 9.

26 Belinda Bozzoli, *Theatres of the Struggle and the End of Apartheid* (Athens, Ohio: Ohio University Press, 2004).

Finally, there is a need to take a closer, critical look at the perception of conflict many interventions work with. In programmes up until 2001, internal armed conflicts were depicted as being fought between a government's army and groups that had taken up arms against the government. This changed quite dramatically with the war on terror. Suddenly we began to hear of new categories of combatants, which transgressed the civilian-military dichotomy. The Iraq war perpetuated the temporary breakdown in the dichotomy. As the Americans entered Iraq, they seemed to think they had won a conventional war against a conventional army. Only slowly did they realize that they were facing an insurgence. After what one of the old hands in counterinsurgence tactics, John McCuen,[27] would have considered a series of strategic mistakes, the American army published their most recent counterinsurgency booklet[28] and began to change strategy. Suddenly it was all about "winning the hearts and minds," securing bases in rebel territory and making alliances with local strong men. In this way, the notion of conflict changed and civilians were included in the thinking about war.

This kind of war, in which the civilian partakes in fighting and is the target of war, is more common than conventional wars. Parts of the civilian population are engaged in armed conflict for a number of reasons and in a number of ways. As the French counterinsurgency expert Roger Trinquier suggested, on the basis of his own experience of Indochina and Algeria, the civilian population is at the heart of modern warfare. "Modern warfare" in his concept is internal armed conflict that involves guerilla tactics and counterinsurgency. Both insurgencies and counterinsurgencies are based on the extensive incorporation of the "local population" in some kind of organizational structure through which people may or may not be provided with arms. In other cases, local people themselves acquire weapons.

Developments in modern warfare therefore challenge the dichotomization between civilians and the military on which DDR are based. The analytical challenge is to ask questions that transcend institutional and legal

27 McCuen, *The Art of Counter-Revolutionary War.*
28 Nagl, foreword to *The U.S. Army/Marine Corps.*

categories and relate to practices. We must ask who are involved in violence, how, and for what reasons, instead of operating with the preconceived notions of combatant and civilian.[29] Thus, some use violence frequently within organized structures; some use violence occasionally; some use violence for economic ends; some use violence when threatened; some order violence; and some follow orders. Each of these categories of the use of violence can characterize a host of different actors such as the military, the police, mafia organizations, paramilitary groups, traditional chiefs, gangs, self-defence units, landowners, political parties, guerillas and militias. The list is in no way exhaustive but indicates that violence, whether in national armed conflicts or inter-communal violence, cannot be captured within the categories of civilian and military.

This means that internal armed conflicts can seldom be understood in the singular, on the basis of the primary, often national conflict alone. The issues at stake – claims to independence, secession, a change of regime, the self-determination of ethnic groups, and the control of essential resources – are "internalized" or interlinked with local issues of conflict, as armed factions involve civilians in local self-defence, cells, vigilante groups, militias and the like. Pre-existing conflicts over land, leadership, water and inheritance are often reframed and magnified, as armed factions are involved in the resolution of such conflicts within families, villages, neighbourhoods and districts. Thus, we may operate with primary and secondary levels of conflict: in the context of (latent) armed conflict, the meaning of local, secondary conflicts is reinterpreted through the lens of the primary conflict, which then provides legitimacy and a means of using (threats of) violence to solve secondary conflicts.[30]

Through the following two case studies of Guatemala and South Africa, we attempt to explore some of these dilemmas in practice by analyzing the genesis, dynamics and variations of armed civilian groups and the attempts to demobilize that have been made.

29 We are grateful to Jennifer Schirmer for posing these questions in a response to an earlier draft.

30 Buur, Jensen, and Stepputat, eds., introduction to *The Security-Development Nexus.*

The Civil Patrols in Guatemala

Thirty-five years of armed insurrection by leftist guerrillas in Guatemala ended with the signing of peace accords in 1996. Apart from a brief period between 1980 and 1983, when guerrillas had substantial support in the population, the military government maintained territorial control throughout the conflict without being able to wipe out the guerrillas. International pressure brought about peace negotiations, which lasted from 1988 to 1996. The counterinsurgency campaign in 1981–83 left 150,000 dead and created huge displacements of population. The united revolutionary guerrilla forces in URNG[31] numbered 6–8,000 at their highest, while the army had 30–40,000 men under arms during the 1980s and 1990s.[32]

In 1982, at the height of the Guatemalan civil war, the army organized the rural population in conflict areas into civilian patrols (PAC, Patrullas de Autodefensa Civil), which became decisive in the army's victory. During 1982–83, between 1 and 1.3 million men, or 15 per cent of the population, were enrolled, mostly in the highland provinces dominated by the Maya-speaking population. When the civil patrols were created, the guerillas controlled many rural districts and had an active support base of at least 350,000 people who were organized as "Irregular Local Forces." The army's civil patrols emulated the guerillas' local organization of supporters.

Using strategic massacres as a means of dividing and displacing the population and cutting off the guerillas from their supporters, the army (re-) incorporated the population by organizing them into civil patrols and supporting them through emergency programmes. Guatemalan officers drew upon French and U.S. experience in Indochina and Algeria in developing a form of organizing the population that was tried out in a campaign against the guerillas in eastern Guatemala in the late 1960s. These experiences were incorporated into the new counterinsurgency programme in 1982. While the previous "National Security" doctrine, which had involved indiscrimi-

31 Unidad Revolucionaria Nacional Guatemalteca.

32 On the eve of the peace agreements, the army figure was 50,000 effectives, but this was probably inflated for the purpose of demobilization. Jennifer Schirmer, *The Guatemalan Military Project: A Violence Called Democracy* (Philadelphia: University of Pennsylvania Press, 1998).

nate killings, had increased support for the guerillas, the new "Security and Development Plan" viewed the indigenous population as potential allies in the longer term. The army could win "their hearts and minds" by securing peace and incorporating the population into a development-oriented state, thus removing the basis of support from the guerilla groups.

The rural population was concentrated in settlements that were large enough to support a civil patrol on guard around the clock. The organization of the patrols was hierarchical (village, district, province), with the top commanders, usually ex-soldiers, being appointed by the army. Most patrols received (old) arms, but not in numbers corresponding to the number of participants. The patrols were defined as "auxiliary forces" under the responsibility of the Civil Affairs section of the army, which had been developed and enlarged greatly as part of the new strategy. Patrols were tightly controlled by army outposts, but later, as the army gained confidence in them, control was relaxed and exercised from provincial army bases.

The patrols served several functions. They provided extensive information on movements within and outside settlements, on "unknown" people in the area and on people suspected of being guerilla informers and supporters. They defended settlements from guerilla attacks and participated in extensive army sweeps, rounding up guerillas and displaced people in the areas beyond army control, and providing labour for the army's maintenance and construction activities. Periods of duty depended on the size of the population, but twenty-four hours per week was not uncommon in the villages. Usually, people would have to pay a fine or provide a substitute if they left for migrant labour elsewhere, and, in general, patrolling had a severe economic effect on the communities due to the restrictions the conflict imposed on labour and mobility.

The patrols were male-dominated, as every man between fifteen and fifty-five had to participate in them. In principle, patrolling entitled them to food for work and other emergency provisions, although these do not seem to have been provided always. Widows in female-headed households had to pay a substitute to do the patrolling – a very concrete illustration of the gendered nature of patrolling, which perpetuated gender inequalities.[33]

33 In other cases, such as the armed conflict between the Peruvian army and the Shining

The principal aim of the patrols was to discipline the population through "self-control." Patrols engaged in cleansing villages by harassing and expelling suspected or non-participating individuals, and it was not unusual for them to be involved in the harassment or killing of people from their own or from neighbouring villages. While participation in the patrols during the first years was usually forced upon villagers, many regarded participation as the lesser of the possible evils. Participation promised a certain degree of predictability and stability in comparison to the situation during the earlier phase of counterinsurgency. To some extent, the patrols fended off incursions by the government army, the stronger of the two parties. The guerillas carried out attacks on the "paramilitaries," as they called the civil patrols, but they changed their strategy after a few years, concentrating on the regular armed forces.

The social effects of the civil patrol regime varied too. Patrol commanders – often younger ex-soldiers – had more power than the civilian authorities, who kept a very low profile during the 1980s since they were targeted by the guerillas. While commanders on the lower rungs of the system were appointed for one or two years of duty by the members of the patrols themselves, they sometimes stayed on for many more years, assuming a more or less permanent role as brokers in security and in economic and political affairs, including the illegal trade in drugs and timber. Commanders also became important in the local practice of justice and settling disputes, sometimes imposing militarized communal sanctions. Local animosities stemming from conflicts over land, women, inheritance, debts, etc., became linked to issues within the national conflict, as parties to the local conflicts called upon allies in the warring factions to threaten or eliminate opponents. Accusing opponents of being guerilla supporters was a frequent means of ending a conflict.

The civil patrols in the Guatemalan countryside owe their longevity and success partly to the fact that the patrols were appropriated as yet another communal brokerage institution. As such, the patrols reinforced the local community vis-à-vis the rest of the world, thus institutionalizing the exclu-

Path (*Sendero Luminoso*), women have often taken over patrolling duties in regions where men migrate on a more or less permanent basis.

sion of strangers. The patrols also reinforced the authoritarian side of local politics by asserting the collective authority of villagers over individuals. Within the constraints of centralized army control and conditions of armed warfare, the patrols served to assert local sovereignty and a certain measure of agency. To the degree that the army was seen as supportive rather than abusive, the patrols were an alliance between the villagers and the army.[34]

Participation in the civil patrols was mandatory until 1985. Then the transition to formal democracy brought about a new constitution that made participation voluntary. The army changed the name of the patrols to Voluntary Committees for Civil Defense, but coerced participation was practised into the early 1990s, although on a diminishing scale. The number of members decreased gradually to 600,000 in the late 1980s,[35] while 200,000 patrollers still had to be demobilized officially when the peace negotiations came to an end in 1996. The final peace accord mentioned very briefly that the remaining PACs should be demobilized within thirty days of the signature and that any link to the army should be cut. However, none of the parties of the peace negotiations were interested in having this complex issue on the agenda; the guerilla organizations resisted any equation between the PACs and their forces, and the international community was against any form of support to the process of demobilization of the PACs, which remained entirely a task of the government.[36]

Given the provisions in the constitution against compulsory patrolling, freedom of association and of movement became important issues for Guatemalan human rights groups and popular movements with international backing. When the former Human Rights ombudsman, de Leon Carpio, became president in 1993, many expected him to disband the civil patrols, a move he had supported during his time as ombudsman. However, soon after his own brother-in-law, a critical publisher, was killed, de Leon changed his official position and began to defend the patrols. They contin-

34 Paul H. R. Kobrak, "Village Troubles: The Civil Patrols in Aguacatan, Guatemala" (Doctoral dissertation, University of Michigan, 1997).

35 According to the army's information, quoted in Schirmer, *The Guatemalan Military Project*, 90. According to other sources, there were 600,000 patrollers in 1989.

36 Wenche Hauge and Beate Thoresen, *El destino de los ex combatientes en Guatemala: ¿Obstaculizadores o Agentes de Cambio?* (Ciudad de Guatemala: Magna Terra Editores S.A., 2007).

ued to have a purpose, he argued, and the issue would be dealt with further in the peace negotiations.[37] Freedom of association and of movement was specifically addressed in the human rights accord of 1994. The government promised not to authorize new civil patrols, and the government's human rights institution was commissioned to investigate accusations of their involvement in human rights abuses and coercion.

Meanwhile, however, the excessive costs of continued patrolling contributed to a general fatigue and caused many patrols to abandon their activities clandestinely, without confronting the army directly by returning their arms and asking for official demobilization. Another reason for maintaining the patrols and the alliance with the army was removed by the increased presence in the 1990s of private and multilateral development agencies. Before this, the army's presence in the villages was the only avenue whereby resources for development projects could be obtained, as well as advice from educated people in civil affairs for any kind of local business.

In the early 1990s, the army tried, with some success, to recast the patrols as communal "peace and development committees" with civil obligations, in order to capture the inflow of international funds for reconstruction and maintain the basic structure and linkages between the army and the villages. Nevertheless, their monopoly was often challenged by competing "committees" formed for different purposes, which proliferated with the increasing number of development agencies working in the countryside.

In 1996, the army promised to disarm and demobilize the remaining civil patrols before the end of the year and the final signature of the peace treaty. The UN mission in Guatemala, MINUGUA, was invited to be present at some of the acts of demobilization, but it did not have the necessary information or means to verify whether all the distributed arms were recollected, or if the army had effectively given up its organic links with rural communities. Disarmament procedures were organized and supervised by the army, and sometimes even the patrollers were obviously army recruits in civilian clothes, acting on behalf of absent patrollers.

37 Joel A. Solomon, *Institutional Violence: Civil Patrols in Guatemala, 1993–1994* (Washington: Robert F. Kennedy Memorial Center for Human Rights, 1994), 50.

Patrollers received a meal and a document thanking them for their service to their country.

However, a few years later a growing movement of ex-patrollers began mobilizing for demands for reparation. In various places the government had offered communal development projects for formerly mobilized villages, but the patrollers increasingly insisted on monetary compensation. Demands developed as an issue of political mobilization during the electoral campaigns of 1999 and 2003, first in support of the party of General Rios Montt, the former president of the 1982 counterinsurgency campaign, but later in support of several parties across the political spectrum as the civil patrollers were considered an important political clientele.

The patrollers themselves engaged in many, sometimes violent mobilizations, blocking roads, taking hostages and invading public offices. In the end, between 2003 and 2006, two consecutive governments paid a monetary compensation of 700–800 US$ to each of 629,000 former PAC members, increasing the state's foreign debts by 25 per cent.[38] As such, the PACs continued as a constant obstacle to the peace process and a potentially destabilizing force during almost ten years after the final peace accords.

Armed Civilians in South Africa

When South Africans went to the polls in April 1994, thirty-four years of conflict between the apartheid regime and anti-apartheid forces officially ended as agreed under a negotiated settlement. The regime realized that it could not win militarily despite overwhelming military force and the deployment of a relatively successful counterinsurgency strategy within the South African townships. Partly as a result of this strategy, most of the violence was carried out by Africans against other Africans who were organized in vigilante groups, self-protection and self-defence units (SPUs and SDUs), and kitskonstables (African auxiliary troops deployed in the

38 Ricardo Saenz de Tejada, *¿Victimas o vencedores? Una aproximación al movimiento de los ex-PAC* (Ciudad de Guatemala: Facultad Latinoamericana de Ciencias Sociales, 2004), 76–77.

townships). Many, if not most, of the human rights abuses were inflicted by these groups.[39]

The popular uprisings became widespread from around 1976, when the regime massacred hundreds of children in the Soweto riots. In the years following 1976, significant changes took place within the government and a new strategy was designed to curb the uprising. This "total strategy," which introduced counterinsurgency measures, was based on the idea that South Africa faced a total onslaught against capitalism, civilization and Christianity. On the one hand, the government tried to attract new non-white allies in the shape of the Indians, Coloureds and urban Africans, through limited political reform. It released resources for a number of development projects and programmes. Gradually, trade unions were allowed to form if they had no political affiliation. The pass laws were abandoned. Through these and other initiatives, the government hoped to "win the hearts and minds" of certain sectors in South African society. On the other hand, the initiatives were accompanied by the increasingly violent suppression of the uprising, including two states of emergency, murder, torture, disappearances, the employment of vigilante groups and paramilitary activities.

Partly as a consequence of this strategy, the violence in the black townships rose dramatically from 1986 onwards, and it did not end in 1990 when bans against the African National Congress (ANC) and other political organizations were lifted. On the contrary, the period between 1990 and 1994 saw some of the most dramatic violence of the entire conflict. This increase in violence, often state-sponsored, led leading ANC figures to call for the formation of self-defence units (SDUs) from 1986 onwards. This call for civilian patrols was also echoed in the other political parties, the Pan African Congress (PAC) and the Inkatha Freedom Party (IFP), and was a result of ongoing violence between ANC, IFP and PAC supporters. Each of the three parties formed civilian patrols called respectively SDUs,

39 Gavin Cawthra, *Policing South Africa: The SAP and the Transition from Apartheid* (Cape Town: David Philip Publishers, 1993); Michael Brogden and Clifford Shearing, *Policing for a New South Africa* (London: Routledge, 1993); Ted Legget, "Performance Measures for the South African Police Service: Setting the Benchmarks for Service Delivery," *Transformation* 49, no. 1 (2002): 55–85.

SPUs (Self-Defence and Self-Protection Units) and TKs (Task Force). Of these groups, we shall focus here primarily on the SDUs and their relationship to the ANC.

Originally, the civilian patrols were formed on an ad hoc basis, but after 1990 the ANC itself became involved in the formation of SDUs. The organization drafted a set of guidelines for the formation of SDUs, entitled "for the sake of our lives." SDUs were therefore endorsed and actively supported by the ANC. For instance, the ANC suggested that Umkhonto we Sizwe (MK, the ANC armed wing) soldiers should become the leaders and trainers of SDUs. However, they were to belong to SDUs as members of the community, not as MK fighters. In some cases, SDUs were armed with weapons obtained from MK arms caches. In other cases, they obtained weapons through theft or by modifying tools.[40]

As the ANC came closer to power, the party was increasingly ambiguous about the SDUs. This became particularly clear when in 1993 the party proposed that the SDUs should disband.[41] Most of them refused. One of the reasons the ANC had this ambiguous relationship with this particular constituency must be sought in the changed political environment in which the SDUs no longer played a part. Furthermore, some of the worst atrocities committed in the name of the ANC were actions of the SDUs. Finally, although the ANC claimed them as their constituency, local interests had always directed the SDUs, and as such the ANC often had little control over them.

In terms of organization, the ANC proposed that the SDUs be organized in military style, with companies, platoons and sections, under the command of the Township Defense Committee. Evidence suggests that the SDUs never acquired either the numerical strength or the organizational

40 The ANC guidelines suggested ways in which tools and the like could be turned into, and used as, weapons (ANC, "For the Sake of Our Lives: Guidelines for the Establishment of SDUs," 1991, www.anc.org.za/ancdocs/mis/trc2g.html).

41 Wilfred Schärf, "Re-Integrating Militarised Youths (Street Gangs and Self Defence Units) into the Mainstream South Africa: From Hunters to Game-Keepers?," Paper presented at the Urban Childhood Conference, Trondheim, Norway, June 1997.

level hoped for by the ANC.[42] They were seldom given weapons,[43] did not wear uniforms and did not receive salaries. There were great regional differences in both strength and organization, and it appears that there were many more SDUs active around Johannesburg and in Kwazulu Natal. In both places, the SDUs were engaged in very violent conflicts with Inkatha and their SPUs.

The SDUs were also indicative of changing generational patterns in South Africa. Young people were increasingly taking over from the older generation in the struggle against apartheid.[44] The average age in the SDUs was about twenty. This was, to some extent at least, a conscious strategy on the part of the ANC, which heralded youth as the lions of the revolution and used them to weaken traditional authority in the townships. The generational pattern became intertwined with gender, as it was predominantly men who patrolled the townships. Most of these men were unemployed or had only the most precarious relationships with the labour market.[45]

SDUs were positioned between local and national politics. The ANC recognized that some of the SDUs were outside their control, but ascribed this to the malign intervention of the apartheid security forces.[46] As men-

42 Reliable figures for how many SDUs were active and their level of involvement are hard to find in the literature. For more details, see Penny McKenzie, "Political Pawns or Social Agents? A Look at Militarized Youth in Soweto," *Ibizo* 3 (Cape Town: Centre for Community Justice, 1996); Sylvester Rakgoadi, "The Role of the Self-Defense Units (SDUs) in a Changing Political Context," Occasional Paper from the Centre for the Study of Violence and Reconciliation (Johannesburg, 1995). Monique Marks, "'We are Fighting for the Liberation of our People': The Justifications of Violence by Activist Youth in Diepkloof, Soweto," *Berkeley Journal of Sociology* 41 (1996–1997): 137–65.

43 Most of the SDUs were not particularly well armed. The SPU, which was affiliated with the IFP, had many more weapons, as the security forces and the Kwazulu homeland police supported the IFP. What has happened to these weapons subsequently is difficult to say with certainty.

44 Belinda Bozzoli, *Theatres of the Struggle*; Clive Glaser, *Bo-Tsotsi: The Youth Gangs of Soweto, 1935–1976* (Portsmouth, New Hampshire: Heinemann, 2000).

45 Lars Buur, "The Sovereign Outsourced: Local Justice and Violence in Port Elizabeth," in *Sovereign Bodies: Citizens, Migrants, and States in the Postcolonial World*, ed. Thomas Blom Hansen and Finn Stepputat, 192–217 (Princeton: Princeton University Press, 2005).

46 ANC, "Submission to the South African Truth and Reconciliation Commission," 1996, http://www.anc.org.za/ancdocs/misc/trctoc.html; ANC. "Second Submission to the South African Truth and Reconciliation Commission," 1997, http://www.anc.org.za/ancdocs/misc/trc2.html (page now defunct).

tioned above, local conflicts also influenced the workings of the SDUs. For instance, the Richmond SDU in the Kwazulu Natal Midlands was largely hijacked by the local warlord, Sifiso Nkabinde.[47]

A number of issues emerge from Nkabinde's history. He and his SDU aligned themselves strategically with almost anybody against anybody to further their (and particularly his) interests. Neither the ANC nor the security apparatus nor the police ever managed to control Nkabinde and his SDU. The ANC and the police both needed Nkabinde to gain access to those parts of Richmond controlled by him and his men. Under Nkabinde's control, the SDU also cleansed its own territory in order to remove resistance to their claim to represent the community and control flows of people and goods into and out of the area. Although this happened with particular virulence in Richmond, the internal struggles to become the only defenders of a community, and thus the only brokers with the surrounding society, often led to violence in many other parts of South Africa, where resistance to the SDUs' control was dealt with very harshly.[48]

This does not mean that SDUs were only involved in local struggles or that the national conflict did not play a part. Rather, when local conflicts in Richmond were reinterpreted within the framework of the national conflict between the ANC and the apartheid regime, they tended to change character, and in this case their violent nature increased considerably. This indicates that although the national political conflict influences the way in which local conflicts are fought, national players are often not able to control them.

When the ANC national leadership called for the disbanding of the SDUs in 1993, this was not followed by any policy to address the young people who were their members. Consequently very few SDUs disappeared, and resentment towards the national leaders in the ANC increased. SDU

47 For a detailed account of Nkabinde in Richmond, see Steffen Jensen, "The Battlefield and the Prize: ANC's Bid to Reform the South African State," in *States of Imagination: Ethnographic Explorations of the Postcolonial State*, ed. Thomas Blom Hansen and Finn Stepputat (Durham, North Carolina: Duke University Press, 2001).

48 Joanna Ball, "The Ritual of the Necklace," occasional paper from the Centre for the Study of Violence and Reconciliation (Johannesburg: The Centre for the Study of Violence and Reconciliation, 1994); Bozzoli, *Theatres of the Struggle*.

members felt that they had fulfilled a crucial role in the struggle against apartheid and helped maintain some kind of order in the townships, where the police either did not want or did not dare to go. The sense of neglect and of being forgotten led to threats to resort to violence. In the words of a Sowetan SDU member: "If it means turning to violence and wreaking havoc in order for our grievances to be addressed, then we will do just that. We have done it before, and we got listened to. Nothing can stop us from doing it again."[49] Among people working with the SDUs after 1993, the greatest fear was perhaps that they would become more entangled in crime or that individual members would resort to criminal activities during a period when crime was viewed with increasing alarm.[50]

Despite these dangers, few attempts to deal with, or demobilize, the SDUs were made, and the conflict between them and the police escalated around the country. One attempt to deal with them took place in Khayalitshia, near Cape Town, from 1994 to 1998, when an NGO, the Urban Monitoring Action Committee (UMAC), decided to engage with them. UMAC identified one of the reasons for the hostility towards the police in the desire of SDU members' to join the police. They wanted to do this for several reasons. Due to their local nature, the SDUs thought they were better equipped to police their own areas, which they knew far better than the police, and the community trusted them more than they trusted the police. Subsequently, UMAC mediated between the police and the SDU in order to reach common ground. Although the police and the ANC government ultimately refused to incorporate the SDUs into the police en bloc, the UMAC project generated a far better understanding between the police and the SDUs. In 1997, the SDUs in the Western Cape formally decided to disband, the only ones in the country to do so. This also led to a fairly successful disarmament of the Western Cape SDUs.

49 Quoted from McKenzie, "Political Pawns or Social Agents?," 31.

50 As Rakgoadi puts it: "Gangs, like political organizations, provide a way of life for many youths because in the absence of employment opportunities, they serve as a support system and personal security. As in gangs, joining a political organization provides one with a sense of acceptance, an identity and a sense of security through bonds of loyalty to a group which vows to protect its members against internal threats. The SDUs served this purpose as well." Rakgoadi, "The Role of the SDUs," 7.

In other parts of the country too, the SDUs demanded to be incorporated into the police. However, since this demand was generally refused, tensions rose in many parts of the country.[51] Several SDUs have maintained their organizations, fighting crime and acting as political brokers, while others have collapsed or turned into criminal organizations. For those who fight crime, as well as being recognized as brokers of state development, it is still an ambition to turn the crime fighting and community politics into formalized livelihoods.

Conclusion

The cases of Guatemala and South Africa display a number of similarities and differences. The similarities may well be general characteristics of armed civilian groups, and the differences point to variations in context and form which have to be taken into account when considering forms of demobilization. Beginning with the similarities, in both cases locality was significant, also for the reasons to fight. Secondly, both groups had a quite slippery relationship to authorities, state or political party. Thirdly, there were complicated links between local conflicts and the national struggle. Fourthly, masculinity played an important role. Fifthly, the collective stood above the individual and to participate in the structures became crucial for individual livelihood. Sixthly, the forms of power produced by and in the conflict endured in the post-conflict society; and finally, in both cases, recognition from the state was imperative in the expressed demands, although in different ways.

This brings us to the differences, because although both groups claimed recognition from the state, the claims were different as the SDUs demanded actual enrolment into the state, while the PAC's demanded increased levels of development support. Hence, the different forms of organization also differed in terms of their relationship to the authorities. To some extent, this relates to the urban nature of South African SDUs compared to the rural PACs. Arguably, the spatial difference also informed the extent to

51 UMAC, *Engaging Militarized Youth*, Final Project Report (Cape Town: 1998).

which the SDUs were specialized in security, or if they performed general ordering and authority tasks like the PACs.

The questions, then, remain. Should such groups of armed civilians be demobilized, who should be responsible and how should it be done? We argue that despite the often faulty processes of present-day DDR programmes, some of the answers to these questions can be found in critically looking at the programmes through the lens of our cases. Firstly, in terms of the question of whether groups should be formally demobilized, our analyses do not come out strongly either against or in favour of demobilization. If in favour, on the one hand, some societal anxieties could be alleviated and the role of often ordinary citizens be recognized, thereby deferring potential protest against a new regime. On the other hand, however, particular forms of masculinity might be reproduced, local conflicts nationalized and deepened and some forms of local power authorized by the programmes. Furthermore, new incentive structures – it pays to be organized violently – might perpetuate violent structures unnecessarily. However, when this is said, it seems to us that demobilizing armed civilians would be a productive enterprise.

How might this be achieved? Firstly, it seems imperative to include the armed civilians in peace talks, at least as an item on the agenda. Secondly, inspiration for how to proceed might be gained from DDR programmes, albeit in modified form. Instead of assembly, a carefully executed registration is imperative. As in conventional DDR programmes, registration must be carried out in conjunction with the civil patrols themselves. The UMAC example shows that it is sometimes necessary to be instrumental in creating representative structures among the armed civilians themselves. This process is somewhat more complicated than in the case of military structures, where there are existing chains of command. This makes registration a very cumbersome process. In the Western Cape, three years passed before the SDUs finally decided to disarm and demobilize.

This implies that registration is not only a first step but also an ongoing process, overlapping other steps. Instead of conventional discharge and reinsertion, agencies ought to view these steps in a more symbolic manner. As both the cases discussed here illustrate, a strong group identity exists as the armed defenders of country and community. Thus, a kind of symbolic discharge and reinsertion may be necessary. Furthermore, symbolic discharge and reinsertion might offer an opportunity to address local conflicts. When armed conflicts are fought in local communities by people in the community, they often involve serious maltreatment of fellow citizens and neighbours. Hence, reinsertion could meaningfully address past abuses by bringing cases before the formal court system or by mediating them locally. Finally, instead of "reintegration" a better approach might be recognition. Combatants do not need to go home, they need to be recognized by the state. Furthermore, contrary to, for instance, UNDP's community approach (communities before individual or collective identities), the cases show that it may be necessary to recognize armed civilians as groups before targeting them as members of communities, families and households.

One possible option that might prove valuable, given the limited reach and resources of many states, would be to formalize these structures of security, but in such a way that the fundamental principles of constitutional democracy are not compromised. There have been successes with this approach in South Africa, where complicated legislative work was initiated to create greater access to justice by recognizing alternative forms of justice, such as conflict-resolution mechanisms at the local level. The South African example illustrates that it is imperative to align these structures of justice within state systems, as well as to recognize existing structures that often involve armed civilians to some extent. Otherwise we might witness, as in the cases of South Africa and Guatemala, more spectacular incidents of violence by SDU or civil patrols turned vigilantes.

The final question to address is, who should be in charge of such programmes. When taking the special conditions into account, it seems that NGOs or other non-state actors with good local knowledge would have comparative advantages in carrying out programmes for armed civilians, although local and national NGOs are likely to have histories of participation in the violent conflicts. Furthermore, existing evaluations of DDR programmes recommend involving representatives of the ex-combatants in the design and planning of the programmes. Governments are ambivalent actors in the context of armed conflict. Governments have vested interests in either sustaining or ignoring the issue of armed civilians, since they themselves have often been involved in the mobilization of armed civilians.

But our cases suggest that it is exactly recognition by the government that armed civilians demand. As indicated by the Guatemalan case, it may be counterproductive if governments are represented by the military which organized the armed groups of civilians in the first place. Finally, contrary to the large-scale DDR programmes, where international agencies have been implicated in direct implementation, international agencies should primarily be engaged in demobilization through consultancy, technical assistance and possibly funding.

References

ANC. "For the Sake of Our Lives. Guidelines for the Establishment of SDUs." 1991. www.anc.org.za/ancdocs/misc/trc2g.html. (page now defunct).

———. "Submission to the South African Truth and Reconciliation Commission." 1996. http://www.anc.org.za/ancdocs/misc/trctoc.html. (page now defunct).

———. "Second Submission to the South African Truth and Reconciliation Commission." 1997. http://www.anc.org.za/ancdocs/misc/trc2.html. (page now defunct).

Anderson, Mary B. *Do No Harm: How Aid Can Support Peace – Or War.* New York: Lynne Rienner Publishers, 1996.

Ball, Joanna. "The Ritual of the Necklace." Occasional Paper from the Centre for the Study of Violence and Reconciliation. Johannesburg: The Centre for the Study of Violence and Reconciliation, 1994.

Ball, Nicole. "Demobilizing and Reintegrating Soldiers: Lessons from Africa." In *Rebuilding Societies after Civil War: Critical Roles for International Assistance*, edited by Krishna Kumar, 85–105. Boulder and London: Lynne Rienner Publications, 1997.

Bozzoli, Belinda. *Theatres of the Struggle and the End of Apartheid.* Athens, Ohio: Ohio University Press, 2004.

Brogden, Michael and Clifford Shearing. *Policing for a New South Africa.* London: Routledge, 1993.

Buur, Lars. "The Sovereign Outsourced: Local Justice and Violence in Port Elizabeth." In *Sovereign Bodies: Citizens, Migrants, and States in the Postcolonial World*, edited by Thomas Blom Hansen and Finn Stepputat, 192–217. Princeton: Princeton University Press, 2005.

Buur, Lars, Steffen Jensen and Finn Stepputat. Introduction to *The Security-Development Nexus: Expressions of Sovereignty and Securitization in Southern Africa*, edited by Lars Buur, Steffen Jensen and Finn Stepputat, 9–33. Uppsala and Cape Town: Nordiska Afrikainstituten and HSRC Press, 2007.

Cawthra, Gavin. *Policing South Africa: The SAP and the Transition from Apartheid.* Cape Town: David Philip Publishers, 1993.

Clark, Kimberly Mahling. "Fostering a Farewell to Arms: Preliminary Lessons Learned in the Demobilization and Reintegration of Combatants." USAID Document: PN-ABY-027. Washington, D.C., 1997.

DAC. DAC *Guidelines on Conflict, Peace and Development Co-operation*. Paris: OECD, 1997.

Danida. *Denmark's Development Policy: Analysis: Partnership 2000*. Copenhagen: Ministry of Foreign Affairs of Denmark, Danida, 2000.

Dolan, Chris and Jessica Schafer. *The Reintegration of Ex-Combatants in Mozambique: Manica and Zambezia Provinces*. Final Report to USAID. Refugee Studies Programme. Oxford: University of Oxford, 1997.

Glaser, Clive. *Bo-Tsotsi: The Youth Gangs of Soweto, 1935–1976*. Portsmouth, New Hampshire: Heinemann, 2000.

Hauge, Wenche and Beate Thoresen. *El destino de los ex combatientes en Guatemala: ¿Obstaculizadores o Agentes de Cambio?* Ciudad de Guatemala: Magna Terra Editores S.A., 2007.

Jensen, Steffen. "The Battlefield and the Prize: ANC's Bid to Reform the South African State." In *States of Imagination: Ethnographic Explorations of the Postcolonial State*, edited by Thomas Blom Hansen and Finn Stepputat, 97–122. Durham, North Carolina: Duke University Press, 2001.

Kingma, Kees. "Demobilization and Reintegration – an Overview." In *Converting Defense Resources To Human Development: Proceedings from an International Conference, 9–11 November 1997*. Report no. 12. Bonn: BICC, 1998.

———. "Demobilization and Reintegration Experiences in Africa." In *War Force to Work Force: Global Perspectives on Demobilization and Reintegration*, edited by Natalie Pauwels, 301–28. Baden-Baden: Nomos Verlagsgesellschaft, 2001.

Kobrak, Paul H. R. "Village Troubles: The Civil Patrols in Aguacatan, Guatemala." Doctoral dissertation, University of Michigan, 1997.

Legget, Ted. "Performance Measures for the South African Police Service: Setting the Benchmarks for Service Delivery." *Transformation* 49, no. 1 (2002): 55–85.

Marks, Monique. "'We are Fighting for the Liberation of our People': The Justifications of Violence by Activist Youth in Diepkloof, Soweto." *Berkeley Journal of Sociology* 41 (1996–1997): 137–65.

McCuen, John J. *The Art of Counter-Revolutionary War*. London: Faber and Faber, 1966.

McKenzie, Penny. "Political Pawns or Social Agents? A Look at Militarized Youth in Soweto." *Ibizo* 3. Cape Town: Centre for Community Justice, 1996.

Meddings, David R. "Civilians at War: A Review and Historical Overview of Involvement of Non-Combatant Populations in Conflict Situations." *Medicine, Conflict and Survival* 17, no. 1 (2001): 6–16.

Nagl, John A. Foreword to *The U.S. Army/Marine Corps Counterinsurgency Field Manual: US Army Field Manual no. 3–24 / Marine Corps Warfighting Publication no. 3–33.5*, by United States Dept. of the Army. Chicago: University of Chicago Press, 2007.

Paris, Roland. "International Peacebuilding and the 'Mission Civilisatrice'." *Review of International Studies* 28, no. 4 (2002): 637–56.

Pauwels, Natalie, ed. *War Force to Work Force: Global Perspectives on Demobilization and Reintegration*. Baden-Baden: Nomos Verlagsgesellschaft, 2000.

Pouligny, Béatrice. *The Politics and Anti-politics of Contemporary Disarmament, Demobilization and Reintegration Programs*. Paris: CERI, 2004.

Rakgoadi, Sylvester. "The Role of the Self-Defense Units (SDUs) in a Changing Political Context." (Occasional Paper from the Centre for the Study of Violence and Reconciliation. Johannesburg, 1995).

Saenz de Tejada, Ricardo. *¿Victimas o vencedores? Una aproximación al movimiento de los ex-PAC*. Ciudad de Guatemala: Facultad Latinoamericana de Ciencias Sociales, 2004.

Schafer, Jessica. "'A Baby Who Does Not Cry Will Not be Suckled': AMODEG and the Reintegration of Demobilised Soldiers." *Journal of Southern African Studies* 24, no. 1 (1998): 202–27.

Schärf, Wilfred. "Re-Integrating Militarised Youths (Street Gangs and Self-Defence Units) into the Mainstream in South Africa: From Hunters to Game-Keepers?" Paper presented at the Urban Childhood Conference, Trondheim, Norway, June 1997.

Schirmer, Jennifer G. *The Guatemalan Military Project: A Violence Called Democracy*. Philadelphia: University of Pennsylvania Press, 1998.

Solomon, Joel A. *Institutional Violence: Civil Patrols in Guatemala, 1993–1994*. Washington, D.C.: Robert F. Kennedy Memorial Center for Human Rights, 1994.

Sørensen, Georg. "Sovereignty, Change and Continuity in a Fundamental Institution." *Political Studies* 47, no. 3 (1999): 590–604.

Stockton, Nicholas. "Accountability in Peace-Building: The Case of the Democratic Republic of Congo." Paper presented at the FAU Conference, Gjerrild, Denmark, March 2005.

Trinquier, Roger. *Modern Warfare: A French View of Counterinsurgency.* Translated by Daniel Lee. New York: Frederick A. Praeger, 1964 [1961].

UMAC. *Engaging Militarized Youth.* Final Project Report. Cape Town: UMAC, 1998.

United Nations Development Programme. *Sharing New Ground in Post-Conflict Situations: The Role of UNDP in Support of Reintegration Programmes.* 2000. http://web.undp.org/evaluation/documents/postconflict_march2000.pdf (accessed 13 June 2013).

United Nations Inter-Agency Working Group on Disarmament, Demobilization and Reintegration. *Integrated Disarmament, Demobilization and Reintegration Standards.* New York: United Nations, 2006.

United Nations. *Disarmament, Demobilization, Reintegration (DDR) and Stability in Africa.* Conference Report, Freetown, Sierra Leone, 21–23 June, 2005. New York: United Nations, 2005. http://www.un.org/africa/osaa/reports/DDR%20Sierra%20Leone%20March%202006.pdf. (accessed 26 May 2013).

United Nations Security Coucil. "The Role of the United Nations Peacekeeping in Disarmament, Demobilization and Reintegration. Report of the Secretary-General." S/2000/101. 11 February 2000.

———. "Report of the Secretary-General on Developments in Guinea-Bissau." S/2000/250. 24 March 2000.

———. "Report of the Secretary-General on Developments in Guinea-Bissau and on the Activities of the United Nations Peace-Building Support Office in that Country." S/2000/632. 28 June 2000.

———. "Report of the Secretary-General on Developments in Guinea-Bissau and on the Activities of the United Nations Peace-Building Support Office in that Country." S/2000/920. 29 September 2000.

Utas, Mats. "Watermelon Politics in Sierra Leone: Hope amidst Vote Buying and Remobilized Militias." *African Renaissance* 4, no. 3–4 (2007): 62–66.

Vigh, Henrik. *Navigating Terrains of War: Youth and Soldiering in Guinea Bissau.* New York: Berghahn Press, 2006.

Vines, Alex. "Disarmament in Mozambique." *Journal of Southern African Studies* 24, no. 1 (1998): 191–205.

Notes on Contributors

Steffen Jensen, b. 1966, is Senior Researcher at DIGNITY-Danish Institute Against Torture. He has published extensively on violent networks, human rights and security in South Africa and the Philippines.

Lars Bo Kaspersen, b. 1961, is Professor of Political Sociology in the Department of Political Science at the University of Copenhagen. His research interests include historical-comparative macro-sociology, state formation processes in Western Europe, war and society and the sociology of war.

Gunner Lind, b. 1953, is Professor of Early Modern History in the Department of History at the University of Copenhagen. He has published extensively on military history and war in early modern Danish history.

Jeppe Büchert Netterstrøm, b. 1972, is Associate Professor of Early Modern History at the Section of History, Arhus University. He has published widely on feuds, crime and state-building in late medieval and early modern Denmark.

Palle Roslyng-Jensen, b. 1944, is Associate Professor of Contemporary History in the Department of History at University of Copenhagen. He has published on Danish military and politics and public opinion during the Second World War and early Cold War.

Robin May Schott, b. 1954, is Senior Researcher. She is a feminist philosopher who has published extensively on issues related to war, gender and sexual violence.

Finn Stepputat, b. 1955, is Senior Researcher at the Danish Institute for International Studies.

Index